American Federalism
and Individual Rights

American Federalism and Individual Rights

Stephanie M. Walls

LEXINGTON BOOKS
Lanham • Boulder • New York • London

Published by Lexington Books
An imprint of The Rowman & Littlefield Publishing Group, Inc.
4501 Forbes Boulevard, Suite 200, Lanham, Maryland 20706
www.rowman.com

6 Tinworth Street, London, SE11 5AL, United Kingdom

British Library Cataloguing in Publication Information Available

Library of Congress Cataloging-in-Publication Data

Names: Walls, Stephanie M., author.
Title: American federalism and individual rights / Stephanie Mora Walls.
Description: Lanham : Lexington Books, [2021] | Includes bibliographical references and index. | Summary: "American Federalism and Individual Rights presents the founding concepts of federalism and individual rights, and facilitates a discussion of their compatibility. Through the lens of policy analysis, the author discovers ways in which federalism has both helped and hindered the protection of individual rights in the United States"—Provided by publisher.
Identifiers: LCCN 2020050859 (print) | LCCN 2020050860 (ebook) | ISBN 9781498589444 (cloth) | ISBN 9781498589451 (epub)
Subjects: LCSH: Federal government—United States. | Civil rights—United States—History. | Individualism—United States. | Liberty. | United States—Politics and government.
Classification: LCC JK311 .W238 2021 (print) | LCC JK311 (ebook) | DDC 323.0973—dc23
LC record available at https://lccn.loc.gov/2020050859
LC ebook record available at https://lccn.loc.gov/2020050860

For my mother, Janet Cutinella, whose passion for politics inspired my own.

Contents

Acknowledgments

Due to the COVID-19 pandemic, I finished this book in a makeshift office space in my dining room. For the first time since grad school, I found myself once again working with officemates. My sixteen-year-old daughter, Lauren, also occupied the dining room for her remote learning, and my thirteen-year-old son, Nick, was just upstairs working on his schoolwork at his desk. I thought it would be difficult to work from home, but it turns out I have raised very polite and considerate officemates. I have never been more appreciative of both kids' strong work ethic and self-sufficiency, for without those things, I do not know that I could have completed my project on time. That is a nice way of saying that they did not need my help with anything school related and left me alone to get my work done. I very much enjoyed our lunch and snack breaks, too. Much love and appreciation to my husband, David, as well, who has always been supportive of my work and (mostly) left me alone so I could meet my deadline!

I am very appreciative of my employer, Bowling Green State University, for granting me Faculty Improvement Leave to work on this project full-time for one semester, and for my colleagues on the Firelands campus for their professional and moral support during this project. I would like to specifically thank our library associate, Nestor Rave, for his research support; my department chair, Dr. Christine Genovese, for scheduling around my leave; and the BGSU Faculty Association for making my leave possible.

Preface

When I began work on this book in the summer of 2018, I could not have known that by the end I would be living through the COVID-19 pandemic. I thought I had a fairly thorough grasp on the policy areas that could be significantly impacted by a federal power structure, and I selected policies to include in this book based on what I thought would be both relevant and interesting. I can honestly say that I never considered a policy scenario that involved the delivery of healthcare in the United States during the spread of a highly contagious virus. Throughout the writing of this book, and surely before, I have been well aware of the ways in which the states can assert their authority over various policy areas and found evidence of that state power across the topics in this book. Even so, it would have been hard for me to imagine a time where the governor of my home state of Ohio would so clearly dictate the terms of my everyday life. Of course, I knew that the state government had power before, but perhaps I was just used to the ways policies varied from state to state. Today, however, I am writing this from my home because my governor told my college to shut down the campus. I am home because my governor ordered me to stay home. During this pandemic, the way policies vary from state to state means that people in one state may have a greater chance of staying healthy while people in another state have a greater chance of contracting a possibly life-threatening virus or having difficulty accessing life-saving healthcare for other emergencies, because the hospitals are over capacity with coronavirus patients. I identify more strongly as an Ohioan than I did when I began writing this book, and federalism is the reason for that. The connection between federalism and the protection of individual rights is not a new topic, though this scenario makes it feel new. The balance of power between the national government and the states dates back to the founding era, and the relationship between federalism and individual rights is as vital to a discussion of American politics now as it was then. The question remains: What exactly is the relationship between federalism and individual rights?

In 2011, the Supreme Court decided the case of *Bond v. United States*.[1] The case involved a Pennsylvania woman, Carol Ann Bond, who had been convicted of violating the Chemical Weapons Convention Implementation Act of 1998, a federal statute, when she attempted to chemically poison her husband's mistress. She appealed her conviction on the grounds that the federal law applied in her case violated the Tenth Amendment and the state of Pennsylvania's ability to regulate this particular issue. In this case, the Court ruled unanimously that Bond had standing to appeal that conviction on the grounds that the application of federal law in this case exceeded the authority of the national government.[2] The Court successively decided in 2014 that Bond could not be charged under the Act.[3] Though this case was infinitely more personal to Bond and her husband and the woman she tried to poison, for our purposes the matter was about federalism and the balance of power between the national government and the state governments. In the 2011 opinion, Justice Anthony Kennedy took the opportunity to state unequivocally that federalism was created with the purpose of protecting individual freedom.[4] His opinion served as a reminder that federalism is not just a matter between the states and the national government, because that relationship has a direct bearing on the freedom of the individual to enjoy the protections guaranteed by the Constitution. Though the correctness of Justice Kennedy's assessment has been debated, I am inclined to agree that the founders intended federalism, as a method of managing sovereignty with a governmental system, to serve as a protection for individual rights. What is unclear is the extent to which this has actually happened.

Federalism is one of the most important principles of American governance, yet it remains one of the least discussed, least evaluated, and least understood beyond academia. While not the "dark continent" of political science it was once considered, American federalism could certainly be understood and appreciated more by both traditional students, lifelong learners, citizens, and observers of American politics.[5] This book is designed to be a resource for those wishing to better understand and evaluate American federalism today. The basic concept of federalism—the division of sovereignty between the national government and the state governments—is integral to the American governmental identity. It also lies at the root of most political conflict and controversy we see in the country today. The founders expected that federalism would advance another significant founding ideological concept: individual rights. This book will not only provide the reader with the foundational information necessary to understand federalism and individual rights, but it will also provide a structure to assess how compatible these two founding ideals actually are.

Introductory courses in American politics routinely cover the principles of American democracy, and it is easy to assume that they all naturally fit together. The founders set out to create a political system based on democratic principles, and they wanted to protect individual rights, establish and preserve equality before the law, and to protect majority rule and minority rights. Though the founders valued these principles, that did not necessarily mean that the principles would all be compatible or mutually reinforcing. The classical liberal theory they rested their assumptions on was not thoroughly tested. The assumption that all people were inherently equal was so unstable that even the people who put those words to paper could not really grasp what those words meant when it came to African Americans and women.

There is a vast literature available on the topic of federalism, and it extends across several disciplines including political science and law. I have worked to incorporate ideas from a variety of disciplines to maximize what is collectively known about the development and implementation of federalism in the United States. There are books and articles both on the history and development of federalism and also on the connection between federalism and public policy dating back several decades to the present. This book intends to bring the history and policy together in a way designed to be evaluative and empowering to the reader. This book addresses both theory and the practical application of the theory. An active and effective American citizen should be knowledgeable about federalism and empowered to use that knowledge to assess the effectiveness of this power distribution and hold both national and state politicians accountable for the way they use that power. While this book does not provide a comparison of how various policy areas have been managed under unitary systems, it attempts to show what has happened in different policy areas under a federal system and whether or not those actions can be construed as advances for individual rights.

In order to better understand the relationship between federalism and individual rights with one book, we will need to proceed with two main tasks: first, we will engage in a short course review of a vast amount of material, including the origins of federalism and individual rights; and second, we will review and evaluate specific policy areas to see what has actually happened in the practice of federalism and its impact on individual rights. Part I of the book will include coverage of both the origins and debate over American federalism, the practice of American federalism since the founding, and a review of individual rights in the United States. Another organizational possibility would have been to provide a more integrative overview of the relationship between federalism and individual rights and how the branches of government have engaged in these matters. I have chosen to present the topics of federalism and individual rights independently as a precursor to my policy discussions so as to bring others into the conversation who may not have working knowledge of either of these fundamental topics. My coverage of federalism reaches back to include some older scholarship, as this is very consistent with what is currently begin taught in introductory-level American government classes. There is an effort to bring in some more contemporary scholarship as well, to give some breadth to this coverage. The separation of these topics is intentional as a building block approach to the content. Part II contains policy-oriented studies in which we will examine the policy areas of civil rights, education, same-sex marriage, and physician-assisted death. In each chapter, we will learn about the policy area, its history with federalism, key policy developments, and apply a three-part test to determine whether or not federalism has been successful in facilitating the protection of individual rights in that policy area. Part III contains the concluding chapters that provide both summary and analysis of the policy studies and ideas for future research of the impact of federalism on the protection of individual rights. We will return to the topic of COVID-19 and discuss some early thoughts about that developing situation and its relevance for federalism and individual rights.

My hope is that this book can be an access point to the understanding of federalism and individual rights for those who are interested in American politics and political culture. These topics can be intimidating to the average observer or student of American politics, and I would very much like for this book to open the door to a broader discussion. For those who study, write, and teach these topics, then perhaps my presentation can be part of the larger discussion of how these concepts relate to one another and help inform future work connecting theory to practice. Whatever the impact, I am happy to be part of the conversation.

NOTES

1. *Bond v. United States*, 564 U.S. 211 (2011).
2. "Bond v. United States." *Oyez.* Accessed March 31, 2020. https://www.oyez.org/cases/2010/09-1227.
3. *Bond v. United States*, 572 U.S. 844 (2014)
4. Severino, "Justice Kennedy: Federalism Exists to Secure Individual Liberty," *National Review*; *Bond v. United States*, 564 U.S. 211 (2011).
5. Kincaid and Cole, "Is Federalism Still the "Dark Continent" of Political Science Teaching?" 877.

Part I

FOUNDATIONAL CONCEPTS

Federalism and individual rights are fascinating and complex topics in the context of American government and political culture. A tremendous amount of work has been done over time to understand the origins and functionality of each of these concepts individually. The importance of these topics is not only evidenced by the amount of research that has been done but also by the treatment they are given in political science education. It is truly impossible to understand or appreciate American government and politics without understanding these core components. While these topics receive ample attention in academic settings, it seems that these topics are not nearly as interesting to others who live in the United States or are otherwise impacted by American politics. It has been particularly difficult to determine conclusively what federalism means to average Americans.

A recent study by political scientist Nicholas Jacobs concluded that most people do not really care much about federalism as long as they get the policy outcomes they want.[1] However, other studies have found that people do care about federalism and that politicians may be able to capitalize on those preferences. One such study by John Dinan and Jac Heckelman found strong connections between partisanship and ideology and the federalism preferences of the general public.[2] Whether people care about federalism or prefer centralized or decentralized policymaking, questions remain regarding how and why people develop those preferences and the extent to which those attitudes directly connect to their desire to protect individual rights. The connection between the principles and practice of federalism deserves closer scrutiny. If citizens, at large, and politicians, in particular, are aware of federalism but unsure of how it relates to other principles of American democracy, or worse, do not care how it relates as long as they achieve their desired policy outcomes, then the long-term health and stability of American democracy could be in question.

There is great value in understanding the functionality of American government and politics, and the study of its components must go beyond a general definitional understanding to a more thorough and integrative assessment of how those components work together. Much of the debate over the meaning of American federalism centers on how it arose and what it meant to the founders. Regardless of the exact definition of federalism or where the American founding falls in the chronology of its development, federalism has always been about moderating power and establishing authority in a way that is most just and organizationally stable. Federalism is based on the idea that multiple actors in a political system can balance the powers of others in that system through a sharing or division of sovereignty.

The core principles of American democracy—majority rule and minority rights, equality before the law, individual rights, separation of powers, and federalism—are assumed to be complementary, but that assumption may not be justified. The emphasis American governance and culture places on individual rights creates a number of societal challenges and inconsistencies, and so the question of the compatibility between individual rights and federalism, in particular, is a logical one.[3] In the United States, the individual is the primary unit of societal measure, and that principle is embodied in the founding documents. The emphasis on the individual, the preservation of individual rights, and the maintenance of a federal system all relate to one another. Specifically, the translation of popular sovereignty into any type of governmental sovereignty could ultimately pose a threat to the freedom of the individual. This possibility stands in contrast to an understanding of federalism as a method of protecting individual rights. Do multiple levels of governance actually serve to protect individual rights or do these multiple levels of governance act as an obstacle to that protection? Are federalism and individual rights truly compatible? Much of this complexity has been overlooked in the current teaching and treatment of federalism in American society. Over the last several years, important work has been done to better seat American federalism in both a historical and theoretical context, and there is even more that we can learn about federalism through studying its relationship with individual rights. It is my hope that this text can add to this discussion and also serve as a bridge to the practical consideration of policy development in a few impactful and timely policy areas.

This part of the book will accomplish three goals that will then facilitate the policy reviews contained in part II. Chapter 1 contains an explanation and summarization of the development and meaning of federalism, what it meant during the founding era, how it was debated, and why it was ultimately settled upon as the political power arrangement for American governance. Chapter 2 addresses the experience of American federalism in the time since the founding, highlighting how it has changed and shifted over the years as a dynamic component of American politics. Chapter 3 provides foundational information about individual rights, their importance in American politics, and an explanation of why the relationship between federalism and individual rights should be closely examined. This part will equip the reader with the foundational knowledge necessary to engage in a systematic review of four policy areas that have been particularly relevant for both the practice of federalism and the protection of individual rights.

NOTES

1. Jacobs, "An Experimental Test of How Americans Think About Federalism," 573.
2. Dinan and Heckelman, "Stability and Contingency in Federalism Preferences," 234.
3. For a thorough discussion of individualism in American society, see Walls, *Individualism in the United States*.

Chapter 1

American Federalism

Origins and Debate

The literature on American federalism is complex and extensive, and the coverage extends across a significant duration of time, reaching back to the American founding. The work that has been done on American federalism can be divided into many subcategories, including historical overviews, efforts to define and identify types of federalism, and studies focused on evaluating the function and performance of federalism. Due to the vast literature, the objective of this first chapter is both ambitious and challenging. This chapter is intended to provide a survey of this information which will result in a general understanding of federalism and open the dialogue over how compatible federalism is with the pursuit and protection of individual rights in the United States. This chapter will utilize a "what, why, how" framework to accomplish this goal. What is federalism? Why was federalism considered an appropriate way to distribute or manage political power in the United States? How did federalism finally take shape in the U.S. Constitution?

Federalism can seem to be a bookish, dated concept that only rings the most distant of bells for many observers and even some practitioners of American politics. Perhaps one read the *Federalist Papers* at some point during their education (or more likely, just one or two of the essays in an introductory political science course) and knows it has something to do with American politics. The idea of federalism as only a footnote to the modern understanding of American politics is ironic on many levels. First, this was a concept that was a significant component of founding era political thought. It was a concept that existed in practice during the colonial era before it was properly identified or understood.[1] It was an arrangement, but not an agreement, that allowed for governance across a large geographic area. It was an organizational and governing idea that filled in the gaps left open when a great distance exists between the government and the governed. The

5

arrangement existed, but it was extremely difficult to articulate and institutionalize in a way that could be acceptable to all parties involved, namely those accorded governing authority. Second, federalism is at the root of most American political conflict today, and as such, has served as a critical factor in this country's development.[2] If there is any question as to the veracity of that statement, one need only consider the historical topic of slavery and states' rights and the challenge of modern issues such as discrimination and abortion.[3] The concept of federalism is thoroughly embedded in the creation and practice of American government and politics, and yet is rarely discussed or understood outside of academic settings. Federalism is a political and organizational concept that is both "everywhere and nowhere" at all.[4]

WHAT IS FEDERALISM?

There are many terms that have been used to describe federalism. When we think of a "textbook" definition, we consider the standard meaning, but what if there are multiple textbook definitions? The exercise of identifying several competing definitions of federalism to illustrate the confusion is not a new one though it remains quite effective.[5] Here is one example of a textbook definition: "A system of shared sovereignty between two levels of government—one national and one subnational—occupying the same geographic region."[6] Another reads: "A constitutional arrangement whereby power is divided between national and subnational governments, each of which enforces its own laws directly on its citizens and neither of which can alter the arrangement without the consent of the other."[7] Or another: "A way of organizing a nation so that two or more levels of government have formal authority over the same land and people. It is a system of shared power between units of government."[8] In just these few definitions, we hear about "shared power," "divided power," and "shared sovereignty." We already have some issues to sort out. To share something is not necessarily the same thing as dividing it, and sovereignty and power are not the same thing at all.

Moving on, one can define federalism as a distribution of "partial autonomy" to the states as the result of a unique American political identity.[9] This identity leads American citizens to see themselves as accountable to both the national government and the government of the state they live in. The grant of partial autonomy allows for a policymaking structure that caters to both of those identities. However, how do we know what proportion of our identity is accountable to which level of government? Additionally, how is one partially autonomous? Isn't autonomy the ability to do what one wants? If one is only partially autonomous, are they autonomous at all?

In order to better grasp the concept of federalism, we must address a few key terms: federal, national, sovereignty, power, divide, and share. The root word *federal* is itself a confusing term, and it has been since the founding.[10] Did "federal" indicate support for states' rights or support of the national government? Even then it was not always clear if it was a reference to federalism and the role of the states or if it was a reference to the national government. During the Constitutional Convention, references to the national government or to national practices were always about those activities and authority that concerned the national government and the people, not the national government and the states. Interestingly, those individuals at the founding who were more in favor of federal provisions (emphasizing the relationship between the national government and the states) adopted the name "Anti-Federalist" after their more nationalist contemporaries took the name "Federalist" during the ratification process.[11] Those who preferred a national government over a truly federal system became known as Federalists, and those who preferred a federal system became known as Anti-Federalists. The legacy of those actions persists today, as Americans still refer to the national government as the "federal" government.[12]

As opposed to a federal government, a national government is one that rules over and is accountable to the individual citizens of that place. In order to achieve a functional federal system, there needs to be some way to establish and enforce both institutional and physical boundaries between the national government and the states and then also among the states.[13] Examples of institutional features that support a federal relationship include equal state representation in the Senate and roles for the states in both the presidential election process and the constitutional amendment process.[14] The presence of clear geographical boundaries between states is necessary in a federal system, as is a recognized governmental structure within each of those states empowered to provide governance within that defined space.

To be sovereign means to have ultimate governing authority. There is no authority higher than one that is sovereign. It is the person or the body who has the final say over any matter relevant to that authority. In the context of modern federalism, sovereignty is considered something that both levels of government possess in some way, but there are many challenges here. First, how does one share or divide something that is ultimate and final? If the national government is sovereign and the states are not, that is a unitary system. If the states are sovereign and the national government is not, that is a confederation. But what power does a national government have if it is not sovereign?[15] Further, and to complicate things even more, if sovereign means having final say, can any democratic government be truly sovereign if it is, by definition, accountable to the people? In this case, the people are sovereign.

Next, is the concept is of power. Power is the ability to compel someone to do something that they would not do of their own accord. Power can take many forms, including political, economic, and social. A sovereign ruler or government will at least possess political power. However, other actors who are not sovereign may still have the ability to compel action. If we are dividing or sharing power, that is not the same thing as dividing and sharing sovereignty. Multiple actors can possess power, but breaking sovereignty into parts is a more difficult task.

A frustrating part of studying federalism is the way "divide" and "share" are used interchangeably and how the use, or misuse, of these words further complicate our understanding of sovereignty. The distribution of power may be described as something quite precise and defined, something that is very collaborative and vague, and everything in between. In the former model, powers are cleanly distributed, the levels of government have a "quota of authority" and a "distinct sphere" in which they act.[16] The decision over which level oversees which issues may be related to perceived efficiency and effectiveness and whether or not there is a need for policy uniformity.[17] This view of federalism is compatible with the recognition of national and state autonomy, as the presence of autonomy would certainly suggest this cleaner divide of specific issues to specific levels of government.[18]

However, federalism can also be described in vague terms wherein there is a high degree of concurrency and a less specific idea of which level is responsible for which types of policy. The language that centers more on "sharing" than "dividing" suggests this more overlapping and fluid arrangement. In this scenario, both levels of government are working together and under a general understanding that the states are responsible for any policy areas that are not expressly mentioned in the U.S. Constitution.[19]

To return to the topic of sovereignty, both the dividing and sharing sovereignty is challenging to sort out, as the national government, the state governments, and the people are all vying for their share. Where sovereignty should be concentrated in a federal system depends upon who you ask. At the time of the founding, the question of where to place the emphasis was a source of contention between the "state federalists" and the "national federalists."[20] Federalism does require that sovereignty reside in more than one place, but there is disagreement about what this actually means for structure and dynamics of a political system.

As Vincent Ostrom states in *The Meaning of American Federalism,* "We are in the presence of a tyranny of words."[21] In this book, I will use the term federalism to describe a system of governance in which sovereignty is divided between the states and the national government. There are other books and articles on federalism wherein the term is used to refer to a political system where the states have more power than the national government. While that is one possibility in a federal system, it is not the only possibility. I will only use the term in the most neutral sense to refer to the division of sovereignty. As I will show, sometimes the national government exerts greater control over policymaking and sometimes the state governments demonstrate greater control. This variation is possible through federalism. Additionally, I will resist using the word "federal" to refer to the national government in order to avoid confusion in the context of this work.

Another component of the federalism discussion focuses on whether or not the federal agreement is between the states and the national government or the people and the national government. This is an interesting part of the discussion that has been largely left out of current consideration of federalism. If the focus is on the sovereignty of the people, then the authority that both levels of government possess derives from the people. In this scenario, a sovereign people delegate power to the national government and state governments and then hold both levels accountable for their actions.[22] There is another perspective on this that has persisted since the founding, and it is the idea of the national government deriving its authority from the state governments because the states came together and agreed to grant that authority. This is known as "compact theory."[23] The more persuasive argument at the founding rested on the concept of popular sovereignty, but it is compact theory that has persisted in influencing modern understandings and applications of federalism.[24]

Purposes of Federalism

Given that federalism is conceptually difficult to explain and practically difficult to implement, one may be inclined to ask why federalism would be a desirable choice. What could be the benefits of choosing a more complicated system? We will deal more specifically with why federalism was the system of choice for the United States later in this chapter, but for now we can address the beneficial purposes of federalism in more general terms. Federalism can both serve to create opportunities and to correct deficiencies in a political system.

There are several ways in which federalism creates opportunities for both the government and the governed. First, the division of sovereignty allows for governments to function more efficiently in geographically large countries. The less physical distance between the government and the governed, the faster information can pass between the two, the faster problems can be solved, and the faster the needs of the people can be met. Second, federalism can provide for more effective governance, insofar as policy created at the state level may be more likely to meet the expectations of that state's residents as opposed to nationally created policy. This can allow for better representation for minority populations who stand a better chance of having their needs met at the state level. Third, federalism can play a role in promoting both individual and group rights.[25] Federalism provides individuals and groups with multiple opportunities to protect their rights, because if they cannot accomplish their policy goals at one level, they can try on the other.[26] It should be noted that, while the expansion of rights is a possibility under federalism, some have argued that this is not the reason federalism was selected as the method of political power distribution.[27] We, of course, will be coming back to this particular topic. Federalism can also reduce the power of majorities through decentralizing the policymaking process. As we will see in the next section, there were pressing concerns about the power of majorities at the time of the American founding.

Federalism can also be utilized to correct political deficiencies that can arise with regard to stability, state strength, and legitimacy. For instance, in countries where there are deep ethnic divides or language barriers, federalism can provide an organizational way to diffuse tensions and prevent violence and discriminatory policy and practices.[28] Federalism can provide a short-term solution and compromise for new nations that are unable to resolve internal power struggles in a way that is definitively victorious for either side. As Rubin and Feeley explain in their article "Federalism in Interpretation," federalism in this case can be seen as a "tragic choice," but it is at least a path forward for emerging nations that may not have another path forward at that time.[29] Federalism can accommodate a wider variety of views than a unitary system can, and that accommodation can at least allow competing groups to coexist.

These general definitions and perspectives on federalism bring us part of the way in answering the question of what federalism is. The other part of this journey requires us to consider the *Federalist Papers* and the work that Alexander Hamilton, James Madison, and John Jay did to explain the concept and provide a rationale for it. The *Federalist Papers* do not tell us everything we need to know about the concept, but it does provide some insight into at least one side of the debate.

The Federalist Papers

The *Federalist Papers* is a series of eighty-five essays that were published in newspapers beginning on October 27, 1787.[30] The public debate in the press over the issue of ratification had already begun with opponents to the Constitution writing essays under pseudonyms like "Cato" and "Brutus" that had drawn direct, public responses from Alexander Hamilton himself.[31] Beginning on October 27, 1787, all essays published as a part of this series were signed "Publius," though we now know Hamilton, Madison, and Jay were responsible for writing these essays. Hamilton bound these essays together in complete volumes in 1788.[32] These essays were intended to advance the cause of ratification and to also provide the theoretical foundation and justification for such a system.[33] There are conflicting reports on exactly how these essays came about. We have a general idea of who authored which essay, but even the authors themselves came into conflict over authorship of specific essays.[34] The extent of active collaboration is debated, and there is evidence that these essays were the result of independent efforts. Our understanding of this process is ultimately significant to how we understand the overall purpose of the documents and their continued importance today.

With regard to collaboration, Madison and Hamilton drew from common information that they had generated and shared during the Constitutional Convention. While they did not necessarily agree during those convention debates, they both utilized notes from those meetings to write their essays.[35] This common source of information would suggest a degree of passive collaboration that could lead to some internal consistency within the essays themselves. Since the essays were bound together in 1788, it would make sense to see them as each part of a larger tract with a coherent purpose and intent. However, later review of these documents and the history of that time period suggests otherwise. While it is documented that Madison referenced some collaboration with Hamilton, he had also been known to comment that the speed with which these essays were published really prohibited a great deal of collaboration, if any.[36] Further, we are pressed to find any evidence that review of the other's work led to revision or modification, suggesting that any collaboration that occurred was superficial at best.[37] The product was a series of essays that were written and disseminated quickly in order for timely impact on the ratification debate with no real effort to edit them individually or as a body of work for clarity or consistency.[38]

What then of the purpose and importance of these essays? The options in this assessment are quite at odds with one another. This collection has been described as an indisputable guide to the meaning of the Constitution that represents the best American political theory as to offer, and it has also been described as a mere series of political writings published to accomplish the political goal of ratification. One purpose seems very noble while the other more practical, perhaps. As for their importance, this varies as well. In the preface to the 1999 reprint of the *Federalist Papers,* political scientist Charles Kesler explains that, at the founding, the *Federalist* was heralded by the likes of Thomas Jefferson as "the best commentary on the principles of government" and "an authority" on American government.[39] Kesler shares that, as recently as the 1961 printing of the *Federalist,* noted political scientist Clinton Rossiter echoed these sentiments calling the *Federalist* "the most important work in political science that has ever been written, or is likely ever to be written, in the United States."[40]

Others, like historian Bernard Bailyn, have cast serious doubt on these claims, stating that these essays do not constitute "an integrated, systematic treatise on basic principles of political theory produced in calm contemplation" as one might think.[41] He calls them "polemical essays directed to specific institutional proposals written in the heat of a fierce political battle.[42] This description notwithstanding, Bailyn agrees with the idea that these words are still impactful in our understanding of federalism because of the way the essays are perceived by others—that they are, in fact, representative of some cohesive body of political theory.[43] He does leave readers with a word of caution as to the relevance of these essays to the modern world, as he sees a tendency for scholars and politicians to rely too heavily on their content to solve problems of the modern era: "the authors of the *Federalist Papers* lived in a preindustrial world whose social and economic problems were utterly different from ours and whose social policies, in so far they had any, if implemented now would create chaos."[44]

The *Federalist Papers* address many topics, including why the current confederacy was not working, specifics about the separation of powers, the branches of government, and the issue of faction. With regard to the specific topic of federalism, we find as many questions as answers. There are a number of essays that touch on the issue of federalism, but no one essay in particular expounds upon its merits. In fact, we find a number of places where the meaning of the word federal is moderated and changed in ways to make it more amenable to a nationalist mindset. Any situation where the national perspective can come to call itself federal suggests a situation wherein the meaning of words is being manipulated to an extent to achieve a certain outcome. Certainly, the *Federalist Papers* were written from a distinct perspective and with a specific agenda, and we see that clearly as it pertains to the subject of federalism. The treatment of federalism in this document has been called "a relatively weak, unenthusiastic, ambiguous defense, and not of federalism as such, but of certain federal elements in a Constitution primarily national."[45]

What is perhaps most noteworthy about the treatment of federalism in the *Federalist Papers* is the extent to which Hamilton and Madison work to transform its meaning into one that compromises the spirit of both federal and national forms of government. What they wish to call "federal" in a new sense is actually a combined or mixed system with both national and federal elements.[46] As one would assume, the emerging "anti-federalist" perspective was skeptical that such a mixed system would be capable of preserving state autonomy and that could persist at all as a governmental system.[47]

Federalism is dealt with specifically in some places and more broadly in others. One essay we can find federalism dealt with more specifically is

Federalist No. 9, in which Hamilton discusses the ways he believes the new political system will protect against faction. It is here that he begins to change the meaning of federalism from a relationship between the national government and the states to simply a reference to any political system wherein there exists "an association of two or more states into one state."[48] He goes on to explain: "The extent, modifications, and objects of federal authority are mere matters of discretion."[49] This represents a significant change in the meaning of federalism and reduces the question of authority to secondary status. This part of *Federalist* No. 9 is critical to this discussion, as it has been credited with shaping how we view and understand federalism today.[50] It has been suggested that this passage was written with the intent of misleading those early Americans who were trying to understand the founding principles and evaluate whether or not this proposed Constitution would advance those principles.[51] Whether or not this wordsmithing was done with intent to manipulate or clarify meaning, it does bring to our attention that this was a dynamic era with regard to ideas and concepts and how they were articulated into a new American vocabulary.[52] Federalism had previously been understood primarily as a way to formalize state sovereignty as part of a confederate agreement, and that is not how the founders intended to execute a federal system. The plan advanced by the Constitution and explained in the *Federalist Papers* was a "new federalism" that actually represented a system that provided a role for the states and the national government.[53] It was not until the establishment and acceptance of this new conception of federalism that the debate developed between the Federalists and Anti-Federalists as we now understand it. The Federalists took the position of promoting the national government in this equation, and the Anti-Federalists then promoted the idea of "divided sovereignty" to strengthen the role of the states.[54]

Understandably, the meaning of federalism was confusing to many, since the meaning was actively changed in the course of this debate.[55] Neither the *Federalist Papers* nor the Constitution promote or develop a traditionally federal arrangement.[56] The term was redefined to match what the Constitution actually did provide for: a system that delegates power to the national government and reserves power to the states. The strategy was to change the meaning of federal to the point whereby the Constitution could be defended as creating a "federal" system.[57]

There is an interesting exercise in isolating and defining "federal" and "national" in *Federalist* No. 39, where Madison sets out to directly address the controversy by establishing how to determine the federal versus national characteristics of a government. First, he contends that one must determine the sources from which its ordinary powers are drawn, the operation of those powers, the extent of the powers, and the authority by which future changes are introduced. He determines that the foundation (the Constitution) is a federal constitution; as to the sources of power, Madison finds the House to be national, the Senate to be federal, and the presidency to be both, as the sources are mixed—both federal and national; the operation of the government is national not federal, but because of the limited jurisdiction over specific enumerated powers, the extent of power cannot be called national; and finally, the amendment process is not completely national or federal.[58] The final assessment, per *Federalist* No. 39, is that the proposed Constitution is "neither a national nor a federal Constitution, but a composition of both."[59]

As part of the justification for this new hybrid version of federalism, we can find commentary that seeks to discredit the previous definition. *Federalist* No. 37 expresses concern that there is no good model of federalism to build on.[60] The main problem with any prior attempts at federal government is that federalism is fundamentally flawed, and the solution in future applications is to make a system that is, in fact, less federal.[61] The *Federalist* is largely critical of federalism, and one is hard pressed to find many examples of federalism being referenced as a positive.[62] The main praise of federalism is that it can provide a path for popular control, "a barrier against central tyranny," and a way to "preserve local administration for local purposes."[63]

Implicit in any discussion of federalism is sovereignty, and we can find many references to sovereignty in the *Federalist Papers*. This is of particular importance to this discussion, because it is the handling of sovereignty that makes the "new federalism" of the Constitution possible. It had been long since established that, by definition, sovereignty was an indivisible concept. If sovereignty is about having ultimate governing authority, then it does not make sense for multiple levels of government to have a legitimate claim to it. There was prior agreement that sovereignty was "absolute and exclusive."[64] The *Federalist* verifies this understanding of sovereignty and agrees that dual sovereignty does not make sense. Rather, in this proposed system, it would be the people who are sovereign. The existence of popular sovereignty would make it possible to have governmental authority executed on multiple levels as long as they each derive their authority from the people.[65]

In the presence of lawmaking on multiple levels, Martin Diamond explains in "The Federalist's View of Federalism," we must distinguish between a league and a government, and that we must have a national government that is empowered by the people not the states. Therefore, legislation at the national level must be over individual citizens, not the states collectively, and then subsequently, legislation at the state level would be over the residents of those particular states.[66] This arrangement provides for a national government with power over the individual citizens, but with limitations, and that would work concurrently with state legislative action. This is conceptually different from a unitary system with consolidated power.[67] This idea of concurrent use of authority of both a limited national government and the state governments emerges as a key characteristic of the "new federalism" in the Constitution, or as federalism now understood.[68]

From a logistical standpoint, the *Federalist Papers* also sought to address the practical matter of how the national government would relate to the states and the general topic of intergovernmental dynamics. Throughout the cumulative document, one can find a few ways in which the authors addressed the desire for this information: through a description of state power, the importance of national power, and the value of separate powers. This last component relates to another important relationship: federalism and individual liberty.

First, the Anti-Federalists were sensitive to the possibility of an undesirably dominant national government. One Federalist strategy to address this concern was to assert that dominant *state* governments were far more likely based on the power they would be accorded by the Constitution. *Federalist* Nos. 16 and 17 were utilized to this end. One argument is based on structural intention and one based on history. First, the *Federalist* argued that "the federal government was designed as a creation of the states; it would depend on the states for its existence"[69] As evidence of this dependence, we find the states in charge of presidential elections, staffing of the Senate, collection of federal taxes, and of course, the retention of "all of the rights and powers not specifically delegated to the federal government."[70] The idea of concurrent jurisdiction could work if the national government perceived its success and survival as being contingent on the stability and integrity of the state governments. Undermining state authority would be a way of the national government undercutting its own potential, and that would not be beneficial.[71]

Second, there is a case made for historical precedent among other federal (but perhaps truly confederal) systems and the observation that in many cases it had been the states that had been dominant over the central government.[72] The argument proceeds that it is actually of more concern to "ensure the power of the national government" as opposed to worrying about the state governments.[73] Beyond these points, Madison uses *Federalist* Nos. 45 and 46 to speak of the important role the states will play due to the larger amount of power reserved to the states than delegated to the national government and for the natural attachment and preference the people will have for the states. He does believe that "the states will remain significant centers of political power."[74]

Naturally, the *Federalist* also takes the opportunity to expound on the necessity of national power and how this would be relevant to the intergovernmental dynamics of this new government. The primary argument in *Federalist* No. 15 rests on the need to bring the individual into a role of political relevance for the long-term health and viability of any political system. Absent a direct relationship between the individual citizen and the national government, a country will suffer through ineffective governance and the constant threat of conflict or even rebellion as there are no ways to moderate the conflicts that can arise when the states (one or many) and the national government disagree. The creation of a national government establishes a formal relationship with and a political role for the individual citizen. Further, individuals can more easily be held accountable than states if there is ever any breach in a political obligation. Lastly, individuals are generally better behaved than groups of people. Allowing individuals to function on their own in a meaningful political capacity can only serve to benefit a political system and elevate the level of behavior of all involved.

Finally, the *Federalist Papers* explain how the separation of powers will create balance within the government and with the role federalism plays there. The federalism described in the *Federalist* was arguably one of concurrence, in that the presence of two levels of authority was intended to reinforce one another, not challenge or negate the other.[75] The health and functionality of this relationship would be dependent on a clear delineation of power and specificity of roles, and this was the intent of the proposed Constitution.[76] Specifically, Madison saw these differing roles arising from the differing relationships each level of government would have with the people: "'The federal and state governments,' wrote Madison in The *Federalist*, 'are in fact but different agents and trustees of the people, constituted with different powers, and designed for different purposes.'"[77]

A final related topic is individual liberty and the role that federalism could or would play in protecting it. As noted in *Federalist* Nos. 9 and 10, there was concern about how to protect minority interests from being dominated by majorities. Since the general belief was that factions were more likely in smaller spaces, Madison actually saw the state legislatures as the main threat to individual liberty and wanted there to be a "constitutional negative" in which the national legislature could effectively veto state legislation. He thought that national politicians would be more moderate and diverse in their views and could balance the more passionate temperaments of the state politicians. The proposal of a "constitutional negative" did not make it through the Convention, however, and Madison's concern for minority rights led him to write *Federalist* No. 10 in which he argued that the complexity and tensions of the new government would have a "moderating effect" on faction.[78] The relationship between federalism and liberty is also mentioned in *Federalist* No. 51, as Publius argues that both republican and federal principles would serve to protect minority interests: "Whilst all authority in it will be derived from and dependent on the society, the society itself will be broken into so many parts, interests, and classes of citizens, that the rights of individuals, or of the minority, will be in little danger from interested combinations of the majority."[79]

When considering American federalism, the natural progression is from "what" is to "why?" At this point, it is clear that federalism was not the simple choice, nor was it clearly defined, or necessarily agreed upon by the political elites of the day. Conceptually, it was challenging to establish, and it required a fair amount of linguistic and mental gymnastics to transform it into something that could be implemented in any kind of meaningful way, so why? Federalism was not the first choice of the Founders as the United States was initially established as a confederation.[80] So, why federalism for the United States?

WHY FEDERALISM?

On the surface, the choice of federalism seems to be the result of "necessity (the existence of the states) and theory (the belief that a republic could not easily be maintained across a large territory)."[81] There are so many questions as to how this scenario developed in the first place. The question of "why?" is so established in the literature on federalism that we have the benefit of multiple approaches to learn from.[82] In her 2010 book *The Ideological Origins of American Federalism*, Alison LaCroix moved the literature on federalism forward significantly by returning the conversation to ideology and the role it played in the development of ideology. She situates her work in the federalism literature by providing a helpful and concise overview of the prevailing approaches, differentiating them both on their content and timeframe foci.[83] Interestingly, the approach that one takes to understanding the origins and development of American federalism leads to different ideas about how the Constitutional Convention fits into this process. If one subscribes to an institutional or republican understanding, the Convention is the culmination of a federalism building process, while constitutional law views the Convention as the beginning of federalism.[84]

LaCroix's objective was to reconnect with the ideological perspective on the development of federalism in a way that did not challenge these other approaches but rather moved the discussion forward in a more comprehensive way. Her work refocuses the discussion on the role of ideology in determining the "meaning and significance of federalism in the founding and ratification periods and places the Philadelphia convention in the broader context of federal thought in the late eighteenth century."[85] LaCroix's approach views the development and application of federalism at the Constitutional Convention as an ideological exercise in which the concept of multilayered government was converted into a plan of action. She makes it possible to embrace both an idea-based and experience-based origin story for federalism. I find the use of ideology in the discussion of "why federalism?" to be extraordinarily useful and wish to take this a step further by applying a typology used in the study of ideology to our pursuit of understanding the development of American federalism.

Ideological Federalism

In *Political Ideologies and the Democratic Ideal*, Ball et al. provide an extraordinarily useful tool for studying ideologies. They propose a definition of ideology that encompasses "four functions" in order to identify whether or not a body of thought is truly an ideology: explanatory, evaluative, orientative, and programmatic.[86] According to Ball et al., any ideology will explain social, political, and economic conditions; provide criteria to determine when these conditions are good or bad; create an orientation or sense of identity; and tell its adherents exactly what they need to do. This final component is the action piece and, according to Ball et al., is the component that is particularly necessary for a body of thought to be considered an ideology. There must be an action component. When we consider the question of "why federalism?" and wish to build a more comprehensive explanation, the application of ideology to this discussion is useful and relevant. While Ball et al. do not use their four functions in this way (and do not identify federalism as an ideology), I would like to apply them in order to guide our discussion and understanding of "why?"

The first function of an ideology is the explanatory function. Ideologies provide an explanation for social, political, and economic conditions to help their audience make sense of the world around them and to provide an explanation for why things are the way they are. There are three main components to the federal explanation of conditions: First, it is difficult to organize and administer large countries due to the challenge of distance and diverse populations; second, people are inclined by nature to organize locally to seek solutions to identified public issues; and third, without institutionalized practices, including those intended to establish procedural and jurisdictional boundaries and to mediate disputes, national governments or state governments can grow too powerful.

First, there is the difficulty that must be overcome in organizing and governing a large country. This is a fact that early Americans of the founding era were well aware of from their colonial experiences, as they had been struggling to find a "workable allocation of authority between the center and the peripheries, between the national government and the states."[87] In fact, prior to 1764, the British Empire functioned in practice much by federal principles.[88] Historian Andrew McLaughlin, in his article "The Background of American Federalism," finds there were key components of a federal system as late as 1760 by way of the clearly established national authority in the British government, the lack of significant Parliamentary legislation over internal colonial affairs, and the colonial control over local matters, such as taxation for internal expenses, the maintenance of colonial representative bodies, and local trade.[89] These arrangements had developed because they made sense and they overcame the issues of distance and diversity.

The second component of federalism's explanatory function is the natural inclination of people to organize locally to solve public problems. Again, it was the colonial experience that demonstrated this fact to the founders. Federalism requires people to engage in "self-governing communities of relationships" and this had already happened on its own "in the townships of New England."[90] Further evidence of these organically occurring relationships and "patterns of order" can later be found in other colonial organizational documents and ultimately in the founding documents of the United States, including the Articles of Confederation and the Constitution.[91] The idea that people would be naturally predisposed to local governance and could also reconcile that level of governance with the presence of authoritative legislation on multiple levels did not originate at the Constitutional Convention but rather was something that had been contemplated and practiced in the years before.[92]

The third component of the explanatory function of federalism deals with the role of institutionalized practices. Specifically, without institutionalized practices, including those intended to establish procedural and jurisdictional boundaries and to mediate disputes, national governments or state governments can grow too powerful. The primary example from the American colonial experience, of course, was the expansion of national power over the colonies. However, this unchecked growth and imposition of power can develop at both the national and subnational level if there is nothing in place to stop it. The British Empire has been identified as "a functioning federal system without a sustaining federal ideology."[93] When the politics of the era changed (namely after the Seven Years' War), there was nothing to stop the British government from consolidating and centralizing power when the leadership determined that such a move would be in the Empire's best interest.[94] The British intent was never to actually divide sovereignty in any meaningful way, and was more centered on administrative decentralization that made logistical sense.[95] Without some type of institutionalized power distribution and constraints on how power is used, either side can begin to act based on their own self-interest rather than in the best interest of the intergovernmental relationship between the two (or more) levels of government.

These three components come together to illustrate how federalism served as an explanation for conditions as they were at the time of the founding, but there is also a need to know exactly how to evaluate those conditions. The second function of an ideology is the evaluative function wherein the ideology provides criteria upon which one can evaluate when conditions are good and when they are bad. For federalism as an ideology, conditions are good when there is some voice given to multiple layers of governance. This division of governmental authority need not be perfectly even, and it most likely will not be. However, each layer of government must have authority over some specific areas determined by geography, subject matter, or some combination thereof. Conditions are bad when sovereignty is limited to just one level of government, whether the sovereignty resides at the national level or at the subnational level.

During both the late colonial and founding eras, the establishment of balance between the national and subnational governments was a primary political goal. The objective had been to build a system that could allow for and sustain both a national government and also subnational governments that could reasonably and independently manage their own internal affairs.[96] This objective was based on the premise that such a balance would yield the most efficient and effective policy outcomes. The idea was to have the "best of both worlds," in which the national government could the "energetic center" that a viable and strong state needs while also protecting local autonomy and identity.[97]

Conversely, from the perspective of federalism, conditions are arguably bad when sovereignty is consolidated to any one level of government. Again, we can see this from a historical view of the colonial experience in which the colonists were offended and troubled by the British interpretation of sovereignty as an absolute concept beginning in the 1760s.[98] The colonists were not upset at the premise of the British government having *any* sovereignty, but they rejected the idea of the British government having *all* of the authority to make binding decisions.[99] The colonists thought the idea of finding a way to create a type of procedural boundary or guideline that might lead to power-sharing was not only possible but would be a positive move.[100] From the federal perspective, the absence of this possibility and the persistence of consolidated national power would be a bad, or undesirable, condition. Moving forward to the ratification debates, advocates for the Constitution would have to make an argument that identified why any consolidation of power was a bad condition, and in their case, were tasked with explaining why the consolidation of power at the state level had not worked.[101] There was also an argument to be made by the Anti-Federalists who warned of an overly powerful national government that would lead to "hardship and inequity" for American citizens.[102] In addition to raising awareness of the dangers of consolidated power, there was work to be done, by the Federalists in particular, to present their concept of federalism and to argue why the granting of authority to multiple levels of government would serve as a path to liberty and a better condition.[103]

The third function ideologies perform is to provide an orientative function whereby they provide their audience with an orientation, or identity, to help them determine their place in their local, regional, or global community. Federalism as an ideology provides individuals with a multi-faceted identity. First, people are to identify as sovereign beings in the political system wherein the government acts at their behest and in line with the wishes they express, primarily through elections.[104] Second, people are to see themselves as residents of the state they live in and have the expectation that their state of residence and the individuals elected to conduct its business will be accountable to the views and preferences of those residents. Finally, people also have a national identity as citizens of the United States. As such, they will have the expectation that their country and the people elected to conduct its business will do so in accordance with the wishes of the people. This complex identity allows individuals to feel empowered in their delegation of authority to multiple levels of government and also to have affection and loyalty to all levels of government.

This notion of ideological orientation goes a long way to addressing issues and tensions surrounding the topic of sovereignty. The sovereignty controversy has largely been about what it is, how it creates accountability, and in how many ways it can exist at one time.[105] This orientation provides answers to these questions and, better yet, is thought to be a naturally occurring view of identity among early Americans, as opposed to something that had to be imposed.[106] This political identity did not need to be created, but rather it needed to be identified and institutionalized into political structures and processes. That is what American federalism does. Perhaps most importantly, this orientation provides the basis upon which Federalists and Anti-Federalists could formalize their common ground: a belief in the regulation and protection of the individual and the use of limited, republican government to those ends.[107]

Lastly, and most importantly, ideologies offer a programmatic function. This function is the plan of action that the people are to implement based upon the explanatory, evaluative, and orientative functions. For federalism as an ideology, the program is a government in which sovereignty resides at multiple levels or is at least distributed to multiple levels on the basis of popular sovereignty and is divided or shared in some way. Federalism can be more complexly defined as an organizationally driven power distribution developed as an ideological plan of action that resulted from a specific understanding of political conditions, a normative evaluation of these conditions, and a specific political identity orientation that were the result of historical experience and circumstance both in the colonies and abroad, European political theory, and a desire among the founders to reconcile past colonial issues with the forward momentum of a new republic.

One of the main political goals of the founding era was finding a way to transform the idea of a federal system into a functional system of governance.[108] This required an acceptance of multi-tiered authority, or multiplicity of lawmaking bodies, the formal delegation (and reservation) of powers in a constitution, and the development of a mediation process.[109] All of this was predicated upon a new understanding of popular sovereignty and the role it would play in a federal system.[110] The federal program, as set forth in the Constitution, provides guidance on matters of both the creation of subject-matter boundaries and the possibility of concurrent jurisdiction.[111] This new federal system, and specifically federalism as a programmatic function, would be both national and federal and contain compromises and flexibility to best meet the needs of the people and their many political identities.[112]

BUT THEN, HOW?

In the pursuit of understanding American federalism, the final question we must ask is: how? How were federal principles ultimately institutionalized in the Constitution? This question is more complicated that it may initially seem, as the founders did not include specific language referencing federalism in the Constitution. There is no section on federalism explaining its implementation nor is there any direct reference to it as a mode of distributing political power. Notably, the concept of federalism as a standalone topic was far more prevalent in the ratification debate that occurred subsequent to actually drafting the document. It is not particularly clear that the concept was vetted as thoroughly prior to the debate.[113] Contrary to modern assumptions about American federalism, there is evidence that the founders themselves— Madison specifically—were skeptical of any real balance between state and national authority or the idea that the Constitution would be able to address or restrain potential power grabs or related problems on either side.[114]

Madison and Hamilton had created arguments to justify the role of the national government and to modify the concept of federalism to accommodate a more activist role for the national government. These efforts created a certain response from Anti-Federalists who continued to see challenges in these new and changing interpretations of sovereignty. The idea of having multiple "supreme legislative power(s)" did not make any sense from a sound political science perspective.[115]

The main arguments of the Anti-Federalists centered on the challenge to the concept of divided sovereignty. How could both the state legislatures and a national congress be sovereign? Could this be a manipulation that would ultimately lead to power consolidation and the demise of state sovereignty? At the Convention debates, James Wilson made the argument that the Anti-Federalists weren't wrong about the concept of sovereignty, but they were wrong about who they thought had it. The new Constitution would not grant sovereignty to either level of government, for sovereignty resided with the people. No level of government could ever become more powerful than the people would want it to be.[116]

The Constitution contains instructions on how power is to be allocated without specifically calling the allocation "federal." Federalism, and specifically American federalism, refers to a general concept with competing and unclear definitions. Simply calling the American government "federal" would not have accomplished as much as just laying out how the powers would be allocated in a way consistent with at least one founding understanding of what federalism actually meant. The establishment of federalism further rested upon the incorporation of a meaningful role for the people so that they could exercise their sovereignty in a way that would keep both levels of government accountable. In the words of historian Gordon Wood: "A consolidated government could never result unless the people desired one."[117] The federalism contained in the Constitution and explained in the *Federalist* could only be made palatable to its detractors by centering sovereignty upon the people, empowering them to elect representatives, and encouraging them to hold those representatives accountable on the state and national level.[118] It was the balance between those who had optimism for the strength and viability of the national government with those who believed in the effectiveness and relevance of state and local government that resulted in the acceptance and implementation of American federalism.[119]

Unfortunately, even after one develops a general understanding of this debate, the Constitution can be an unwieldly tool to manage and implement federalism. Since the document does not clear spell out the division between state and national power, federalism became and continues to be a course of conflict and dispute.[120] The nature of federalism as a product of "ingenious and expedient compromises" makes it very difficult to simply point to one "single, logical blueprint for federalism in the Convention debates or the Constitution.[121] As a result, we shall point our fingers at as many things as we must to figure out in which constitutional phrasing this federalism lies.

Federalism in the U.S. Constitution

Generally speaking, American federalism is thought to have shaped the political landscape such that the states can manage their day-to-day affairs, the national political scene can accommodate and has interest in state issues, and the national government can maintain sovereignty over national matters.[122] The application of a broad nationalism supported leaving a power to tax, the power to regulate commerce, and to provide for the national defense to the national government.[123] The Constitution also contains provisions for state power so that the states can tend to "governing everyday American life."[124] A focused review of the U.S. Constitution will provide the details of how these powers are distributed. With regard to the powers available in the Constitution, we speak in terms of the powers *delegated* to the national government and those powers *reserved* to the states.

With regard to national power, the Constitution contains different types of power: expressed power, implied power, and inherent power. Expressed powers are those contained in Article 1, Section 8 of the Constitution. This section lists twenty-seven powers that Congress may specifically exercise. Further, the national government is empowered with implied powers. Implied powers are created by the Necessary and Proper Clause, contained in the same section. This clause allows Congress to "make all laws which shall be necessary and proper for carrying into execution the foregoing powers"[125] This means that any powers that can be tangentially linked to any of the listed powers can be protected as constitutional exercises of national power. That national government also has inherent powers or powers that "are necessary to ensure the nation's integrity and survival as a political unit.[126] These powers are drawn from broadly worded constitutional language that suggests members of the national government are responsible for the general welfare of this country. These powers have been established over time through the practice of American governance. Common examples of inherent powers are regulating immigration and the ability to acquire land.[127]

An additional clause that was considered an important "win" for broad nationalists is the Supremacy Clause contained in Article VI. This clause states that "this Constitution, and the Laws of the United States which shall be made in Pursuance thereof; and all Treaties made, or which shall be made, under the Authority of the United States, shall be the supreme Law of the Land"[128] In practice, this means that if any state or local law comes into conflict with a national law, the national law will stand and the state or local law will be struck down. This clause preserves the national government's power over the states if they come into conflict.

Even with these generous provisions for national power, the Constitution does reserve a number of powers to the states along with opportunities to participate in and influence politics at the national level, including equal representation in the Senate, a role in selecting the president by way of the Electoral College, and a role in amending the Constitution.[129] In fact, the states' role in the amendment process is so important that the process has even been likened to a "hostage" situation wherein the process is not functional without state cooperation.[130]

Beyond these examples, we can see general references to the reservation of powers to the states in the Constitution. One of the clearest examples is the Tenth Amendment which was agreed to during the ratification process, though not formally added until afterward. This amendment formally states that any power that is not specifically delegated to the national government by the Constitution is reserved to the states. The Tenth Amendment opened to the door to what are called "police powers" that can be carried out by state governments. Police powers refer generally to a state's ability to manage its internal affairs, including matters of health, morals, safety, and general welfare of the people of that state.

Further, the Constitution provides for interstate relations, also called horizontal federalism, in which the states are permitted to work together in direct, collaborative relationships. Article IV of the Constitution speaks directly to the relationship among the states and contains the Full Faith and Credit Clause. This clause requires each state to honor every other state's public acts, records, and judicial proceedings. The Constitution also facilitates the creation of interstate compacts, which are agreements "among two or more states to regulate the use or protection of certain resources."[131]

Concurrent powers are also considered as a benefit for the states. The most common example of a concurrent power is the power of taxation, and both state and local governments and the national government are able to tax. The existence of this concurrent power leaves open the possibility that there may be instances when it is appropriate for states and localities to pass laws that are already addressed at the national level. While this does leave open plenty of room for conflict, it can also be seen as beneficial, in that federalism leaves open multiple planes on which to solve problems and address public issues.

While these references to the Constitution may not represent an easy "blueprint" for federalism, per se, they do allow us to see into the overall plan for national and state powers. Perhaps it would have been easier to understand had the founders provided more explicit language regarding the presence of federalism in this new political system. However, it would most likely have been infinitely more difficult to broker a final deal between the Federalists (favoring broad nationalism) and the Anti-Federalists (favoring narrow nationalism). This treatment of the issue allows enough ambiguity in interpretation, that even after ratification both sides had reason to believe that the Constitution could support their position. In fact, in the American experience, we have seen both sides come out ahead at varying points in history.

The what, why, and how of American federalism provides us with a starting point to explore how federalism developed after the ratification of the Constitution. There is no doubt that these are difficult questions to answer, particularly if an additional goal is to provide some representative overview of the ways they have been addressed. However, understanding the complicated and competing terminology, the politics of the founding era, and the various approaches to understanding why and how federalism was implemented enhance our ability to appreciate the concept. This information allows us the opportunity to develop a more thorough understanding of federalism that will ultimately facilitate our assessment of the relationship between federalism and individual rights.

NOTES

1. Murrin, "1787: The Invention of American Federalism," 21.
2. Robertson, *Federalism and the Making of America*, 1.
3. Ibid.
4. LaCroix, *The Ideological Origins of American Federalism*, 1.
5. Reagan and Sanzone, *The New Federalism*, 16–19.
6. Sidlow and Henschen, *GOVT 10*.
7. Dye and Gaddie, *Politics in America*.
8. Edwards and Wattenberg, *Government in America: People, Politics, and Policy*.
9. Rubin and Feeley, "Federalism and Interpretation," 170, 179.
10. Ostrom, *The Meaning of American Federalism*, 70.
11. Krislov, "American Federalism as American Exceptionalism," 14; Storing, *What the Anti-Federalists Were For*, 15.
12. Krislov, "American Federalism as American Exceptionalism," 14.
13. Ibid., 11.
14. Ibid.
15. Ostrom, *The Meaning of American Federalism*, 78.
16. McLaughlin, "The Background of American Federalism," 215.
17. Rubin and Feeley, "Federalism and Interpretation," 171.
18. Ibid., 175.
19. Hail and Lange, "Federalism and Representation in the Theory of the Founding Fathers," 367.
20. Ibid., 372.
21. Ibid.
22. Beer, "The Rediscovery of American Federalism," 86.
23. Ibid.
24. Ibid.
25. Robertson, *Federalism and the Making of America*, 5; Tarr and Katz, "Introduction," 4; This premise will be the focus of Part 2.
26. Robertson, *Federalism and the Making of America*, 5; Tarr and Katz, *Federalism and Rights*.
27. Riker, *Federalism*, 14.
28. Orvis and Drogus, *Introducing Comparative Politics*, 264–265.
29. Rubin and Feeley, "Federalism and Interpretation," 188.
30. Kesler, "Introduction to The Federalist Papers," ix.
31. See Kesler's introduction for discussion over the choice of pseudonyms.
32. Kesler, "Introduction to The Federalist Papers," xiii.
33. Ibid., xiv.
34. Ibid., xii–xiii.

35. Ibid., xii.
36. Ibid.
37. Bailyn, *To Begin the World Anew*, 101.
38. Ostrom, *The Meaning of American Federalism*, 70.
39. Kesler, "Introduction to The Federalist Papers," ix.
40. Ibid.
41. Bailyn, *To Begin the World Anew*, 103.
42. Ibid.
43. Ibid.
44. Ibid., 104.
45. Diamond, "The Federalist's View of Federalism," 56.
46. Storing, *What the Anti-Federalists Were For*, 32.
47. Ibid.
48. Hamilton et al., "Federalist No. 9," *The Federalist Papers*.
49. Ibid.
50. Diamond, "The Federalist's View of Federalism," 24.
51. Ibid.
52. LaCroix, *The Ideological Origins of American Federalism*, 217.
53. Ibid., 217–218; Storing, *What the Anti-Federalists Were For*, 32–33.
54. Storing, *What the Anti-Federalists Were For*, 33.
55. Ibid.
56. Diamond, "The Federalist's View of Federalism," 22.
57. Ibid., 33.
58. Hamilton et al., "Federalist No. 39," *The Federalist Papers*; Diamond, "The Federalist's View of Federalism," 35–37.
59. Hamilton et al., "Federalist No. 39," *The Federalist Papers*; Diamond, "The Federalist's View of Federalism," 41.
60. Diamond, "The Federalist's View of Federalism," 40.
61. Ibid.
62. Diamond, "The Federalist's View of Federalism," 51; Ostrom, *The Meaning of American Federalism*, 75.
63. Diamond, "The Federalist's View of Federalism," 53; Diamond further correctly points out that this third "advantage" really speaks more to decentralization than federalism (56).
64. Bailyn, *To Begin the World Anew*, 115.
65. Ibid.
66. Diamond, "The Federalist's View of Federalism," see also *Federalist* Nos. 15 and 39.
67. Ostrom, *The Meaning of American Federalism*, 85.
68. Ibid.
69. Bailyn, *To Begin the World Anew*, 114.
70. Ibid.; U.S. Const. amend. X.
71. Wood, *The Creation of the American Republic, 1776–1787*, 529.
72. Diamond, "The Federalist's View of Federalism," 43.
73. Ibid.

74. Ibid., 48.

75. Bailyn, *To Begin the World Anew*, 120.

76. Ibid.

77. Wood, *The Creation of the American Republic, 1776–1787*, 546.

78. Bailyn, *To Begin the World Anew*, 123.

79. Hamilton et al., "Federalist No. 51," *The Federalist Papers*; Diamond, "The Federalist's View of Federalism," 61.

80. Ostrom, *The Meaning of American Federalism*, 77.

81. LaCroix, *The Ideological Origins of American Federalism*, 2.

82. Ibid., 5; Beyond these approaches, there have been many efforts contained in the literature of political science, history, economics, and others to explain the origins of the United States' Constitution and its principal components. This portion of the chapter should not be construed as an exhaustive treatment of the topic but rather a framework to understand the development and acceptance of a federal structure.

83. LaCroix, *The Ideological Origins of American Federalism*, 5.

84. Ibid.

85. Ibid.

86. Ball et al., *Political Ideologies and the Democratic Ideal*, 5.

87. Greene, *Peripheries and Center*, 198.

88. McLaughlin, "The Background of American Federalism," 215.

89. Ibid., 216.

90. Ostrom, *The Meaning of American Federalism*, 57.

91. Ibid.; LaCroix, *The Ideological Origins of American Federalism*, 20–21.

92. LaCroix, *The Ideological Origins of American Federalism*, 101.

93. Murrin, "1787: The Invention of American Federalism," 21.

94. Ibid., 21, 26.

95. Ibid., 22.

96. Greene, *Peripheries and Center*, 198.

97. Ibid., 206–207.

98. LaCroix, *The Ideological Origins of American Federalism*, 37.

99. Ibid., 95.

100. Ibid., 103.

101. Bailyn, *The Ideological Origins of the American Revolution*, 351.

102. Storing, *What the Anti-Federalists Were For*, 15–16.

103. Bailyn, *The Ideological Origins of the American Revolution*, 351.

104. Murrin, "1787: The Invention of American Federalism," 36.

105. LaCroix, *The Ideological Origins of American Federalism*, 70.

106. Rubin and Feeley, "Federalism and Interpretation".

107. Storing, *What the Anti-Federalists Were For*, 5.

108. LaCroix, *The Ideological Origins of American Federalism*, 135.

109. Ibid., 9, 135.

110. Murrin, "1787: The Invention of American Federalism," 36.

111. LaCroix, *The Ideological Origins of American Federalism*, 175.

112. Storing, *What the Anti-Federalists Were For*, 12.

113. Wood, *The Creation of the American Republic, 1776–1787*, 525.

114. Ibid.
115. Ibid., 527.
116. Ibid., 530–531.
117. Ibid., 531.
118. Ibid., 545.
119. Robertson, *Federalism and the Making of America*, 22–23.
120. Ibid., 19.
121. Ibid., 31.
122. Ibid.
123. Ibid., 19.
124. Ibid., 31.
125. U.S. Constitution, art. I, sec. 8.
126. Sidlow and Henschen, *GOVT 10*, 55.
127. Ibid.
128. U. S. Const. Art. VI.
129. Robertson, *Federalism and the Making of America*, 2.
130. Krislov, "American Federalism as American Exceptionalism," 17.
131. Sidlow and Henschen, *GOVT 10*, 57.

SUGGESTED READINGS

Bailyn, Bernard. *The Ideological Origins of the American Revolution.* Cambridge, MA and London: The Belknap Press of Harvard University Press, 1967, 1992.

Hamilton, Alexander, James Madison and John Jay. *The Federalist Papers.* ed. Clinton Rossiter New York: New American Library, 1961.

LaCroix, Alison L. *The Ideological Origins of American Federalism.* Cambridge, MA: Harvard University Press, 2010.

Ostrom, Vincent. *The Meaning of American Federalism.* San Francisco, CA: ICS Press, 1991.

Robertson, David Brian. *Federalism and the Making of America.* New York and London: Routledge, 2012.

Chapter 2

American Federalism in Practice

If anything is clear about the practice of American federalism, it is that very little is clear. Or rather, every explanation on its own is clear, but when taken all together, things get a bit murky. While this chapter does not aspire to describe every one of these explanations, it does provide coverage of the dominant themes and perspectives. Some approaches to explaining federalism are historically based, while others are conceptually based. This is not unusual in the study of political science, and this chapter attempts to reflect that balance. Developing a familiarity with the practice of federalism in the United States will provide some further perspective in understanding what the founders were trying to accomplish, and it will also provide a broader foundation upon which we will build an understanding of individual rights, both in theory and practice.

The next steps forward after the ratification of the Constitution were challenging, as the people of the era still were not entirely sure what this power structure would look like or even what to call it.[1] What they could not have known then was the contentious role federalism would persistently play in American politics moving forward.[2] What they surely knew, however, was the confusion that already existed over the terminology used. The word "federal" had been used as a synonym for "confederal" and an antonym for "national" during the Constitutional Convention.[3] During the ratification debates, those who supported ratification (and thus a stronger basis of power for the national government) had snagged the term "Federalists" for themselves and left the proponents for states' rights with the term "Anti-Federalists."[4] To this day, we refer to the national government as the "federal" government, and so this shrewd move made long ago by the Federalists continues to shape our understanding of these key terms and confuse the matter of who was for what all of those years ago.[5]

Given this backstory, it comes as no surprise that the study and assessment of American federalism has been as varied as the scholars who have taken on these tasks. Many have accepted the challenge of describing federalism in practical terms that consider the experience of American federalism. One of the preeminent scholars of federalism, Daniel Elazar, made tremendous contributions in this regard. His understanding of federalism allocated power to the national government in a more conservative way, in that the national government need only be concerned with the exact powers delegated by the Constitution, any matters of national security and foreign affairs, any issues that arise "between the constituent entities of the federal system," and providing any and all needed support that the states require "in matters of national concern."[6] However, not all scholars would agree with this assessment, and the reality of American federalism has not always followed these standards. This chapter is the somewhat abbreviated story of what happened after ratification. The U.S. Constitution established a federal system, but it was only through practice that we would come to develop some understanding of what that meant.

American federalism has been described in so many ways, and these descriptions speak to the complexity of the concept. Elazar described federalism as a partnership and covenant among the levels of government designed to "foster a special unity among them."[7] Others have described federalism as a system that utilizes a "flexible wall of separation and cooperation between national and state authorities and structural protection for the states in the national system."[8] The Senate, Electoral College, and amendment processes are cited as examples of protections the states enjoy.[9] In order to unite these somewhat different images of how federalism has been characterized—both as a wall and a covenant, we can think of federalism as a method of power distribution that provides "unity without uniformity" in that it both unites the national government with the states while preserving room for flexible and unique problem-solving and decision-making.[10] As a model for federal systems moving forward, the founders created a system that connected federalism with democracy in an indelible way.[11]

Beyond these somewhat abstract descriptions, we can understand American federalism by way of its structural features: namely, a written Constitution that is the supreme law of the land, the existence of subnational political entities that each have legislative authority, some degree of divided or shared sovereignty among these levels of government, a role to play in law enforcement on each level, and courts empowered with judicial review to ensure compliance with constitutional principles.[12] These features were clear and understood at the founding. A general sense of the nature and structure of federalism gives us some basis for understanding the starting point for the implementation of American federalism. However, changing political culture over time would prove to be a challenge and source of stress on this system.[13]

The existence of federalism signals a division of sovereignty, but there is no idea or guarantee of that division being equal. The question of the exact balance of power between the national government and the states is another important piece of the puzzle in understanding the experience of American federalism. There is an argument to be made either way regarding which level of government enjoyed a greater share of sovereignty immediately after ratification. This ambiguity makes it difficult to sort out, however, and the uncertainty of the founding era has led to uncertainty in the modern era.[14] In *The Development of American Federalism,* William Riker wrote: "If the inventors themselves had understood exactly what they had invented, we could hope to answer these questions more easily."[15] They were mostly clear about the ends: protecting some understanding of liberty, establishing a stable and sustainable governmental system, and learning from past experience both as British colonies and as a fledgling confederacy.[16] The means, which we now know as federalism, ended up being a collection of "overlapping" powers and responsibilities that would create an unending source of conflict and a method for cooperation and coordination between the national government and the states.[17]

EARLY SUPREME COURT DECISIONS

These overlapping powers and the competitive environment that federalism created provided the Supreme Court with opportunities early on to establish powers for the national government and to mediate disputes between the national government and the states. These opportunities represent the beginning of the interpretive record of constitutional federalism. This role for the Supreme Court is counted as an "elemental constitutional foundation of federalism."[18] These early decisions would serve to reinforce the powerful position of the national government, suggesting a balance of power that tipped in its direction.

The first such case was *Marbury v. Madison,* decided in 1804. This case involved the creation of new judicial positions by Congress and the appointment of judicial officials by exiting President John Adams before the end of his term. When newly appointed Secretary of State, James Madison, declined to serve the appointment papers to William Marbury, a justice of peace appointee, Marbury petitioned the Supreme Court to compel delivery of the papers. Marbury's ability to directly appeal to the Supreme Court by way of original jurisdiction was provided by the Judiciary Act of 1789. This case became significant, not with regard to Marbury's outcome, but because the Supreme Court used this case to declare the Judiciary Act of 1789 unconstitutional. It found that this law went beyond the scope of permissible legislation regarding court jurisdiction and came into conflict with what the Constitution established as matters for original jurisdiction. This established the power of judicial review and would serve as the basis for mediating future constitutional disputes between the states and the national government.[19]

The 1819 case of *McCulloch v. Maryland* would require the Supreme Court to consider both the Supremacy Clause and the Necessary and Proper Clause when mediating a dispute between the national government and the state of Maryland.[20] After Congress created the Second National Bank in 1816, the state of Maryland levied taxes on banking transactions in the state, but the cashier for the Baltimore branch, Edwin McCulloch, would not pay them. The state court contended that the creation of the bank was unconstitutional, as it was not an enumerated power of Congress in the Constitution. The Supreme Court had to decide if Congress was in the bounds of its constitutional authority to create the bank in the first place, and if so, whether or not Maryland would be allowed to tax its operations. In a move that would advance the position of the national government, the Supreme Court ruled that Congress did have the constitutional authority to create the bank by way of the Necessary and Proper Clause, and that as such, Maryland was in violation of the Supremacy Clause by levying a tax as a consequence and a way of inhibiting lawful government action.

A third case from this early era that is important to the formalization of national power is the 1824 case of *Gibbons v. Ogden*.[21] This case involved the application of the Commerce Clause to an issue involving the national government and the state of New York. Thomas Gibbons, who was a steamboat operator with a federal coastal license, appealed to the Supreme Court when the state of New York had ruled that their regulation of ferry routes between New York and New Jersey superseded the authority of the national government. New York had granted a ferry route to Aaron Ogden, who had successfully sued Gibbons on those grounds in state court when Gibbons began servicing that route. The Supreme Court ruled that the Commerce Clause granted authority to the national government over interstate commerce, including steamboats. Thus, New York could not create laws that would control interstate navigation. This set an important precedent for the exclusive role the national government would play in the regulation of interstate commerce.

From these early decisions, it would appear that the balance of power was very much how Hamilton and Madison and other Federalists wanted it: tipped decisively in the direction of the national government. Of course, the story does not end here, and the overall objective of pulling together a coherent view of American federalism requires us to survey both the historical and conceptual literature.

STUDYING AMERICAN FEDERALISM: ERAS, EVENTS, AND DECISIONS

Over the course of the United States' history, there has been a succession of events and developments that have shaped the trajectory of American federalism. Among those include the Civil War and desegregation, the Great Depression and the New Deal legislative program, the development of communication technology, and globalization.[22] While these events and developments are commonly known, the connection to federalism is perhaps not as readily apparent. The circumstances that the American people find themselves in at any given point in time have influenced their expectations for governmental power—how it is allocated and exercised. The history of federalism reveals many situations that have resulted in the further strengthening of national power.[23] The Civil War is but one example of this. Where the Civil War began, however, and where it ended show a violent and dramatic struggle between those who wanted a stronger national government and those who believed the states' affairs should be left alone to allow the institution of slavery to persist.

Based on the early rulings of the Court, the constitutional power of the national government seemed to be prevailing over preferences for state power; however, not enough time had passed to truly establish this dominance to the extent of "lock-in" before the crisis of slavery emerged as a politically salient issue. In his 2000 article, "Federalism and Decentralization: Ownership Rights and the Superiority of Federalism," Albert Breton describes lock-in as the entrenched assignment of constitutional powers. The way constitutional powers are assigned or owned in a federal system is the product of both the prevailing conception of rights and also historical circumstances and events. As a result, the conception and distribution of power is subject to evolution and change over time. This process can fall into a condition of lock-in whereby tradition takes over as the prevailing influence and can discourage further change or progress and is most likely a pattern that is advantageous to one side.[24]

Had the tradition of national dominance been more established, the Southern states might not have felt so empowered to assert their claims of states' rights and ultimately secede from the Union. Breton contends that the stronger the tradition, the more consistent with the original understanding (in this case, a stronger national government), and the more stable the political system.[25] Due to the events of the Civil War, we can assume then that not enough citizens perceived there to be a strong tradition of national authority in place. This perception left the possibility open for the states to challenge the power of the national government. The "uncertainty regarding the nature of the ownership rights governing the division of constitutional powers between the federal government and the states" opened the door to a violent civil war.[26]

The success of the national government in settling this war over slavery and states' rights started the clock anew to find a "new normal" in balancing national power and state power. The ratification of the Thirteenth, Fourteenth, and Fifteenth Amendments represented a significant step in formalizing the power of the national government to determine the nature of rights for all citizens. The Fourteenth Amendment specifically provided the basis for equal treatment regardless of one's state of residence.[27] This also represented a very challenging time for those Americans who believed that the national government was now on a trajectory to violate states' rights in a number of policy areas. There was a sensitivity that the balance of power attempted through the Constitution was not balanced at all at this point in history. History tells us that, even with the Reconstruction Amendments in place, there was still a great deal of racism to contend with in the South and significant groupings of people across the spectrum who believed that federalism had suffered a substantive setback as a result of the Civil War. Decades later, we would see these exact concerns emerge in the 1896 case of *Plessy v. Ferguson*.[28]

This case involved a Louisiana state law entitled the "Separate Car Act," that mandated racial segregation on passenger rail cars. Based on the belief that the Fourteenth Amendment's Equal Protection Clause would invalidate any such law mandating segregation, Homer Plessy—a man who was one-eighth African American but qualified as black under state law—tested the law by taking a seat in a "whites only" car. He was arrested and his conviction was upheld at the state level. When the Supreme Court heard this case, the determination was made that, while the Fourteenth Amendment was intended to create equal protection of African Americans before the law, it was not intended to enforce any notion of social equality or engagement between the two races. The decision denied Congress of the ability to enforce the Fourteenth Amendment beyond a very limited interpretation of legal equality.[29] Further, it was determined that racial segregation alone did not constitute discrimination as long as the accommodation provided to each race was comparable. This rationale established the Separate but Equal Doctrine that held for almost sixty years.

Another significant historical event that shaped the expectations and reality of federalism in the United States was the Great Depression and resulting New Deal legislative plan. The stock market crashed on October 29, 1929, and led to one of the most devastating downturns the American economy had experienced. The previously localized efforts to address poverty were not adequate to deal with the scope and magnitude of American poverty at this juncture. When elected by a decisive majority in 1932, Franklin Roosevelt came into office with the objective of providing relief to the American people and the American economy. He is credited with accomplishing that through an aggressive agenda built from legislation and executive orders.[30] The time from the New Deal era until the 1950s has been described as the "high point" of cooperative federalism in the United States.[31] The magnitude of this national crisis required a cooperative response and was able to unify both national and state authorities behind a number of programs that needed both national and state funding and administration to succeed. Examples include the Federal Emergency Relief Administration, the Social Security Act, and the Fair Labor Standards Act.

Described as the "last distinctive period of American federalism," the years covering the civil rights era, the Great Society, and beyond into the 1970s, featured continued growth of national power that was upheld by Supreme Court.[32] Beginning in the 1950s and continuing into the 1960s, the Supreme Court took opportunities to expand the role of the national government in a number of policy areas, including criminal justice and race relations.[33] There was a general political awareness of the level of cooperation needed for the successful implementation of policy, and this awareness was institutionalized in several ways. One example was the creation of the U.S. Advisory Commission on Intergovernmental Relations (ACIR), which would go on to produce numerous insightful and prescient reports and recommendations over the next several decades.[34] This cooperative spirit helped with the financial challenges of implementing policy at the state and local level, and it also worked very well to address the major issues of this era, including racism, poverty, and the environment.[35]

A highly impactful court case from this era that embodied the spirit of nationally led action on policy issues was *Brown v. Board of Education* decided in 1954.[36] This case overturned the precedent set in *Plessy v. Ferguson* and decided that racial segregation, even in the presence of "equal" facilities, did represent discrimination and was a violation of the Fourteenth Amendment. This decision thereby made racial segregation illegal and unconstitutional. Unfortunately, enforcement was a long and slow process and showed how damaging local control could be for sensitive social issues.[37]

Due to the specific nature of civil rights issues and the division between the states on issue of segregation and discrimination, state autonomy and the desire to preserve it because linked to racism and support for discriminatory practices.[38] In the case of civil rights, it was impossible to make an argument for keeping meaningful authority at the local level without making an argument for racist policies. The national policy was morally right, and the local policies were morally wrong. National power was used as a tool to overcome state and local authorities who were depriving citizens of their constitutional rights.[39] The passage of the Civil Rights Act of 1964 would further reinforce this idea that the national government had to step in to right the wrongs at the state and local level. Overcoming this distinction would be a challenge for states' rights advocates in the years following this era.

The mid-1960s saw the development of President Lyndon Johnson's Great Society legislative plan which included the creation of the Medicare and Medicaid programs. Both of these programs were created to facilitate health-care coverage for vulnerable populations. Like the civil rights policy of the era, these programs became another source of tension between the national government and the states.[40] After several decades of national dominance and nationally led cooperative policy plans, the desire to shift power more deliberately back to the states began to gain momentum.[41] This shift was encouraged by a number of other circumstantial factors in the economy, political culture, and global politics that were all pointing to less governmental action and intervention.

Before this movement could gain too much momentum, however, the national government again took the lead in a policy area, this time with environmental policy. The nature of this agenda required a level of cooperation as the other social policies had.[42] The arguments for national action on behalf of environmental needs followed a logic that had been used with other social matters: the issue was an important public matter that could not be easily contained to one geographic jurisdiction, be it a city or state, and the national government already had the constitutional authority to regulate commerce.[43] Most pollution came by way of production externalities that industries were not taking responsibility for, so regulation of those externalities would very easily link to the concept of business regulation. From the perspective of cooperative federalism, national involvement on environmental policy made a great deal of sense, though there would be pushback for decades to come.

The era beginning in the 1970s and ending with the September 11, 2001, terrorist attacks can be more difficult to describe because there is not one unifying theme as we have seen in earlier eras. There are a number of factors that impacted the way federalism functioned during this time, including a growing desire to reduce the role of government combined with the reality that the national government had become quite involved in the regulation and administration of a number of policy areas. It has proven much easier for the role of the national government to grow than to be scaled back, and so any call to make cuts immediately raises the questions of how and where the reductions should take place. While cooperative federalism was not satisfactory to all, there was no doubt that by the 1970s American federalism was very nation centered. This orientation would impact the trends in federalism even as the preferences of American political culture began to shift. These impacts can be identified with regard to the persistent role of cooperation in federalism, the emphasis on intergovernmental relationships, and the idea of coercion.

It has been observed that the overall cooperative nature of federalism declined in the 1970s and 1980s as the national government engaged more actively in preempting state laws.[44] Even when federal statutes were used to limit state regulations (and thus, in theory attempting to reduce the role of government in private business), they represented a more aggressive stance in favor of national power rather than leaving the state legislatures to determine the regulatory environment appropriate for their own states. Nevertheless, the idea of cooperation continued to appeal as a feature of intergovernmental relations as it would at least keep the states in the conversation. Cooperation in this environment has been described as "defensive" on the part of the states as they worked to "accommodate the inevitable without caving in to the insufferable."[45] The national government would continue to lead on policy through the 1970s as the states became more responsible for administration and implementation.[46] American federalism continued to rely on nation-centered intergovernmental relations through the 1980s but to a lesser extent.[47] This focus on keeping the peace via balancing intergovernmental relationships represented a more serious issue for federalism and a significant concession that had taken place decades before.[48]

The enumeration of national powers in the Constitution was no longer viewed as an obstacle to exercising national authority in a wide range of policy areas. Both the courts and American political culture had shown to be quite tolerant of this expansion of power over the previous decades. Even as citizens began disengaging from party politics in the 1970s, their representatives in the federal government continued to feel empowered to make policy in a great many areas.[49] As the power of these politicians grew, so also grew their disconnection from the state and local officials due to the breakdown of the party organization and its ability to connect politicians across the levels of government.[50] The federalism of this era allowed for the assertion of national power and influence but did not eliminate the possibility for state and localities to grow in their power as well. The challenge of this, however, is that growth was now expected to happen at the behest of the national government, not the request of the states, and this could certainly be viewed as a compromise of federal principles.[51]

At the beginning of the 1990s, federalism was still viewed as more nation centered than state-centered, though not as activist as it had been a few decades earlier.[52] As the decade progressed, the backlash against nation-centered policy grew among politicians on both sides of the aisle. The preference for state-level policymaking and the shifting of power from the national government to the states, devolution, was reflected in congressional legislative initiatives. This shift was also reflected in Supreme Court decisions that were focused on limiting the power of the national government.[53] There has been ongoing debate since that time, however, regarding exactly how observable, meaningful, and lasting this shift was.

The Unfunded Mandate Reform Act (UMRA) of 1996 is an example of legislation designed, in theory, to limit the power of Congress to create policy the states would then have to pay to implement. This legislation was credited with at least trying to create institutional limits on congressional authority.[54] The UMRA created procedural requirements that would make it difficult for Congress to pass on expensive regulations without funding, and it also required bureaucratic agencies to formally assess the impact of administrative mandates before they could be implemented.[55] However, this legislation contained a number of exceptions and required specific actions in order for it to actually be applied. Congressional mandates that were exempt from the UMRA included any mandates intended to prevent discrimination, establish the conditions of grant money, and any regulations that did not necessarily have a fiscal impact.[56] In addition to these exceptions, the effectiveness of the UMRA was further diminished because it did not establish any automatic procedures. The application of this law required a member of Congress to formally state during congressional proceedings that a specific mandate was out of order. That motion would then have to be sustained by a majority of members in that particular chamber.[57] Essentially, Congress passed a law that would empower the body to limit its mandate authority if it chose to do so. This act did not stop the passage of mandates nor did it settle any questions or cement any formal shift in power to the states. If anything, it continued to demonstrate the power and influence of national legislative authority over any general commitment to the principle of devolution.[58]

The attacks of September 11, 2001, would shift the nation's focus to national security, which had been a task squarely in the purview of the national government since the founding. After that day, there was renewed confusion about the responsibilities of the national government and the states.[59] The challenge involved reconciling the traditional role of the national government in security matters with the "highly localized" nature of the terrorist attacks and renewing a type of cooperative federalism that would provide for the needs of the directly affected cities and states.[60] There was evidence that devolution was woefully inadequate in dealing with unprecedented security challenges.[61]

Aside from the logistical challenges of addressing a national threat with localized responses was the clear expectation that the national government would take the lead, consistent with traditional expectations of American federalism. Historically, the national government took the lead in times of crisis, and that expectation was still intact in 2001.[62] Unfortunately, neither level of government seemed particularly keen to provide leadership or money to quickly and effectively deal with homeland security. All of the arguments made by states' rights activists in favor of more state authority went silent, and the national government was slow in generating a clear and cohesive plan as well.[63] The people themselves had inconsistent and shifting expectations about which level of government should assume the more dominant role. Public support for the national government increased at the time of the attack but again declined in the years following.[64] By 2005, public opinion in favor of state and local government had returned to higher levels seen before 2001.[65] All of these factors came together to create the rather difficult problem of homeland security in a post-attack, post-devolution federal system.

Unfortunately, it did not take long for some perennial issues of federalism to re-emerge, including coercive regulatory federalism and unfunded federal mandates.[66] The federal government was generous with financial aid to the localities like New York that were directly hit, but that aid came with restrictions on how it could be spent.[67] The creation and imposition of new homeland security regulations did not consistently come with funding, which caused financial problems for the states.[68] The catastrophe of Hurricane Katrina would come along just a few short years later and reveal all of the persisting weaknesses of addressing national problems with a decentralized approach.[69]

One of the challenges to American federalism in light of these tragedies was learning to think beyond the concepts of centralization and decentralization to find a new approach to federal organization.[70] In order to meet the needs of the people with regard to security and more, the American system of federalism would need a path beyond the "opportunistic" form it had shaped into.[71] Certainly, the objectives of homeland security would be difficult to meet with political actors focused on their own individual policy agendas. The need for intergovernmental cooperation was very apparent, but as history has demonstrated, that can be easier said than done. We will pick up on the themes of American federalism today toward the end of this chapter.

STUDYING AMERICAN FEDERALISM: THEMES AND DEBATES

Beyond a review of the history of American federalism is the attempt to study and explain it conceptually. This task has proven to be as complicated as the lived experience. Many scholars of political science and law have developed terminology to help teach and explain the concept of federalism, and like the history, not all of these approaches can be documented here. This chapter will continue its treatment of the federalism experience with a survey of some of the broader themes and debates in the study of federalism: dual versus cooperative federalism, centralized versus decentralized federalism, and the costs and benefits of federalism.

The discussion of dual versus cooperative federalism concerns the matter of interpreting what a division of sovereignty actually means in practice. If by dividing, we mean that "the federal and state government have been able to either to divide responsibility among their separate jurisdictions, with each responsible only for its own share of the divided responsibility," then we are referring to dual federalism.[72] If, however, if we mean "to divide the works of government cooperatively, sharing responsibility in specific programs, with all units directed toward common goals that extend along the entire share of concurrent powers," then we are describing cooperative federalism.[73] Though these two interpretations of federalism are generally accepted on a definitional basis, there has been disagreement as to when and how often we have actually observed each of these interpretations in practice. First, we will further explore what these terms mean, and then we can examine some of the debate over when they have occurred.

The idea of dual federalism is based on a desire to preserve specific policy areas for state control so as to limit the power of the national government. Dual federalism can prevent the creation and imposition of uniform rules that may not account for state and local preferences.[74] Historical evidence of dual federalism has been identified by way of specific policy areas that have been largely left to the states to regulate, including elections, family law, and criminal law.[75] Edward S. Corwin, in 1950, defined dual federalism as a circumstance in which the national government exercises specific enumerated powers and both levels of government enjoy sovereignty over their "respective spheres" thus denoting political equality.[76] This is not to be understood as a collaborative relationship but rather a tense relationship.[77]

On the contrary, cooperative federalism describes a relationship between the states and national government that is rooted in the sharing of resources, authority, and responsibility. This notions rests on a specific understanding of governmental powers and responsibilities that regards them all as "concurrent and overlapping" and therefore impossible to separate into distinct spheres.[78] The state governments and the national government are not at odds with one another but are partners who are on the same team and wish to create and implement policy for the betterment of all at the state and national level.[79] The presence of cooperation should not necessarily be construed to mean a singular institutional structure, as the states are empowered to create their own policymaking structures. However, cooperation can be understood in terms of information sharing and coordination to achieve policy goals.[80] Cooperative federalism can also be understood to accommodate concurrent state power and does not necessarily mean that the national government has more or less authority over the states. The focus here is on the coming together of both levels of government to address identified public issues in a way that maximizes and shares resources, credit, and blame.[81]

Beyond the challenge of identifying and defining these types of federalism, there has been a great deal of debate as to when these types of federalism have been utilized. First, we have the position that dual federalism came first and then transitioned to cooperative federalism.[82] This argument is largely based on the observable shift of specific policy areas from the state level to the national level, such as civil rights, safety and workplace regulations, and corporate law.[83] The competing theory is that dual federalism never really existed, and that American politics dating back to the 1800s displayed a great deal of cooperation among national, state, and local government across policy in all levels of formation and implementation.[84] The reason for this was practical, in that it was simply never viable to divide policy with such clear and precise lines. This level of rigidity never worked and therefore never was.[85]

Next, we can discuss federalism in terms of the centralization or decentralization of policymaking. If the significant policymaking decision are made "exclusively through the machinery of the central government" then we consider that a centralized system. A decentralized system will engage in policymaking whereby "decisions are made, partially at least, through the machinery of local governments."[86] The degree to which federal policymaking is centralized can be considered as points along a continuum from centralized to decentralized. A review of the federalism literature shows, however, a tendency toward centralized policymaking that can be traced back to the founding era.[87] It should be noted that there is a strain of thought that attempts to address the concept of decentralization as a concept separate from federalism. We will deal with this more later in the chapter. For the time being, I am addressing decentralization and centralization in the context of American federalism.

In the course of American political history, there have been a number of both centralizing and decentralizing forces that have impacted where significant decision-making takes place. Regarding centralizing forces, we can identify examples over time that have enforced the idea of the national government taking the lead in policymaking.[88] First, the Constitution establishes a direct relationship between the national government and its citizens, which limits the leverage the states have in controlling the national government.[89] This direct relationship was further strengthened when the Seventeenth Amendment was ratified in 1913. Prior to this amendment, Senators were chosen by the state legislatures, and the Senate was intended to represent state interests. The Seventeenth Amendment changed the method of electing senators to a direct popular vote, and provided another linkage between the people and the national government.[90] Second, the Supreme Court has functioned as a centralizing influence by way of several decisions made from 1964 to 1992.[91] During this time, federal judges across the ideological spectrum consistently interpreted the Commerce Clause, the Supremacy Clause, and Congress' spending power in a way that promoted the centralization of significant decision-making to the national government.[92]

A third centralizing influence on American federalism has been the organizational and procedural changes in the political party system. Once considered decentralized, the party system of the past was thought to grow from state and local preferences. This was due in large part to the absence of a unified party ideology with no easy way to create and impose one.[93] This decentralized party structure was celebrated as "the main protector of the integrity of states in our federalism."[94] However, even as William Riker was writing this in 1987, the political party system had been changing for several years. This change began in earnest after the 1968 Democratic presidential nomination period revealed a number of problems and inconsistencies in the party's processes. These issues led both major parties to develop stronger national organizations while also yielding more power to their members in the electorate to make the nomination decisions.[95] The political system has since grown to accommodate an increasing number of interest groups, political action committees, and a growing number of partisan and divisive media outlets.[96] Without a decentralized party system to maintain "the guarantee to the states in the federal bargain," federalism has naturally centralized. Along with the decline of distinct state and local party politics, we have seen a decline in the connection between members of Congress and the states and districts they represent. Due to the growth of the individually oriented campaign and fundraising efforts, an aspirational politician does not necessarily need strong party roots in the region they wish to represent, if at all.[97] Rather than viewing themselves as a representative of a state or district in a national legislature, more and more representatives see themselves as national politicians. Changes in campaign finance have also made them pervious to influences beyond their specific constituents. We will come back to the topic of centralization later in the chapter when we discuss American federalism today.

Regarding decentralizing forces, we can identify examples over time that have enforced the idea of the state governments taking the more dominant role in meaningful decision-making and policy implementation. A few examples of decentralizing forces include the need for state and local buy-in for effective policy implementation, the role of public opinion, and the role of states in creating meaningful opportunities for political activity. First, from a practical perspective, it has always been important for states and cities to agree with federal policy initiatives and objectives, because they are quite often the ones with the administrative responsibility of implementation.[98] In order to enhance that buy-in, it is logical to shift decision-making toward those people who are actually on the frontlines of policy implementation to increase ownership and accountability. Even if we can quantitatively say that federal expenses have increased over time that does not necessarily mean that the states have lost significance for implementation.

Second, we have seen the powerful role that public opinion can play as a decentralizing influence. At the very least, the dissatisfaction of the people with federal government activity can lead to a change in rhetoric. We saw this position influence President Ronald Reagan in the 1980s, when he utilized a noted amount of states' rights rhetoric and expressed a desire to reduce the size of the national government. Moving into the 1990s, the candidates in the 1992 presidential election and the 1994 congressional elections tapped into the public sentiment that was growing weary of uniform policies decided at the national level.[99] The Republicans' "Contract With America" represented a move to take public opinion on the centralization of American federalism and turn it into legislative change toward decentralization.

Third, states have taken it upon themselves to create processes and institutions that have made their internal political activities as meaningful, if not more, than national policymaking. One example of this is the creation of direct initiatives.[100] Most states have some process in place to turn specific issues over to the voters, whether it is through a petition process or through legislative referral. In fact, many states have used this route to bypass the federal regulations that make marijuana illegal. We will discuss the power of these initiatives more in chapter 7 on physician-assisted death. Another example is the empowerment of state governors to be more powerful and significant leaders in their respective states with the regard to the general public and their state's legislative process.[101] The importance of gubernatorial authority has certainly been amplified during the COVID-19 pandemic.

If we consider centralization as a continuum, then there are further assessments to be made regarding how centralized or decentralized American federalism has been at any given point in time. One perspective considers decentralizing forces as an intended counterbalance to centralizing forces, the effect of which serves to stabilize the federal system.[102] This perspective hinges on the assumption that we can easily discern decentralizing activities from centralizing activities and then make strategic decisions on which to utilize. However, other perspectives on the topic emphasize the difficulty involved in accurately gauging which activities are centralizing or decentralizing. For instance, a seemingly centralizing activity in which the federal government has taken the lead in creating an impactful policy program might actually be decentralizing, in that it provides a path for state and local governments to act on that issue. It could be that the states wished to act sooner but were slowed by other local political pressures or restrictions which the national action alleviates.[103] The New Deal legislative program has been used as an example in this regard as it freed states from private interests that had stopped more expansive social programs at the state and local level.[104]

Another perspective on the role of balance in a federal policymaking structure is found in the 1987 book by Daniel Elazar, *Exploring Federalism.* Elazar suggests moving beyond the ideas of centralization and decentralization and toward a matrix model where there is no center and no periphery.[105] In such a model, political connections and communications are many and varied without a rigid hierarchical structure in place. This model allows for decision-making to occur in ways that make sense to the various players depending on the policy matter.

The concept of decentralization in a federal system has created some disagreement and debate in the federalism literature, and this debate impacts how we assess the costs and benefits of federalism. Essentially, you can have decentralized political structures without having a federal system, and that many of the costs and benefits of federalism are actually costs and benefits of decentralization with no reference to sovereignty and the division thereof. For instance, a cost that is commonly attributed to federalism is the occurrence of interjurisdictional spillover, wherein a member of one community is able to access a benefit intended for people of another geographic jurisdiction.[106] However, one could argue that this type of cost is truly a cost of decentralization that could be experienced in a unitary system with decentralized policymaking, not just a federal system.[107]

From a federal perspective, strictly understood then, the main cost of federalism is the cost of enforcing the "ownership rights that pertain to the assignment of powers."[108] The federal judiciary was intended to be the arbiter of federalist disputes in the American political system. We have already reviewed a number of court cases that illustrate this function. Though the federal courts are part of the national government, they have always been intended to function in an independent manner in assessing the behavior of both the national government and the states.[109] Since ownership rights are not automatically self-enforcing, they must be enforced by someone. The need for enforcement is considered a cost of federalism.[110]

When we consider the benefits of federalism, we encounter a similar tension with regard to what is truly responsible for the benefits: federalism, specifically, or decentralized policymaking, generally? A benefit that is commonly credited to federalism is policy innovation and experimentation, but technically this could happen in a unitary system whereby the subnational governments are empowered to innovate.[111] In addition to state-level policy experimentation, there can also be the presence of vertical competition to benefit the people. This is a situation in which both the national government and state governments are both working to provide a service, regulation, or redistribution and has been identified as a benefit unique to a federal system.[112] There may be a time in which both levels of government are working on a particular policy, but ultimately the people will show a preference based on which level of government is providing the service more effectively.[113] The duplication or overlap of services is a temporary feature of vertical competition and will eventually resolve in the people's best interest.[114]

Federalism has been described and explained in many ways, and we have looked specifically at federalism through the dual versus cooperative lens, the centralized versus decentralized perspective, and by way of its costs and benefits. These explanations layer on top of the historical experience of American federalism. The study of federalism is a complicated undertaking, with knowledge of the historical development and the conceptual treatment equally important to its understanding. In recent years, more work has been done to reconcile the changes in the American political system with the foundational knowledge we have amassed about federalism over the years.

AMERICAN FEDERALISM TODAY

There have been countless attempts to understand and explain federalism over the years, and this book aspires to be just one of many ways to bring the information together and assess the practice of federalism in the United States. First, we must decide whether federalism is a static concept reinforced by institutional practices, or if modern American federalism is, in Joseph Zimmerman's words, "complex and metamorphic."[115] If the concept and practice of federalism is truly metamorphic, then we need to be cognizant of those changes and make sure that our ways of assessing the effectiveness of federalism are changing as well. If we accept the dynamism of federalism, then the question arises as to whether or not modern federalism is consistent with the founders' intent.[116] Of course, there is always the follow-up question: Does it matter if the practice of modern federalism is consistent with the founders' intent? It seems that if the founders were that sure they had a perfect formula for federalism, they would have written it out more specifically.

The history of federalism in the Unites States demonstrates that it requires cooperation to work effectively but it also naturally cultivates conflict.[117] To achieve stability, federalism requires both levels of government to be strong, active participants in the policymaking and implementation process.[118] As the distinction between national matters and state and local matters blurs (if it was every truly there at all), modern federalism requires a broader more integrative conceptualization.[119] It is through this lens that we can consider the themes and issues of American federalism today.

In 2009, law professor Robert Schapiro developed this type of conceptualization in his book, *Polyphonic Federalism: Toward the Protection of Fundamental Rights.* Schapiro provides a path forward for the consideration of modern American federalism that seeks to be compatible with the reality of American politics.[120] Polyphonic federalism focuses on the interaction between the different levels of government and the concurrence of power that we now find in most policy areas.[121] Since polyphonic federalism is about these relationships, it supports the notion that modern federalism is dynamic and thus able to change, adapt, and problem-solve in innovative ways.[122] When we consider federalism as a fluid concept and focus our attention on the mechanics of the relationship between the national government and states, the pressure to identify federalism as one "type" or another eases. While modern federalism has been described as featuring both cooperation and conflict, we do not necessarily need to tease these apart. Rather, we can let them coexist in a way that will promote the "substantive goals" of federalism: efficiency, participation, and liberty.[123]

Related to the polyphonic conception of federalism is the study and implementation of optimal intergovernmental relations. In 1987, Elazar wrote that the "essence of federalism" could not be identified solely through the examination of American political institutions. The essence of federalism was actually about the "institutionalization of particular relationships among the participants in political life."[124] Based on this idea, we can learn about the connection between the theory and practice of federalism through the study of intergovernmental relations. The connection of theory to practice by way of intergovernmental relations is logical, but it need not represent a clean departure from earlier methods of studying and understanding federalism. I am hesitant to draw a distinct line between what has been called "new style" versus "old style" federalism.[125] The reconceptualization of federalism as the study of intergovernmental relations is very useful and allows our study of federalism to move forward in concrete and constructive ways. However, I do not think it should lead to an abandonment of constitutional federalism or the desire to understand what the objectives of the founders were. That knowledge is still significant to the understanding of federalism today, whether we find the modern practice of federalism to be compatible or incompatible with it. When Michael Raegan and John Sanzone discussed the "new federalism" in the early 1980s, they were correct to identify the focus on practice and relationships in federalism. After decades upon decades of federal cooperation and the tensions that been generated, it made—and continues to make—a great deal of sense to learn about intergovernmental relations so that scholars and practitioners can ultimately make normative judgments about how to optimize efficiency and responsiveness to the people.

The study of intergovernmental relations allows us to consider and analyze which policies should be administered at what level. When we decide to relieve a federal agency of some administrative responsibilities by shifting to them the states, what additional challenges do we create by way of monitoring and oversight?[126] From the perspective of the states, how should they proceed to protect their autonomy, ward off federal preemption, and navigate the changing political environment with regard to accountability and coordination with the national government?[127] These are important questions, among countless others, that the study of intergovernmental relations allows us to explore. However, the study of theoretical federalism continues to be a needed touchstone when formulating normative assessments of federalism that are based on both constitutional principle and practical considerations of efficiency. While the richness and complexity of the federalism literature can be challenging to sort through, the nature of it should not render it useless in the modern context. The study of intergovernmental relations is important but should not subsume or be conflated with the study of federalism as a foundational principle of American governance. There are many challenges that American federalism faces today, and both approaches are needed to find the most suitable path forward. Among these challenges is the threat and reality of centralization in American politics.

As we previously reviewed, the centralization in American politics can be observed through the centralization of political parties and the centralization of power in Congress. Both of these instances of centralization create problems for federalism. The centralization of political parties creates a threat because it has served to inhibit the diversity and uniqueness of ideas and the accountability of the representatives to their constituents. The expansion of congressional authority poses a threat as the power encroaches on any sense of legislative and bureaucratic autonomy for the states.

First, the functionality of federalism is affected by the changing nature and role of political parties in American politics.[128] In 1964, political scientist, William Riker, identified political parties as the main peripheralizing force in American politics.[129] He explained that the founders had created both centralizing and peripheralizing (decentralizing) institutions to facilitate the existence of a federal system. Riker recognized that while the founders did not explicitly create a party system, the parties would ultimately be highly significant in countering the centralizing forces that would prove historically dominant.[130] He contended that this peripheralizing role was contingent upon the decentralized nature of American political parties, as this was the nature of party organization when he was writing in the 1960s and in the years prior. Riker believed that parties (and their ideas, and goals, and accountability) were kept local because there was not any good way to unify either party ideology or organization.[131] Further evidence of this peripheralizing balance was the fact that only a nationally oriented party organization would allow a president to "count on substantially complete support from his partisans in Congress," and it was a "well-known fact" that this was not possible.[132] Therefore, because no president could unify congressional partisans with ideology, he would always need to utilize bargaining and this would maintain the significant role and balancing power of the states.[133] Riker called the decentralized American party system "the main protector of the integrity of states is our federalism."[134] The times would change, however, and the party system would gradually cease to perform this role.

In 1986, the ACIR published a report entitled, "The Transformation in American Politics: Implications for Federalism," wherein they described a rather disturbing scenario for the future of federalism. Since that time, all of the concerns expressed in the report have proven to be legitimate and the contributing phenomena described have all become markedly worse. The report was predicated on the assumption explained by Riker decades before that the decentralization of the political parties in the United States had been vital to the maintenance of federalism.[135] Their concern regarding the veracity of this claim by the mid-1980s stemmed from the Supreme Court's 1985 ruling in the *Garcia v. San Antonio Transit Authority* case which stressed the role of the political process, and not the courts, in protecting states' rights.[136] In the report, under the authorship of the then ACIR Director of Communications, Bob Gleason, the ACIR proceeded to lay out its rationale for why this reliance on political process may be problematic for the future of American federalism.

The report argued that most of the institutional means to regulate national power were practically gone at that point, including the role of the states in the Electoral College, the means for electing U.S. Senators, and the interpretation and application of the Commerce Clause and Necessary and Proper Clause.[137] Further, the commission contended that since the 1960s, the political machines had "withered away" and the major party organizations were now better described as "national party confederations" paired with "centralized political mobilization."[138] They identified six root causes for this change, including the growth of independent voters, the erosion of state and local party control over messaging and candidate selection, television, interest groups, campaign finance, and the nationalizing of the party organization.[139] Since the time that report was released, all of these factors have only increased in significance and to an extent that the members of the advisory commission may not have imagined. The ability to unify party ideology and party organization through the media today has served to create a level of executive influence over Congress that represents a great departure from the system Riker observed in the 1960s. It may be worth noting that the ACIR was eliminated in 1996, when its funding was cut from the federal budget.

This action removed any institutional method for observing and improving the relationship between the states and the national government moving forward.[140]

Second, the functionality of American federalism has been impacted by the growth of congressional power. It has been said that even those credited with writing the Constitution who strove to preserve and promote the role of the national government would be quite surprised by the power Congress has.[141] In his 2008 book, *Contemporary American Federalism,* Joseph Zimmerman explains the three significant roles that Congress plays which make it such a dominant force in the American federal system: facilitator, inhibitor, and initiator.[142] Congress facilitates through appropriating money for state use, it inhibits state action through its preemptive powers, and initiates by enacting standards that set parameters for new state regulatory actions.[143] While the Constitution was not written to expressly create these roles, it was written in a way that facilitated the gradual growth of congressional power in these realms.[144] There is certainly nothing contained therein to stop it.

The centralization of American politics by way of the party system and congressional power is easily observed, however, the impact of this centralization is debated. While the centralization of politics appears to generate some deleterious effects for federalism, there is the competing perspective that the growth of national power does not necessarily mean the states must lose power.[145] The ability of all government to expand its sphere of influence and activity allows power to grow on all levels.[146] Much of this debate is further influenced by normative assumptions of what federalism *should* look like—should the states be more powerful or should the national government be more powerful, and it is safe to say that there is no consensus on this matter.[147] Further, the challenge these centralizing forces present does not settle the issue of how the national governments should relate to the states, cooperatively or competitively, and we still must grapple with competing theories here as well.[148] This is an area polyphonic federalism can be of help to us, perhaps in how we perceive congressional power in the broader federal system. Pragmatic federalism could be another way, wherein the national government takes the dominant role, but its relationship with the states is interdependent and productive.[149]

Beyond the issues of centralization, modern American federalism faces additional challenges including when and how to identify consensus, the increasing size and diversity of the country, and matters relating to establishing and understanding the modern concept of state identity. First, deciding where and how to resolve an issue of public policy is infinitely easier when the preferences of the people are known and line up largely in support of one position. In a federal system, we not only have the task of identifying the policy preferences of the people, but then we also have to determine the best way to create and implement those policies. As the people, both citizens and politicians, move in a similar direction regarding both the "what" and "how" of public policy, they demonstrate consensus.[150] When consensus is observed, this means that the people wish to deal "with a series of core issues in generally agreed upon ways."[151] We have examples in the past where this type of consensus has been established with regard to such things as equality, and we can observe a commitment that is seen across the board, politically and personally.[152] When this type of consensus is established, the decision to make policy at the national level can be logical and maybe even easy. But what if it is hard to determine? Certainly, there are rarely, if ever, issues that all Americans agree upon. When we refer to consensus then, do we truly just mean a large and established majority? Where is the cutoff, and what happens to policymaking if there is too thin a margin between those in favor and those against?

The growing size and diversity of the United States poses another challenge to modern American federalism. While these matters are not new and have certainly been aided by technological advances in communication and information dissemination, the size and diversity of this country continue to strain a democratic system that, ideally, is responsive to its citizens.[153] One advantage of the decentralized policymaking structure that federalism can facilitate is its ability to tailor policies to the preferences of various subsets of the population, provided of course, that they are living in the same geographic area. However, what if you have interests that represent a decent percentage of the population, but they are spread out over a larger area? How does federalism work to address these specific concerns if the states do not provide an adequate venue to do so?

Lastly, modern federalism faces the challenge of establishing and understanding a modern conception of state identity. At the height of the civil rights era, the promotion of state identity became synonymous with promoting and maintaining oppressive policies that were desired by a regional populace. How do states move past this idea and make an argument for a state-specific policy that does not tap into themes of discrimination and oppression? One way is to consider states having identifiable interests in contrast with the national government.[154] These interests can be unique to those state-level political institutions, and not just a reflection of what the people want or what the politicians and bureaucrats personally want. Those interests and preferences would be reflective of what is best for the long-term strength and viability of the states.[155]

This list of challenges is by no means exhaustive but rather provides examples of why we must always be thinking constructively and creatively about federalism in this country. Regardless of the amount of research and theorizing and observing that has been done over the years on the topic of

American federalism, the scenery is always changing. American federalism is dynamic, and the issues that arise require new solutions and applications so that federalism can remain the relevant and most effective approach to managing power and decision-making in this country.[156]

CONCLUSION

American federalism is a complicated concept that is largely studied and understood by observing and assessing how it has developed over time. We are able to build knowledge regarding the intent of federalism from the founding documents and supporting material from that era, and then use that foundational information to inform those observations and assessments. Of course, this is not a simple exercise either and the varying trends in the studying and teaching of federalism reflect the complexity involved. One challenge to the scholarship of federalism is that it occurs in a variety of academic and professional realms, including political science, law, political philosophy, and economics, and these various disciplines to not consistently overlap.[156] I have tried to bring these perspectives together into this summary with the hope of creating a useful survey of information that might enhance the understanding of federalism among those who wish to better understand how it impacts American politics and political culture.

Federalism is rife with uncertainty, and as Larry Gerston writes in his book *American Federalism: A Concise Introduction*, it is open to interpretation, it is inconsistent, incomplete, and always changing in response to the world around it.[157] It is also fluid and adaptable and a way to navigate through a jumble of public policy issues and competing principles of American democracy that were adopted and implemented at the same time federalism was formalized as a method of political power distribution so many years ago.[158] There is no doubt that the citizens of a federal political system are deeply impacted by the policymaking and implementation that happens at all levels of governance.[159] Depending on the preferences of the citizens and the political actors, we see some issues addressed at the state level, some at the national level, and then always face the possibility of rethinking everything in the event of a judicial challenge or if the consensus changes. Taken alone, federalism is complex enough, but it is not the only founding principle of American democracy that we find in the U.S. Constitution. The purpose of this book is to see how well we can reconcile it with the preservation and promotion of the individual. Before we are ready to see how federalism has impacted public policy and the protection of individual rights in the United States, we need to make one more stop to learn more about the role and history of individual rights in American politics.

NOTES

1. Alexander, "The Measurement of American Federalism," 100.
2. Ibid.
3. Krislov, "American Federalism as American Exceptionalism," 14.
4. Ibid.
5. Ibid.
6. Elazar, "Opening the Third Century of American Federalism: Issues and Prospects," 19.
7. Elazar, *Exploring Federalism*, 5.
8. Krislov, "American Federalism as American Exceptionalism," 11.
9. Ibid.
10. Ibid., 15.
11. Elazar, *Exploring Federalism*, 108.
12. Corwin, "The Passing of Dual Federalism," 3.
13. Gleason, "The Transformation in American Politics: Implications for Federalism," 3–4.
14. Riker, *The Development of American Federalism*, 136.
15. Ibid.
16. Katz, "United States of America," 296.
17. Ibid.
18. Walker, "The Advent of an Ambiguous Federalism and the Emergence of New Federalism III," 271.
19. *Marbury v. Madison*, 5 U.S. 137 (1803).
20. *McCulloch v. Maryland*, 17 U.S. 316 (1819).
21. *Gibbons v. Ogden*, 22 U.S. 1 (1824).
22. Katz, "United States of America," 311.
23. Schapiro, *Polyphonic Federalism*, 2.
24. Breton, "Federalism and Decentralization: Ownership Rights and the Superiority of Federalism," 10–11.
25. Ibid., 12.
26. Ibid., 13.
27. Zimmerman, *Contemporary American Federalism*, 191.
28. *Plessy v. Ferguson*, 163 U.S. 537 (1896).
29. Rutherglen, "The Thirteenth Amendment, the Power of Congress, and the Shifting Sources of Civil Rights Law," 1552.
30. "Franklin D. Roosevelt," *White House*.
31. Katz, "United States of America," 311.
32. Kincaid, "From Cooperative to Coercive Federalism," 140.
33. Walker, "American Federalism from Johnson to Bush," 115.
34. Kincaid, "From Cooperative to Coercive Federalism," 140.
35. Ibid.
36. Brown v. Board of Education, 347 U.S. 483 (1954).
37. Schapiro, *Polyphonic Federalism*, 47.

38. Ibid., 49.
39. Kincaid, "From Cooperative to Coercive Federalism," 142.
40. Katz, "United States of America," 312.
41. Schapiro, *Polyphonic Federalism*, 47.
42. Kincaid, "From Cooperative to Coercive Federalism," 143.
43. Ibid.
44. Ibid., 148.
45. Ibid., 146.
46. Walker, "The Advent of an Ambiguous Federalism and the Emergence of New Federalism III," 271.
47. Walker, "American Federalism from Johnson to Bush," 105.
48. Ibid.
49. Kincaid, "From Cooperative to Coercive Federalism," 149.
50. Ibid.
51. Walker, "American Federalism from Johnson to Bush," 118.
52. Ibid., 117.
53. Schapiro, *Polyphonic Federalism*, 1; see also Cole et al., "Devolution: Where's the Revolution?" and Conlan, "From Cooperative to Opportunistic Federalism," for a discussion of these actions.
54. Posner, "Unfunded Mandates Reform Act: 1996 and Beyond," 53.
55. Troy, "The Unfunded Mandates Reform Act of 1995," 139–140.
56. Posner, "Unfunded Mandates Reform Act: 1996 and Beyond," 54.
57. Ibid.
58. Ibid., 71.
59. Eisinger, "Imperfect Federalism," 538.
60. Ibid., 537.
61. Ibid.
62. Ibid., 538.
63. Ibid., 542.
64. Kincaid, "From Cooperative to Coercive Federalism," 169.
65. Ibid.
66. Ibid., 181; Roberts, "Dispersed Federalism as a New Regional Governance for Homeland Security," 416.
67. Kincaid, "From Cooperative to Coercive Federalism," 181; Eisinger, "Imperfect Federalism: The Intergovernmental Partnership for Homeland Security," 540.
68. Roberts, "Dispersed Federalism as a New Regional Governance for Homeland Security," 416.
69. Scavo et al., "Challenges to Federalism: Homeland Security and Disaster Response," 83.
70. Ibid.
71. Conlan, "From Cooperative to Opportunistic Federalism," 667.
72. Elazar, "Federal-State Collaboration in the Nineteenth-Century United States," 222.
73. Ibid.

74. Schapiro, *Polyphonic Federalism*, 3.

75. Ibid., 35.

76. Corwin, "The Passing of Dual Federalism," 4.

77. Ibid.

78. Katz, "United States of America," 312.

79. Elazar, "Federal-State Collaboration in the Nineteenth-Century United States," 194.

80. Ibid., 221.

81. Zimmerman, *Contemporary American Federalism*, 200.

82. Ibid., 9.

83. Schapiro, *Polyphonic Federalism*, 36–37.

84. Elazar, "Federal-State Collaboration in the Nineteenth-Century United States," 192.

85. Ibid.; see also Zimmerman, *Contemporary American Federalism*, 8.

86. Riker, *The Development of American Federalism*, 137.

87. Ibid.; Alexander, "The Measurement of American Federalism," 101.

88. Katz, "United States of America," 307.

89. Riker, *The Development of American Federalism*, 137.

90. Alexander, "The Measurement of American Federalism," 100.

91. Walker, "The Advent of an Ambiguous Federalism and the Emergence of New Federalism III," 272; Walker, *The Rebirth of Federalism*, 173–205.

92. Walker, "The Advent of an Ambiguous Federalism and the Emergence of New Federalism III," 272–273.

93. Riker, *The Development of American Federalism*, 219.

94. Ibid., 221.

95. Walker, "The Advent of an Ambiguous Federalism and the Emergence of New Federalism III," 272.

96. Ibid.

97. Elazar, "Opening the Third Century of American Federalism," 14.

98. Walker, "The Advent of an Ambiguous Federalism and the Emergence of New Federalism III," 272.

99. Ibid., 273.

100. Katz, "United States of America," 302.

101. Ibid.

102. Alexander, "The Measurement of American Federalism," 110.

103. Elazar, *Exploring Federalism*, 198.

104. Ibid.

105. Ibid., 199.

106. Breton, "Federalism and Decentralization: Ownership Rights and the Superiority of Federalism," 3.

107. Ibid.

108. Breton, "Federalism and Decentralization," 14.

109. Ibid.

110. Ibid., 16.

111. Ibid.

112. Ibid., 7.
113. Ibid.
114. Ibid., 8.
115. Zimmerman, *Contemporary American Federalism*, 187.
116. Katz, "United States of America," 316.
117. Ibid., 311.
118. Ibid., 316.
119. Schapiro, *Polyphonic Federalism*, 97.
120. Ibid., 92.
121. Ibid., 95.
122. Ibid., 92, 95.
123. Schapiro, *Polyphonic Federalism*, 92.
124. Elazar, *Exploring Federalism*, 12.
125. Reagan and Sanzone, *The New Federalism*, 3.
126. Zimmerman, *Contemporary American Federalism*, 195.
127. Ibid., 199.
128. Katz, "United States of America," 317.
129. Riker, *Federalism*, 87.
130. Ibid.
131. Riker, *The Development of American Federalism*, 219.
132. Ibid.
133. Ibid., 220.
134. Ibid., 221.
135. Gleason, "The Transformation in American Politics," 2.
136. Ibid., 1.; *Garcia v. San Antonio Transit Authority*, 469 U.S. 528 (1984).
137. Ibid.
138. Ibid., 2.
139. Ibid., 2–3.
140. Katz, "United States of America," 314.
141. Zimmerman, *Contemporary American Federalism*, 188.
142. Ibid., 192.
143. Ibid.
144. Ibid.
145. Glendening and Reeves, *Pragmatic Federalism*, 32.
146. Ibid.
147. Ibid., 51.
148. Ibid.
149. Ibid., 63.
150. Gerston, *American Federalism*, 9.
151. Ibid., 10.
152. Ibid., 9–10.
153. Nugent, *Safeguarding Federalism*, 57.
154. Ibid., 24.
155. Ibid., 25.
156. Ibid., 7.

157. Gerston, *American Federalism*, 16–17.
158. Ibid., 13.
159. Ibid., 14.

SUGGESTED READINGS

Elazar, Daniel J. *Exploring Federalism*. Tuscaloosa, AL: The University of Alabama Press, 1987.

Nugent, John D. *Safeguarding Federalism: How States Protect Their Interests in National Policymaking*. Norman, OK: University of Oklahoma Press, 2009.

Riker, William. *The Development of American Federalism*. Norwell, MA: Klewer Academic Publishers, 1987.

Schapiro, Robert A. *Polyphonic Federalism: Toward the Protection of Fundamental Rights*. Chicago and London: The University of Chicago Press, 2009.

Zimmerman, Joseph F. *Contemporary American Federalism*. Albany, NY: State University of New York Press, 2008.

Chapter 3

Individual Rights

The American political system is based on a number of democratic principles that have come together to create a unique political culture and environment. At the time of the founding, there was a need to institutionalize these principles into a political structure so that they could be easily understood and implemented. Along with the desire to create a method of power distribution that would be acceptable to a broad portion of the population was the objective of creating a system based on the importance and primacy of the individual. Assumptions and beliefs about human nature and the role and capabilities of the individual would serve as the foundation for this objective and would go on to make many components of the American political system, both logical and practical. In this chapter, we will build on what we know of federalism to learn about the role of the individual in American political culture. Our ultimate goal is to establish, at this point in time, whether or not federalism and individual rights are compatible concepts or if they have worked at cross purposes. In order to conduct this assessment, we will need to understand both American federalism and individual rights.

As with chapters 1 and 2, the goal herein is to provide the reader with an opportunity to learn about a broad and complex topic in a more condensed form. Any meaningful understanding of American politics is greatly enhanced by learning about the importance of the individual in American political culture. In order to accomplish this goal, we will be learning about the importance of individual rights by way of a historical and theoretical approach extending back to the founding era. We will learn some about the political theory that inspired the founders and the ways individual rights were institutionalized in the documents and practices of the national and state governments. We will then review some of the ideas and perspectives related to the relationship between individual rights and federalism, as there has been considerable work done regarding the compatibility of these two concepts. This review will position us to evaluate different areas of policy to see how well federalism has worked to protect the rights of individuals in the United States.

THE INDIVIDUAL IN THE FOUNDING ERA

The founding of the United States provided many opportunities to utilize political theory that was thought to be experimental and even controversial. The political theory that inspired the founders was rooted in classical liberal ideology with its focus on limited government, the need for consent among the governed, and the political necessity of individual rights. Classical liberalism was and is an ideology that has specific ideas about human nature, and these ideas represented a great departure from earlier conceptions. The individual in classical liberal thought is reasonable and rational, capable of learning from experience and improving their condition. People are essentially equal in their capabilities and potential and so the possibilities are far greater than in past European feudal systems where upward mobility was not possible nor justified. While the founders relied on several theorists for their foundational knowledge and thinking about the individual, we will focus our attention on two significant thinkers: Thomas Hobbes and John Locke. This brief review of classical liberal theory, as it pertains to the individual, will help us in our pursuit of understanding the relationship between individual rights and federalism.[1]

Hobbes is considered the first liberal theorist and is credited with developing social contract theory. He wrote in the 1600s while he was in exile from England. Locke also wrote in the 1600s and built upon Hobbes's theory to develop classical liberal theory as we understand it today. As we would come to expect from later ideological work, these early theorists were focused on issues of human nature, morality, and the role and expectations of the individual in a social context. For our purposes, we are particularly interested in their thoughts on the individual and ultimately find these theorists in agreement that people naturally exist in an individualistic condition. This premise serves as the cornerstone for the ultimate program of classical liberalism—the application of the theory in practice.

In *Leviathan*, Hobbes's focus is on determining the best type of state to serve the long-term interests of the people. While the individual is not his primary concern, he must turn his attention to this matter as it is the condition of the individual within and outside of society that supports his idea for state development. He proceeds based on the natural inclinations and condition of people, which he is quite pessimistic about. Hobbes believes that the natural human condition is quite violent and contentious. His development and description of this condition is significant for the development of individualism, and ultimately individual rights. Among the characteristics that Hobbes identifies are the human capacity for knowledge and reasoning, the ability to consent, the love of competition, and the natural equality that exists among individuals.

Hobbes is not known for his fondness of democracy, and in no way advocated for such a system. However, he provided some acknowledgment and understanding of the individual that would go on to be significant to others. His characterization of human nature, at least in some respects, provides the groundwork for later, more expansive, views of the individual as a significant political figure. First, Hobbes believed that human beings were capable of reason and could learn from experiences and then apply those lessons to future choices. Since people have the capacity for reasonable decision-making, they have the ability to grant meaningful consent to one who might rule over them in order to provide safety and security. Hobbes considers reason to be a tool used by individuals to arrive at their own conclusions rather than exhibiting a dependency on others for information.[2]

The ability for the individual to consent to a particular government, and the resulting creation of governmental authority over the people, provides further support for the politically significant role of the individual. While Hobbes describes the state of nature as one free from any type of government or societal restrictions on free will, this is not a pleasant condition. People will reason their way to a better and safer situation by consenting to an absolute ruler who can establish order and rules that they are then compelled to live by. Consent connects to the individual in two ways. First, the decision to grant consent to govern is completely voluntary. Second, the ruler can only have governing authority by way of this individual consent.

Additionally, Hobbes identifies some natural tendencies in human behavior relative to seeking power. He believes people channel their self-interest and individual identity into a willingness to engage in contentious relations with others. This willingness allows individuals to function in politically significant ways. Hobbes's thoughts on power connect to the individual because more power leads to a greater capacity to provide for oneself. In a natural state, this innate desire for more power and a higher quality of living puts one into competition with others—one of the causes of conflict that Hobbes identifies.[3] Lastly, Hobbes acknowledges a natural equality that exists among people. It is this equality that makes life so difficult as the state of nature, but it also allows people to move forward in a safer, and ultimately more representative way. Hobbes's idea of equality is not rooted in an assumption that people are all the same, but he also does not believe significant differences in capabilities are likely either.[4]

A second significant figure for the development of individual rights is John Locke. Born in 1932, Locke's education and career did not immediately lead to politics and political theory. Locke was trained as a medical doctor and only became a political figure when his primary patient became a politician. Locke, like Hobbes developed his theories of governance based on his beliefs about the natural condition of people as individuals. We look primarily to his *Second Treatise on Government* for these ideas. Unlike Hobbes, Locke believed that there is a moral standard, natural law, that compels certain behavior, even in the absence of government and formal societal connections. Even with natural law, however, Locke argues that people wish to leave the state of nature because there is no impartial judge to execute the law and mediate violations of the law. The establishment of a social contract and a formal governing body creates a higher quality of life and allows for these tasks to be delegated to the government.[5] We find many arguments in favor of individualism in Locke's writings, and these are the points that were particularly persuasive during the American founding era, including natural equality among people, the inability to subordinate another or be subordinated, the use of reason, the existence of natural rights, the nature of labor and private property, the role of consent, and the nature of political society.[6]

The first characteristic that is important to us here is the state of natural equality that exists among people. This equality of capability and aptitude thus entitles all people to comparable levels of power and authority.[7] The individual authority that equality grants, however, does not extend to authority or dominance over others, and it cannot be surrendered to another.[8] Locke also bases his views of the individual on their ability to utilize reason in decision-making. This is significant because it empowers the individual in their dealings with others and with the government. Since the individual is primarily rational, as opposed to emotional, they can be expected to learn from experience and to change course based on those lessons learned. Locke's assertion of natural rights forms another important component of his argument in support of the individual. He identifies the natural rights of "life, health, liberty or possessions" and contends that these are rights that all people have by virtue of being human.[9] Since these rights are naturally occurring and not granted by government, the violation of these rights by a government can provide legitimate grounds for the individual to rebel against such a state. Locke's views on labor and property are significant for this study, as well. People have ownership of their own bodies, and so when they mix that labor with any item, the ownership extends to that item. At that point, we have a legitimate claim to that item, and it becomes our private property.[10]

Lastly, we see Locke's emphasis on the importance of the individual with regard to consent and the nature of political society. Due to the natural freedom that people possess, any decision to leave the state of nature is made freely and the granting of consent to another for purposes of governance is also made freely.[11] While the state of nature is not quite as dire for Locke as it was for Hobbes, it is still not an ideal condition. It remains logical to leave it as long as the ensuing social contract provides for the ongoing protection of natural rights.

Hobbes and Locke contribute to the general understanding of the individual as one who is inherently equal to other people, who utilizes reason to arrive at legitimate decisions and conclusions, who has power over themselves and the ability to transfer authority to another body, should reason lead them to make that decision. Both of these theorists describe individualism as a metaphysical condition that must be reconciled with a political system that preserves and protects the individual while providing the safety and security needed for a long and productive life. For the founders, these ideas served as the justification for a number of procedures and provisions deemed necessary for a viable political system that featured the individual as the center of the political world they were working to construct. Next, we can look to see where in the Constitution we find provisions intended to protect the individual and their rights.

INDIVIDUALISM IN THE CONSTITUTION

The U.S. Constitution does not represent the first attempt to institutionalize these beliefs about the individual, as we can see evidence that the Declaration of Independence and the Articles of Confederation sought to protect the individual as well.[12] For our purposes, however, we will limit our attention to the Constitution as it is the document that institutionalized federalism in the American political system. The Constitution also represents a renewed commitment and reconceptualization of how a government could incorporate and protect individual rights.[13] The preservation of individual rights in the Constitution emphasizes the importance of this concept to the founders and also serves to make the point that the preservation of individual rights would require formal provisions and structure.[14] We find this emphasis in terms of protections for individuals and their rights.[15] Examples can be found in the denials of power to the national government, the structure of the national government, and in the national government's grants of power.[16]

First, the Constitution contains specific denials of power to the national government in order to protect individual rights. Examples include the use of the writ of habeas corpus which prevents individuals from being held by the government without demonstrating that there is cause to do so; prohibitions against the use of bills of attainder, which prevent the legislature from passing punitive laws targeting an individual or group; and prohibitions against ex post facto laws, which prevent the legislature from retroactively applying laws and penalizing people for committing acts that were legal at the time they were committed. Another prime example, of course, is the ultimate inclusion of the Bill of Rights to the Constitution, with the goal of more specifically delineating freedoms that would be protected against encroachment by the national government.

Second, we find individual rights protected through structural and procedural provisions contained in Articles I through III of the Constitution and explained in *Federalist* No. 10.[17] Specifically, the individual is protected through the creation of a mixed government that functions by utilizing checks and balances of power. James Madison explains in this essay the human inclination to group into factions based on shared perspectives on specific issues. We should be protected from minority factions by majority rule, but Madison dealt directly with the potential of majority factions who might be prone to deprive the minority of their rights. He believed that mixed forms of governance would deal effectively with this possibility and ensure the protection of all individuals' rights.[18]

The grants of power in the Constitution take the form of both expressed and inherent powers and are another way the individual is protected. The expressed powers listed in Article I, Section 8 of the Constitution are powers that were identified to be related to issues of national significance, wherein it would not be desirable or beneficial to the nation or its individual citizens to have a great deal of variation. The Supremacy Clause provides stability to this claim by making the Constitution and the federal laws that are created by its authority supreme over state laws in the event of a conflict. Though the Supremacy Clause can be interpreted to tread on state authority, it provides a method through which the national government can protect the individual citizens from state actions that may create policy detrimental to the rights of the people.[19] Additionally, the national government provides for inherent powers necessary for the long-term viability of the nation that also serve as individual protections, such as powers related to the general welfare and the common defense of the people.[20] Lastly, the Constitution reserves powers to the states to deal with "ordinary concerns," which can also be viewed as additional protections for the individual. Such powers were reserved to the states with the "firm expectation that the states would wield their power in ways consistent with individual liberty."[21]

These many provisions serve as the constitutional foundation for individual rights and freedoms in the United States. However, it is the variation in implementation that has led to the question of compatibility between federalism and the protection of individual rights. It has been argued that the effective protection of individual rights would indeed come down to the functionality of federalism, specifically: Would federalism serve to limit the powers of both the national government and state governments? Would state governments honor their obligation to protect individual rights in areas they were sovereign over? Would the Bill of Rights be able to serve as a protection for individual rights at the national level?[22]

To the extent that the states were reserved powers not expressly delegated to the national government, they were empowered by the Constitution to use their own state constitutions to identify and protect individual rights. Though the Bill of Rights is now thought of as the main protection for individual rights, that has not always been the case. Historically, the Bill of Rights was limited to the activities of the national government, and the states were empowered to create their own state constitutions to set protections at the state level.[23] Years before U.S. Constitution was drafted, many states were already at work establishing rights for their own citizens.[24] These early state-level declarations of rights would serve as a model down the road for a national bill of rights.[25] After the founding era, the states were encouraged in various ways to actively engage in the identification and protection of individual rights, though the trend would later turn toward the role of the national government. Though the states have always had the legal ability to expand our understanding of individual rights, there is not a large tradition upon which to draw from.[26]

INDIVIDUAL RIGHTS AND FEDERALISM

The question of the compatibility between federalism and individual rights has been asked and answered, so why ask it and try to answer it again? The simple answer: because things are always changing. Our understanding of federalism changes over time, and even at one given point in time, different scholars have different opinions. Given the nature of federalism, it is difficult and probably controversial to say definitively that any of these takes are wrong. So, why is the question asked in the first place? The question can be controversial because not everyone agrees federalism was intended to serve this purpose. One of the arguments for having a federal system is that it allows sovereign power to exist closer to the people and can limit the power of the national government, presumably to protect freedoms and rights. But has this worked? Even with a federal system, the preservation of rights has not always been successful and we have seen variation in protections based upon time, place, who is seeking the rights protection, specifically which rights they would like protected, and which level of government has taken the lead on the policy. If the division of sovereignty between the national government and the states has served to protect individual rights, then we can say that the concepts are compatible. However, if that division of sovereignty has somehow served to inhibit or violate individual freedom and rights, then we can conclude that these founding principles of American democracy may be at cross purposes, at least at some points in time and in some policy areas. We may find, given the subjectivity of both federalism and individual rights, a mixed bag of results.[27]

How then do the concepts of individual rights and federalism relate to one another? To the extent that the Constitution was created to establish a lasting form of governance based on generally agreed upon principles, the compatibility of these principles is very important to the lasting success of this political system and its ability to stay true to those founding concepts. The importance of this question has long since been established and recognized.[28] This book is but one attempt to answer the question and to be part of this larger, ongoing conversation. The difficulty encountered when dealing with this question has made it the subject of some controversy.[29] Since there are so many ways to define the concepts and interpret founding intent and documents, even if we can agree that there is tension between federalism and individual rights, we still might not agree on why there is tension or what can be done to address it. It is my contention that disputes over the nature of rights is one contributing factor to this tension.

The Nature of Individual Rights

When we consider the concept of a right, whether it is a natural right or a right granted by a government, we are referring to something that an individual is entitled to do. It is an activity that an individual can engage in freely or an activity or procedure that is promised if and when an individual person wishes to engage in it or if circumstances call for it. That basic concept is clear, though deciding which activities qualify may not be quite as clear. When we layer on the concept of federalism, the situation can grow more complicated. In a federal system, each individual is both a national citizen and state resident, subject to the jurisdiction of both the national and state government.[30] It is understood that one purpose of a federal system is to institutionalize balance and, arguably, to create a system of governance that can adequately deal with both national and state concerns, culture, and preferences. How then do rights fit into this understanding? If any significantly sized group of people contend that an activity should be protected and classified as a right, then does it make sense for a right to only be protected in some places? The argument has been made that by conceding that an activity is a right, it should not be limited in its protection.[31] Based on this perspective, it would seem that the tension between federalism and rights is irreconcilable, as federalism facilitates a variety of policies and rights protection would appear to "require universal standards and uniform treatment."[32]

There is another side to this coin, however, as we are left with the issues of deciding which activities should be protected and exactly how many people (and at what level) need to support this decision to make it legitimate. For instance, if a majority of people nationally are in favor or classifying an activity as a right, but the matter only enjoys minority support in a particular state, is it legitimate to impose that decision on the state? What about the minority view in that state?[33] The American political system values both majority rule and minority rights. Given the numerous challenges that these issues present, the ability to protect rights at the national and state level can be viewed as an opportunity to develop a more expansive view of rights. However, allowing for the creation and protection of rights on multiple levels can help individuals deal with obstacles they encounter in the process of gaining national recognition.[34] In the course of American history, there are examples of rights protection playing out in a multitude of ways.

In "The Past and Future of the New Judicial Federalism," G. Alan Tarr identifies three eras of rights protection in the United States.[35] During each era, the expectation changed for where and how rights would be protected. The initial expectation from the founding was that the states would take lead in protecting individual rights through the use of their constitutions.[36] The second era featured the expectation that the national government, by way of the federal courts, would take almost full responsibility for protecting individual rights.[37] This era lasted from roughly the 1930s to the 1970s.[38] The third era, which Tarr identified in the 1990s, features components of both eras. The national government was still dominant with regard to civil liberties law, but the states had begun reasserting their power to utilize state constitutions as a method of protecting rights.[39]

This shifting of responsibility and activity over time is indicative of the tension that has existed between the states and the national government on this matter since the founding. It had been the hope and expectation of the Anti-Federalists, in particular, that the states would be ready, willing, and able to use their sovereignty to protect the rights of the residents of their respective states through the use of their state constitutions. The states appeared up to this task, as the states' constitutions typically featured their own declarations of rights.[40] The states had already begun this practice under the Articles of Confederation, so there was reason to be optimistic that the states would embrace this responsibility and also be effective in the protection of individual rights. Unfortunately, the ongoing issue of how to identify rights would plague American politics through the Civil War and beyond.

Given the nature of slavery and the pervasive racism that caused and perpetuated that institution, the end of the Civil War was the beginning of a new challenge to American federalism and the protection of individual rights. The states could not necessarily be trusted to consistently protect the rights of

African American citizens, and thus the Thirteenth, Fourteenth, and Fifteenth Amendments were necessary to compel compliance with the end of slavery and the recognition of African Americans as citizens.[41] This shift of responsibility to the national government would open the door to other actions regarding matters such as child labor, workers' rights, in addition to issues of racial discrimination and oppression.[42] Through the doctrine of selective incorporation, the Supreme Court established a path to apply the Bill of Rights to state actions.[43] Moving into the twentieth century, the Supreme Court took on the issue of free speech but did not have any guidance from the states on how to proceed. There was "no body of state-court free speech law" that could be utilized in creating a national standard that might be acceptable and organically developed at the state level, as the state courts had busied themselves primarily with property and business cases.[44]

Following the same trend of devolution and decentralization that was observed in other sectors of American politics in the 1970s, the focus began to shift somewhat to the potential of state declarations of rights in providing individuals with protection.[45] However, it has been argued that, through the end of the 1990s, the states as a whole had not taken on the cause of promoting civil liberties in any meaningful way.[46] While this shift may seem positive from a rights perspective, it created conceptual challenges for the relationship between federalism and individual rights. The shift of responsibility to the national government made sense given the nature of rights and the need for standards and fairness. However, creating one path to rights protection bypassed one of the important assumptions made about federalism in the first place—that it would create many paths and opportunities for rights protection.[47] The acceptance and promotion of the national government as the better protector of individual rights challenges one of the justifications for dividing sovereignty between the national government and the states in the first place.[48]

The state courts have missed opportunities over time to rely on state constitutions for civil liberty protections, and thus have not gained significant experience in doing so.[49] This has historically left the federal courts to move forward on such matters with limited, if any, documented guidance from the states. The federal decisions have then served as guidance for the states, as it has been observed that state judges have been more likely to apply the Supreme Court's reasoning to state decisions even when not directly compelled to do so.[50] Again, this is not necessarily problematic from a rights perspective if the end result is the protection of individual rights, and we have no reason to assume that state constitutions would be interpreted in a more rights-affirming manner than the Bill of Rights.[51] It is also not likely at this juncture that the state courts will take the lead in applying state constitutions as the primary protection for individual rights.[52]

Founding Perspectives

Given the nature of the relationship between individual rights and federalism and the tension that it has historically displayed, it is worthwhile to consider what the initial expectations were for this relationship. Revisiting the founding era and the evidence of those expectations will serve to further build our understanding of this relationship. *Federalist* No. 51 is commonly mentioned in this regard, as it is one primary source we can point to that explicitly claims that the division of power that defines a federal system could be expected to better protect individual rights.[53] This expectation grew from the founding belief that limited government was part of the political plan needed to protect the individual, and federalism was one way that government power could be contained.[54]

Of course, there was not just one "founding perspective," and the debate between the Federalists and the Anti-Federalists provided an opportunity to air out some of the conceptual conflict that these perspectives had with one another. Both the Federalists and the Anti-Federalists knew that threats to individual liberty were real and of concern, but they disagreed as to where the threats were likely to come from.[55] The Anti-Federalists believed that the greatest threat to individual liberty was a national government that would be distant from the people and more likely to assume more power than was necessary or appropriate.[56] Government authority closer to the people would be more protective of those individuals and less likely to engage in tyrannical policy making and implementation.[57] The Federalists, however, contended that greatest threat existed at the state level where local majorities would have a better chance at depriving individuals of rights.[58] The national government could actually overcome those local threats due to the larger array of interests represented at the national level, the quality of politicians that national politics would draw, and by taking issues that were truly national in nature from state and local politicians who did not have the nation's interest in mind but rather their own locality.[59]

Types of Individual Liberty

How we conceive of liberty goes a long way to determining what types of right protection are most effective and appropriate. Given the theoretical foundation of the American political system, we do take liberty in any sense to mean individual liberty, and its preservation is arguably the priority of the government on both the national and state level.[60] There is nothing inherently individualistic about federalism, but the preservation of individual rights is a feature of the American brand of federalism. The establishment of a federal system was made possible by a belief that individual freedom would be best protected by distributing powers to both the national and state governments, and the actions of both levels of government would be guided by the ultimate and supreme value placed on individual liberty.[61]

By virtue of the subjectivity involved in the identification and prioritization of individual liberties, we will not likely discover a strict pattern that governmental decision-making follows in this study; sometimes a state or states may do a better job of protecting individual rights and sometimes the national government may be more active.[62] The hope is that it all balances out in the end with the goal of individual freedom coming out ahead.[63] It is not assumed, however, that such an aggregate assessment would be a satisfactory measure of the American experience and the success of the national and state governments in protecting individual rights across the board. As we will see, the focus on individuals and the protection of their rights can sometimes get lost in the federal debate over which level of government should be doing what.

A belief in both federalism and the preservation of individual rights rightfully leads us to question any government action that intervenes with individual activity if it is not properly rooted in constitutionally granted power.[64] It has proven easy to lose sight of individual liberty as a goal, however, and become distracted by a preference for either national or state authority and action that is somehow separated from that prior concern. In his book, *Grassroots Tyranny*, Clint Bolick contends that disputes between the national government and states that concern individual liberty should always be resolved with a "preference in favor of liberty," regardless of which "side" that lands us on.[65] There are different conceptions of liberty that are relevant to this discussion, and they include federal liberty, positive liberty, and negative liberty. Understanding these various takes on liberty gives us an advantage in navigating debates on this and related topics and provides the foundation upon which varying proposals to protect liberty are built.

Federal liberty is a term used to describe freedoms individuals expect to have by agreement.[66] In a political system based on classical liberalism, we would expect the components of the agreed upon liberty to be predicated on natural rights and then broadened to encompass whatever rights are deemed appropriate for that particular country. Whatever the parameters for the understanding and application of individual freedom are, they can be understood in positive and negative terms. Both conceptions of liberty are consistent with the establishment of natural rights in liberal thought and the acknowledgment of nation-specific rights as provided for in the definition of federal liberty. Negative liberty means that the individual is most free when they are left alone. In the American context, we would understand negative liberty to mean limiting government action to the bare minimum so as to maximize the space the individuals have to make their own choices.[67] However, this limited governmental action can have unintended consequences, because limited governmental interference in individual affairs can actually increase the possibility of private interests interfering in individual affairs.[68] Positive liberty is based on the idea that the protection of individual rights may require "affirmative governmental conduct."[69] It is the notion that the government, at either the national or state level, may need to interfere in individual affairs to actively provide for freedom. It may be the case that individuals need help to be free, and laws that deal with matters of discrimination, education, and the environment are examples of policy areas that could benefit from this understanding of liberty.[70]

There is debate as to which type of liberty the founders had in mind. Clearly, the idea of federal liberty fits easily, as they were influenced by social contract theorists. The idea of protecting and expanding upon the idea of natural rights and formalizing those rights in a binding constitutional document is clear and supported by the historical record. However, whether the founders were more focused on promoting negative or positive liberty is debatable.[71]

Compatibility of Individual Rights and Federalism

There are varying perspectives that are useful in assessing the relationship between individual rights and federalism. First, it is important to establish that, regardless of which relationship we ultimately find to me more persuasive, these topics were closely related in founding thought.[72] The establishment of a federal system and the division of sovereignty that it entails would have been difficult to fathom without the underlying emphasis on and belief in the primacy of the individual and individual sovereignty.[73] It is through the classical liberal conception of the individual that one can develop any argument for disseminating meaningful political power more broadly. A less optimistic view of human nature would almost surely lead to the concentration of power among the few, as we would feel far less confident in the ability of most people to responsibly manage political power. Federalism provides many more seats at the table of substantive political decision-making.

Second, it is the primacy of the individual and the individual's capacity for intelligent and rational thought that creates the tension in a federal system. Though the founders believed that individuals were given due protection for their natural rights and were capable of rational and reasonable thought, they were not under any illusion that individuals were perfect or naturally altruistic. They recognized that any government, at any level, had the ability to expand its powers beyond an acceptable level out of a desire to promote a specific agenda or set of objectives that might benefit a certain group of individuals. This could certainly happen at the state level, as Madison repeatedly expressed concerns that smaller governing bodies could have a heightened potential of violating minority rights.[74] Thus, the national government had a role to play in addressing the potential for tyranny at the state level.[75] Given the historical experience of the colonial era, the dangers of an overly powerful national government were known. The founders also recognized that state governments could be both "bulwarks of liberty and oppressors of liberty," and so tried to focus their attention on the preservation of individual liberty for all against government encroachment.[76] The government, any government, consists of a group of people who at any time might lose sight of which policies are truly advancing liberty for all and which policies may only be advancing liberty for some. Federalism was designed to be the method to balance these many needs.[77]

Third, we must remain mindful that these concepts have been and remain controversial in the scholarship of federalism. The historical record show that the political saliency and institutionalization of these concepts were both established during the founding era, but what remains controversial is how compatible these concepts truly are.[78] Does federalism provide a hostile or hospitable environment for the protection of individual rights? We can review the arguments for and against the compatibility of federalism and individual rights in the United States.

Federalism and the Protection of Individual Rights Are Compatible

There is the persisting view that individual rights and federalism are compatible with one another, though that compatibility may require routine maintenance.[79] Further, individual rights and federalism have been viewed as complementary concepts that have been able to accomplish more together for democracy and civil society than they ever could on their own.[80] We can identify in the scholarship of federalism a number of arguments to support this side of the debate, including the connected and interdependent nature of the concepts, the dynamic between the national government and state governments to create balance to advance individual freedom, and the empowerment of the states to balance other states' policy prerogatives.

First, individual rights and federalism are compatible because the concepts are connected and are interdependent. They are mutually reinforcing ideas. Federalism developed because of the belief in the primacy of the individual and the resulting concept of popular sovereignty.[81] Federalism can then serve the purpose of protecting and reinforcing individual rights.[82] This is a view that has been affirmed by the Supreme Court.[83] Political power was not divided and shared with the states simply for the sake of doing so, but specifically in order to promote and protect the rights of the individual. Further, the individuals, with their rights and freedoms, exist in multiple coalitions at various times—sometimes in the majority and sometimes in the minority.[84] Federalism allows for individual protection in the many capacities that individuals may find themselves. Federalism provides a path by which individual rights, understood at times as group rights when like-minded or affiliated individuals come together with related concerns and needs, can be protected.[85] Further, federalism expands the opportunity for individual rights protection. Specifically in instances where desired legal protections are not provided at the national level, individuals can make their case at the state level with the hope that protections can be established in some state or multiple states.[86] In this way, we can observe states as being able to provide for a "diversity of preferences" in a way only a federal system would allow.[87] It takes more than the simple articulation of rights in a list to provide for their protections. The federal governmental structure and distribution of political sovereignty facilitate the protection of individual right.[88]

Second, the dynamics between the state governments and the national government can adapt and function in a few ways to create the power balance needed to protect individual rights. One example of this dynamic is the empowerment of the national government to intervene to protect the individual if the state is a threat to individual rights. This can be observed when the state governments (one or several) are engaging in policies that are construed as limiting individual rights and the national government asserts itself in order to protect those rights against state infringement.[89] During eras of American history, particularly during the civil rights era of the twentieth century, the Supreme Court used its power to make "individual rights synonymous with federal guarantees" when it became apparent that such intervention was necessary to advance the cause of civil rights.[90] This particular dynamic has been described as "non-cooperative," because it requires more drastic and compelling action to bring about faster changes rather than working with the states in a more incremental manner. However, the adjustment or shift toward national power was made possible by federalism and resulted in advances for individual rights.[91] The Fourteenth Amendment made it possible for the national government to protect individual rights from state laws and practices that were designed to limit them.[92]

Another way this dynamic can shift occurs when the states are empowered to push back against the national government if one or more states perceive that the national government is either violating or not doing enough to protect individual rights. Federalism gives the states a way to advance the cause of individual rights and freedoms in a way that is consistent with the culture and expectations of those particular states.[93] Individual rights can be protected by the states in any instance in which the national governments seems less likely to protect them, and provides a method to legitimize opposition to any potentially repressive national government practice.[94] It is not necessary for all states, or even a majority of states, to push back in this way for it to be an effective method of protest and rights protection. Even a few states seeking to expand individual rights protection in a policy area can be an effective method of limiting the power of the national government. A virtue of American federalism is its potential to limit the exercise of national government power, and we can observe that directly when the states shift the power balance their way in the name of protecting individual rights.[95] Federalism opens the door to this possibility.

We can also observe the shifting dynamic function to protect individual rights is when the states and national governments work together to protect individual rights. This has become a growing area of interest in federalism as we see various interest groups and organizations work to build national consensus on a variety of policy issues.[96] Beyond the traditional idea of either the states protecting the individual from the national government or the national government protecting the individual from the states, the idea of a more collaborative "polyphonic" approach has been proposed that perhaps provides even more opportunities for the expansion of individual rights protections.[97] The concept of polyphonic federalism is based on the idea that individual rights are best protected when there is "overlap and concurrence of state and federal authority" and is open to positive notions of liberty in which both levels of government would be empowered to create policies to help individuals be free as opposed to limiting government intervention.[98] One source of limitation on the protection of individual rights can be found in faulty policy implementation. Active cooperation between the national government and the states can lead to the best outcome for individual rights, as there is a shared agenda and plan for implementation.[99]

Lastly, we can argue for the compatibility between individual rights and federalism based on the ability the states have to provide individuals with protection from other states' oppressive policies. From this perspective, we can view states as "sanctuaries" for specific individual rights, as federalism permits them the political autonomy to create policy based on local norms within a limited jurisdiction.[100] Citizens who feel oppressed by, or are simply dissatisfied with, one state's laws can more easily "escape" to another state in a way they could not if such a law existed at the national level.[101] It is reasonable to believe that, due to the element of competition that can arise among states for both resources and people, a state would not want to lose significant portions of its population. If people can move to a neighboring state to avoid unjust policies, this could place pressure on individual state legislatures to reconsider such policies.[102]

Federalism and the Protection of Individual Rights Are Incompatible

The arguments for the compatibility of individual rights and federalism are compelling, but they only tell part of the story of how these concepts have been perceived over time. There is another body of thought that argues that federalism and the protection of individuals rights are not compatible for several reasons, including the lack of a conceptual link between individual rights and federalism; the acknowledgment of rights as fixed concepts in liberal society; the historical failure of American federalism to protect individual rights; and the erosion of federalism to superficial debates about ideology and states' rights.

First, individual rights and federalism are incompatible because there is no conceptual link to connect them. There is very little evidence to support the notion that the founders selected a federal organization to preserve liberty, nor is there evidence to believe that such a thing would have motivated their decision-making. William Riker, in his book *Federalism: Origin, Operation, and Significance*, unapologetically characterizes the connection between federalism and individual freedom as a "widely asserted fallacy" about federalism.[103] He found it highly unlikely that the founders would have been overly interested in "provisions for the distant and not clearly foreseen future" and would have been far more interested in setting up a stable government in that particular moment.[104] Riker did entertain the possibility that the founders could have believed that federalism would provide for freedom, but still asserts that the connection between federalism and freedom is "objectively false."[105] As further evidence of this disconnect, we have observed other federal systems succumb to dictatorship.[106] Thus, federalism was not an automatic path or protected system that would preserve individual freedom. If it were, then dictatorships would not have been able to emerge from federal systems. Additionally, there has been no consistent relationship between either level of government and the protection of rights. The protection of individual rights seems to be dependent on the issue, the time period, and the mood of the courts. There are times when the national government has moved to protect certain individual rights, but then there are other times when the national government has expanded its powers so as to deny individual freedom.[107] Further, the national government has acted at times to decrease the powers of the states only to change course in other times. All of this variation is not evidence of adaptability but rather is evidence of an arbitrariness of action that does not constructively or consistently link the presence of federalism with the preservation of individual rights.

A second argument for the incompatibility of individual rights and federalism concerns the definition of rights and how it is construed under federalism. In a liberal society, rights begin as a fixed notion in the state of nature that include life, liberty, and property. Under a social contract, the responsibility of rights protection is transferred to an agreed-upon government and then other rights can be developed that are rooted in those natural rights. As such, rights in a liberal society are fixed in nature and are not variable. The importance of individual rights protection and the consequences of those rights not being protected make rights as a variable concept a difficult idea. However, this variability is exactly what federalism allows, and it has been considered a disadvantage of such a system.[108] The mobility of the American population has exacerbated the deleterious effects of this variability, in that individuals can and do experience different levels of protection for their rights depending upon what state they are in.[109] This creates a challenge as most citizens associate the rights they enjoy with being American, not necessarily with being an Ohioan or a Texan. While it is true that the expansion and application of natural rights into more specific terms can be challenging due to how individual prioritize various activities, once an activity is identified as a right, it arguably should be a right for all Americans and not just residents of a specific state.[110] If an activity is protected as a right, then it should be a right for all citizens. If an activity is not protected for all, then it is not truly a right.

A third argument for the incompatibility of individual rights and federalism concerns the extent to which it has not consistently worked. We have evidence aplenty of individual rights being violated, and there is a general concern that we can observe no consistent pattern of federalism actually protecting the individual.[111] There are reasons to doubt the states' ability to protect the individual as well as reasons to doubt the national government. One of the commonly cited advantages of federalism is the increased responsiveness of local government, but we have no reason to connect responsiveness to the protection of rights.[112] Indeed, it may be the will of a local majority to oppress another group of people, and so responsiveness could actually lead to a more rapid deprivation of individual rights. The primary example of the states failing to protect individual rights centers on matters of race and discrimination, and these matters have raised serious misgivings about how well states are positioned to protect individual rights.[113] As such, there are large subsets of the American population who have seen or experienced states using their sovereignty to perpetuate discrimination in the areas of "voting, accommodations, education, and employment," and view states as obstacles for the protection of individual rights.[114] There have then been damaging carry-over effects from the state level to the national level when the majority of a state disagrees with the majority of the nation and are able to advance their policies in their particular state.[115] The example of race can be used again here when we see that racist and discriminatory policies at the state and local level served to disadvantage and penalize generations of African Americans who were not able to avail themselves of the same social, economic, and educational opportunities as their white counterparts.[116] There has been a national price to pay for these policies, indeed. On the other hand, we also have evidence of individual rights violated by the national government. Robert Schapiro cites many examples of the Supreme Court making decisions that run contrary to the preservation of individual rights, including cases involving guns in schools, women and violence, the preservation of intellectual property, and work conditions.[117] He contends that the national government, by way of federalism, has been provided with the opportunity and has taken advantage of same to deprive the individual of rights protection.[118]

Fourth, we can argue for the incompatibility between individual rights and federalism by way of current interpretation and application of federal principles. Namely, that the federalism of the founders has been lost and reduced to ideological battles and "states' rights" claims that depart from the original premise of federalism: the protection of individual rights. In *Grassroots Tyranny*, Clint Bolick contends that all current explanations or justifications are devoid of "the original purpose of federalism as promoting individual liberty."[119] He argues that political liberals are in favor of expanded national authority but are really just interested in whichever level of governance is more likely to advance social or economic equality; while political conservatives have become accustomed to defending states' rights as "an end in itself" instead of focusing on the protection of individual rights as an end.[120] With regard to ideological battles, Bolick believes that both liberals and conservatives have chosen their preference for state or national outcome based purely on a desired policy outcome and without any fidelity to federalism as an organizational principle or the protection of liberty.[121] Liberals have become more associated with the protection of national power since the New Deal era,[122] and this connection was strengthened through the civil rights era and Great Society legislative agenda. The national government was able to move the ball downfield with regard to more liberal policy initiatives, but that does not mean that liberals would be disinclined from advancing state initiatives that are consistent with liberal policy initiatives. It was not about a preference for national or state power; it was a preference for which level was willing and able to get something done in a particular policy area.[123] Conservatives have become more associated with federalism by way of a supposed desire to utilize state power to effect policymaking, but even this association is challenged and compromised in modern times as more conservatives see productive pathways forward for their own policy agendas by way of the national government.[124] The whole idea of "states' rights" as a topic of federalism is another reason why the concepts of individual rights and federalism have proven to be incompatible over time. Bolick calls the concept of states' rights an oxymoron, as "states don't have rights. States have powers. People have rights. And the primary purpose of federalism is to protect those rights."[125] However, instead of focusing on individual rights, discussions of federalism have turned their focus to preserving majority will at the local level, which may or may not serve to protect individual rights. In fact, we already know that the founders thought the risk for rights violations would grow as the size of a government and its jurisdiction would diminish.[126] The idea that a discussion of the preservation of federalism would rest on the idea that smaller government is better comes into direct conflict with founding notions of how best to protect individual liberty. This shows that, for at least some advocates of federalism, the defense of the concept has departed the realm of individual rights to center on an ill-conceived notion of states' rights. Federalism, properly understood, should always function to protect individual rights. The purported advantage of federalism is the number of ways it can facilitate this protection, but people have lost sight of this overarching goal and its connection to federalism.[127]

We find coherent arguments in the scholarship of federalism literature that support both the compatibility and incompatibility of federalism and the protection of individual rights, but what about a scenario in which the compatibility could depend on the symmetry of the states' and the national government's goals and objectives? Perhaps there are yet other factors to consider when attempting to determine the compatibility of these concepts. Specifically, the idea of issue and agenda symmetry has been put forth as an additional lens through which we can evaluate individual rights and federalism. As Charles Tarleton explains in "Symmetry and Asymmetry as Elements of Federalism: A Theoretical Speculation," symmetry is important in understanding the functionality of a federal system. He defines symmetry as "the level of conformity and commonality in the relations of each separate political unit of the system to both the system as a whole and to the other component units."[128] States in a symmetrical system would have the same relationship to the national government as other states, and they would all be interested in similar solutions to a common set of identified public problems.[129]

An asymmetrical system would be comprised of states that feature different "interests, character, and makeup" which would separate it from other states and the national system, taken as a whole.[130] Tarleton explains that, while the conventional wisdom regarding diversity and federalism suggests that a federal system is well-suited for a diverse population, this may not actually be the case.[131] An increase of diversity in a country can lead to asymmetry if that diversity is not evenly distributed or if the nature of the diversity varies from one place to another. In the presence of asymmetrical relations, either among the states or between the states and the national government, the likelihood of federal–state conflict increases.[132] Such a system might actually be better suited for unitary governance, as the level of diversity can actually prove to be too difficult for federalism to handle.[133]

Thus, a federal system is appropriate for a symmetrical federal relationship, and a unitary system is appropriate for an asymmetrical federal relationship. Regarding the functioning of federalism in the United States, Tarlton observes that it has varied in relation to the symmetry of the federal relationship. When and where there have been divisive issues, the symmetry has been diminished.[134] Based on this assessment, a federal system is not either functional—meaning it facilitates the protection of individual rights, or not functional—meaning it does not. Tarleton suggests we look to see how symmetrical or asymmetrical the relationships are between the states and the states and the national government to determine how functional the system is. If a federal system, like the United States, is often characterized by asymmetrical relationships (and it has been suggested be Riker that it is), then one would question if federalism is actually the best path forward in the protection of individual rights.[135] In the context of these ideas, it certainly is logical to ask the question.

CONCLUSION

The individual and the preservation of individual rights were of paramount importance to the founders, and we now have a better understanding of the ideas that inspired the protection of individual rights in the American political system. The extent to which federalism serves to protect individual rights is debatable, with highly credible and respected scholars weighing in on both sides. Regardless if one sides with the perspective that the concepts are compatible or not, we have always had, and continue to have, a political system in the United States that purports to value, implement, and protect a federal system and individual rights. We can further engage in a discussion of this relationship through the examination of specific policy areas, and there is no shortage of topics to choose from.

In part II, we take an in-depth look into specific policy areas that have been significant, controversial, and impactful for the lives of Americans, the protection of individual rights, and the integrity and sustainability of this federal system. Every person who lives under a federal system has an interest in the functionality of federalism and whether or not it is serving to accomplish the objectives for which it was implemented. In the American context, we can make the argument that federalism was implemented—at least in part—to facilitate the protection of individual rights. In the political climate of the early 2020s, our ability to assess the functionality of federalism and its relationship to individual rights is of particular value. We are dealing with a number of divisive issues and a global pandemic crisis. Per Tarlton and others, federalism may not actually be the best path forward in such an environment. Yet, it is the power distribution that the United States has, so how does this work most effectively and efficiently? How do the American people move forward as a nation and find solutions to the many identified public issues? If we are unable to find some answers to these questions, the challenges that face the United States will only become increasingly daunting and the future of federalism more compromised.[136]

NOTES

1. For a more thorough treatment of these influences, see Walls, *Individualism in the United States.*
2. Hobbes, *Leviathan*, 42.
3. Ibid., 80–81.
4. Ibid., 103.
5. Locke, *Second Treatise of Government*, 69.
6. Walls, *Individualism in the United States*, 28.
7. Locke, *Second Treatise of Government*, 13.
8. Ibid., 25.
9. Ibid., 14.
10. Ibid., 27.
11. Ibid., 77.
12. Walls, *Individualism in the United States*, 74.
13. Ibid., 77.
14. Ibid., 80.
15. Ibid., 77; McDonald, *Novus Ordo Seclorum*, Ch. 5.
16. Ibid., 77.
17. Ibid.
18. Ibid.; Hamilton et al., *The Federalist Papers*, 46–47.
19. Walls, *Individualism in the United States*, 78.
20. Ibid.
21. Bolick, *Grassroots Tyranny*, 45; 51–52.
22. Ibid., 53.
23. Beasley, "Federalism and the Protection of Individual Rights," 101.
24. Ibid., 102.
25. Ibid.
26. Tarr, "The Past and Future of the New Judicial Federalism," 68.
27. D'Alemberte, "Rights and Federalism," 124.
28. Tarr and Katz, "Introduction," ix.
29. Ibid., xii.
30. Ibid., x.
31. Ibid.
32. Ibid.
33. Ibid., xi.
34. Ibid.
35. Tarr, "The Past and Future of the New Judicial Federalism," 64.
36. Ibid.
37. Ibid., 65.
38. Ibid.

39. Ibid.
40. Tarr and Katz, "Introduction," xii.
41. Ibid., xiii.
42. Ibid.
43. Ibid., xiv.
44. Tarr, "The Past and Future of the New Judicial Federalism," 66, 68.
45. Tarr and Katz, "Introduction," xiv.
46. Tarr, "The Past and Future of the New Judicial Federalism," 69.
47. Yarbrough, "Federalism and Rights in the American Founding," 70.
48. Ibid.
49. Tarr, "The Past and Future of the New Judicial Federalism," 72–73.
50. Ibid., 77; Latzer, *State Constitutions and Criminal Justice*, 10–161.
51. Tarr, "The Past and Future of the New Judicial Federalism," 76.
52. Ibid., 78.
53. D'Alemberte, "Rights and Federalism," 123; Hamilton et al., "Federalist No. 51," *The Federalist Papers*.
54. Bolick, *Grassroots Tyranny*, 5–6.
55. Yarbrough, "Federalism and Rights in the American Founding," 60.
56. Ibid.
57. Tarlton, "Symmetry and Asymmetry as Elements of Federalism," 864.
58. Yarbrough, "Federalism and Rights in the American Founding," 61.
59. Ibid., 61–62.
60. Elazar, *Exploring Federalism*, 95.
61. Bolick, *Grassroots Tyranny*, 178.
62. Kreimer, "Federalism and Freedom," 69.
63. Ibid.
64. Bolick, *Grassroots Tyranny*, 181.
65. Ibid., 183.
66. Elazar, *Exploring Federalism*, 97.
67. Schapiro, *Polyphonic Federalism*, 7.
68. Kreimer, "Federalism and Freedom," 68.
69. Schapiro, *Polyphonic Federalism*, 8.
70. Ibid.
71. For an argument supporting positive liberty in the founding era, see Walls, *Individualism in the United States*.
72. Bolick, *Grassroots Tyranny*, 42.
73. Ibid., 15; Berger, *Federalism*, 52.
74. Bolick, *Grassroots Tyranny*, 38.
75. Ibid., 39.
76. Ibid.
77. Ibid., 42.
78. Tarr and Katz, "Introduction," ix.
79. Zuckert, "Toward a Theory of Corrective Federalism," 76.
80. Elazar, "Federalism, Diversity, and Rights," 7.
81. Zuckert, "Toward a Theory of Corrective Federalism," 81.

82. Pickerill and Chen, "Medical Marijuana Policy and the Virtues of Federalism," 24.

83. Ibid., 29; J. O'Connor, *New York v. United States*, 505 US 144, 181–182 (1992), quoting *Coleman v. Thompson*, 501 U.S. 722, 759 (1991).

84. Elazar, "Federalism, Diversity, and Rights," 2.

85. Ibid., 6.

86. Robertson, *Federalism and the Making of America*, 5; Tarr and Katz, "Introduction."

87. Pickerill and Chen, "Medical Marijuana Policy and the Virtues of Federalism," 27.

88. Ibid., 28.

89. Kreimer, "Federalism and Freedom," 68.

90. Kincaid, "From Cooperative to Coercive Federalism," 143–144.

91. Ibid., 144.

92. Katz, "United States of America," 310.

93. Pickerill and Chen, "Medical Marijuana Policy and the Virtues of Federalism," 29.

94. Kreimer, "Federalism and Freedom," 67–68.

95. Robertson, *Federalism and the Making of America*, 4.

96. Schapiro, *Polyphonic Federalism*, 47.

97. Ibid., 7.

98. Ibid., 8, 106.

99. Ibid., 106.

100. Kreimer, "Federalism and Freedom," 66.

101. Ibid., 70.

102. Ibid., 71.

103. Riker, *Federalism*, 13; for another argument against the compatibility of freedom and federalism, see "Federalism and Freedom: A Critique," by Franz L. Neumann in *Federalism: Mature and Emergent*, edited by Arthur W. MacMahon.

104. Ibid., 14.

105. Ibid.

106. Ibid.; He uses the examples of the Soviet Union, Germany, Brazil, and Mexico.

107. Bolick, *Grassroots Tyranny*, 76.

108. Howard, "Does Federalism Secure or Undermine Rights?" 22.

109. Ibid., 23.

110. Robertson, *Federalism and the Making of America*, 171–172.

111. Ibid., 172; Schapiro, *Polyphonic Federalism*.

112. Kreimer, "Federalism and Freedom," 69.

113. Ibid.

114. Robertson, *Federalism and the Making of America*, 172.

115. Riker, *Federalism*, 158.

116. Ibid.

117. Schapiro, *Polyphonic Federalism*, 6.

118. Ibid.

119. Bolick, *Grassroots Tyranny*, 7.
120. Ibid.
121. Ibid., 15.
122. Ibid., 74.
123. Ibid., 15.
124. Ibid.
125. Ibid., 17.
126. Ibid., 23; *Associated General Contractors of California v. City & County of San Francisco*, 813 R.2d 922, 929 (1987).
127. Bolick, *Grassroots Tyranny*, 76.
128. Tarlton, "Symmetry and Asymmetry as Elements of Federalism," 867.
129. Ibid., 868.
130. Ibid., 869.
131. Ibid., 874.
132. Ibid., 871.
133. Ibid., 872.
134. Ibid., 873.
135. Riker, "Federalism," 158.
136. Bolick, *Grassroots Tyranny*, 9.

SUGGESTED READINGS

Katz, Ellis and G. Alan Tarr, eds. *Federalism and Rights*. Lanham, MD: Rowman & Littlefield Publishers, Inc., 1996.

Kreimer, Seth F. "Federalism and Freedom." *The Annals of the American Academy of Political and Social Science* 574 (2001): 66–80.

Locke, John. *Two Treatises of Government*. London: Cambridge University Press, 1988 (1698).

Walls, Stephanie M. *Individualism in the Unites States: A Transformation in American Political Thought*. New York, NY: Bloomsbury, 2015.

Yarbrough, Jean. "Federalism and Rights in the American Founding." In *Federalism and Rights*, edited by Ellis Katz and G. Alan Tarr. Lanham, MD: Rowman & Littlefield Publishers, Inc., 1996.

Part II

FEDERALISM AND POLICY

The debate over founding intent and the relationship between federalism and individual rights is nearly impossible to resolve as long as we can point to something in the founding documents and supporting literature to back up each perspective. What I propose in this section is to take the debate over how compatible federalism and individual rights are and seat it within a discussion of policy development and implementation. I have selected four policy areas based on considerations of how old or new the policy area is, how relevant it has been for federalism, and to what extent it affects the enjoyment of individual rights. I chose two older, more established policy areas—civil rights and education—and two newer policy areas—same-sex marriage and physician-assisted death.

Civil rights policy development provides both the opportunity to look far back into American history and to learn about a policy area that would dramatically shape the general understanding of individual rights in other policy areas. Education policy is also a policy that dates back into history and also has a vast impact on all Americans as students then as parents. The second two policy areas I selected are newer and do not have as extensive a history: same-sex marriage and physician-assisted death. Both of these policy areas are examples of morality policy, which pose a special challenge in a federal system. The policy development in each of these areas has their own unique arcs and rests at various levels of government today with different potential for protecting individual rights moving forward. Each of these policy areas allows us to learn more about the functioning of federalism in its relationship to the protection of individual rights.

One challenge in this type of review and analysis is finding a basis upon which to determine the effectiveness of federalism in protecting individual rights. In many ways, the answers to the questions designed to address this matter really just lead to more questions and more discussion. Understanding the nature of this pursuit, I have created a three-part test to answer the main question: On the topic of XXX, does federalism advance or diminish the protection of individual rights? The test comprises the following three questions:

(1) Are individual rights on this topic currently protected somewhere in our political system?

- *Yes, at the state level.*
  This indicates an advancement for individual rights, as this would not be possible without a federal system. The individual rights in question could face threats in the future by a nullifying action by the national government.

- *Yes, at the national level.*
  This indicates a possible advancement for individual rights, depending on whether or not the issue originated with the states. If it originated with the states, and is now protected nationally, then it would represent an advancement of individual rights. If it originated with the national government, then we cannot say for sure that federalism should be credited for the protection. In any event, it could still face challenges if states take actions to inhibit the protection or if the federal courts take nullifying action.

- *No, at no level are individual rights currently protected on this issue.*

(2) Is there reason to believe that this protection was enhanced through federalism as demonstrated by issue mobility between levels of government to seek protections for individual rights? Was the issue able to find the "cracks"?[1]

- *Yes, this issue has moved from one level of government to the next with some sort of protective action taken after the move.*
  Federal mobility to achieve or expand protections would be a sign that federalism has advanced the protection of individual rights.

- *No, this issue has only been dealt with on one level.*
  This could be a sign of advancement of individual rights if it has been resolved at the state level but may still face challenges down the road. If it has been resolved at the national level, without state actions, then it is hard to credit federalism solely for the protection.

(3) Is there reason to believe that this protection will be lasting in a federal system as demonstrated by issue symmetry between the states and the national government or among the states?

- *Yes, there is reason to believe that most if not all states have a similar position on this issue and that position is similar to the national position, and the position is in favor of the protection of individual rights.*

  Issue symmetry would provide the most stability in a federal system, and thus most likely to provide consistent protections for individual rights.

- *Yes, there is symmetry, but it is unified against the protection of individual rights on this issue.*

  This would be bad news for the individual right in question, though federalism may not necessarily be to blame for the deprivation of rights protection.

- *No, there is reason to believe that there are significant variations as to the policy positions and prioritization of this issue from state to state and/or between the states and the national government.*

  This could go either way. Certainly, any extant policy protecting individual rights in this policy area are vulnerable, as asymmetry creates conflict and tension on the issue until it can resolve one way or the other.

How one answers each of these questions will depend solely on their independent analysis of the circumstances evaluated in each policy area. To aid in this assessment, I conduct my review of each policy topic using a similar structure. Each chapter features an introduction to the policy area, including some history of the topic in the context of federalism, and a discussion of how I am defining liberty in that policy and what it means for individual rights to be protected in that policy. Second, I engage in a focused review of policy development in that policy area that has been significant for American federalism, with an identification of important themes and a few key examples, including legislative acts, judicial decisions, and also executive action and citizen action, where relevant. Third, I present a discussion of that policy area today, and that includes an identification of persisting issues and how they are dealt with in a federal system. Lastly, I apply my three-part test and determine if federalism has served to advance or diminish individual rights in that particular policy area. My final assessment of the effectiveness of federalism in protecting individual rights in each of these areas is simply that: my assessment. It is my hope that each reader will reflect thoughtfully on these questions and arrive at their own conclusions that may or may not line up with my own.

It is important to note that a book of this nature cannot possibly endeavor to provide a comprehensive overview of each of these policy areas. Instead,

I have aspired to provide the reader with the highlights that I believe make an evaluation in the context of individual rights protection possible. Of course, in doing so, I risk the accusation of providing a discussion that is both too broad and too limited in scope. Indeed, there is so much more to know about these policy areas than what is contained herein, and I would strongly urge the reader to explore the "Suggested Readings" listed at the end of each chapter to learn even more about the featured policy topics.

NOTE

1. Grodzins, *The American System.*

Chapter 4

Federalism and Civil Rights

This chapter begins our exploration of select public policy issues and how they relate to the topic of federalism and individual rights. Our first topic is broad and of great historical significance to the United States: civil rights. For the purposes of this chapter, we will limit our treatment of civil rights to matters concerning Americans of African descent and other persons of color who have suffered a loss of individual rights on the basis of their racial identification. While this is a policy area that has been researched at great length and is admittedly an ambitious topic for just one chapter of this book, it is particularly appropriate and meaningful for our task at hand. Civil rights, as a political and legal matter, served and continues to serve as one of the greatest tests American federalism has navigated, with varying degrees of success.[1] Our specific interest deals with the extent to which federalism has provided for or impeded the protection of individual rights in this realm. Though equal treatment and equal freedoms enjoy widespread support today, the ways in which we provide for and maintain such equality is still difficult to agree upon.

CIVIL RIGHTS

At the time of the founding, the concept of civil rights was not yet developed because the need was not yet realized. The focus at that time was to develop the specific civil liberties that would be recognized and protected under the proposed system of governance with an understanding that both the structure of the government and the distribution of powers would serve to maximize protections. The concept of civil rights developed over time, as civil rights deal with the extent to which all people actually enjoy the liberties that are

89

set forth for all. Though one could make a case the founders were well aware that the enslaved population would not be enjoying any civil liberties, this topic was left for another day.

As we have previously discussed, the issue of formalizing individual rights was contentious at the founding. The provisions contained in the original text of the Constitution were ultimately unsatisfactory to the Anti-Federalists who wished to see a listing of freedoms that would be protected from infringement by the national government. The proposal drew inspiration from the state-level bills of rights that protected individuals from infringement by state governments.[2] Of course, none of these protections were extended to the enslaved population. In fact, the Constitution was designed to provide further protections to the states who wished to perpetuate the institution of slavery in the United States until such time as the states would decide for themselves to terminate it. Though the document does not formally establish slavery, it "implicitly recognized" its existence and, in doing so, preserved the ability of the states to maintain and regulate it.[3] It was the belief of the slaveholding states, then and for decades to come, that slavery was a matter of state governance and regulation.[4] This belief would form the foundation of states' rights doctrine for the foreseeable future. This doctrine would challenge the ability of Congress to extend any authority over slavery by way of the Commerce Clause, deny all black people—regardless of their status as free or enslaved—the ability to hold citizenship, and would argue vehemently for slaveholders' rights to maintain ownership of their enslaved people regardless of location.[5] Though the Constitution articulated none of this, the document was understood to protect the institution of slavery by way of informally reserving the matter for the states.[6] This matter would ultimately lead to war between the slaveholding states and the national government, and its resolution would come to represent a highly significant moment in the federal relationship and the ultimate test of American federalism.

The matter of civil rights today, specifically the extent to which African Americans are able to enjoy the civil liberties that are promised to all, continues to be one of contention and debate. Though we understand civil rights to be a matter of inclusion and extension, the observable and persisting racial disparities keep American society and culture connected to a highly discriminatory past.[7] Even after the passage of significant pieces of civil rights legislation and binding Supreme Court decisions, these racial disparities persist in a variety of ways.[8] We will explore ways that federalism has allowed civil rights protections to develop and progress, but it is not clear that federalism has been of great help in protecting individual freedom by way of civil rights policy. While federalism is able to provide multiple venues for problem solving and policy making, it can also be argued that federalism creates obstacles as well. These obstacles may be particularly challenging for marginalized populations to overcome.[9]

Civil Rights and the Individual

With regard to individual liberty, the next step is to establish what it means for the individual to be protected relative to civil rights policy. Given the nature of civil rights and our operational definition, it seems that liberty exists here in a positive sense. While there are areas of individual action that we can speak of in negative terms, that is, in terms of restricting governmental activity so as to promote individual freedom, the issue of civil rights does not fit into this model.[10] Civil rights address the inability of certain individuals to enjoy freedoms that are identified and protected by the government, and so it is implied that there is someone actively restricting individual action. Relief in this instance would have to take to the form of positive governmental action in order to stop the people who are stopping the other people from enjoying their freedoms. "Affirmative governmental conduct" has been deemed necessary to protect some individuals against rights infringement by other individuals, whether that infringement has been done in a private or public capacity.[11] Though opponents of civil rights progress have cited the protection of their own individual rights in matters of slavery, racial segregation, and racial discrimination, the individuals of concern for our study are clearly African Americans.

The United States, through its Constitution, has already acknowledged the primacy of individuals and the protections afforded them.[12] Once freedom and citizenship were extended to the formerly enslaved, those protections were arguably extended as well and, as such, require positive action on the part of both levels of government.[13] The perpetuation and legitimacy of federalism would depend upon its ability to support and promote the connection between individual liberties (which it was created, in part, to protect) and civil rights (the enjoyment of those liberties by all).[14]

Civil Rights and Federalism

The connection between civil rights and federalism is ingrained in the American experience and worthy of general historical consideration before we look more specifically at federalism and civil rights policymaking. The existence of civil rights as a political and legal concept can be traced back to the end of slavery and the ratification of the Reconstruction Amendments. While it is true that African Americans had no access to American civil liberties prior to the Civil War, there was also no legal expectation that they would. Only after that expectation was established, and then violated, could modern ideas of civil rights develop. Generally speaking, we associate the protection of civil rights with the national government and the defense of slavery and racial discrimination with states' rights doctrine. It is safe to say that civil rights has been traditionally protected at the national level when they have been protected at all. The national government has been more aggressive in civil rights policymaking at some points and less aggressive at others which could suggest some policy mobility in the federal system over time, but only if we assume that the states moved in to fill the void in maintaining and protecting civil rights, when the national government has stepped back. This may be a reach, though, and we can explore this more when we talk specifically about civil rights policy development. However, in times when the states have not been interested in actively protecting civil rights, this can and has been justification for the national government to step in to protect those individual rights. Thus, federal policy mobility can be seen in that regard.

When we consider the relationship between federalism and civil rights, we must confront the tension on the topic regarding which level of government is best suited to ensure access to civil liberties. The idea of "old federalism" or federalism as it was once understood centered on the objective or preserving regional culture or differences, but this may not hold when certain values or issues build national consensus.[15] At such time that this type of consensus develops, the implementation of a uniform national policy can be compatible with federalism, particularly in the case of civil rights, which are based upon the constitutional American value of individual rights.[16] However, even in light of this connection, the argument is made that the implementation of any uniform policy for any purpose undermines federalism and its ability to protect individual freedom. This perspective is rooted in the belief that any effort at uniformity and centralization comes at a cost to the individual, even if the stated goal is to protect the individual.[17]

In her article "Federalism and Rights in the American Founding," Jean Yarbrough discusses African American civil rights as a significant political issue that has inadvertently served to undermine American federalism.[18] Since several state legislatures proved to be the main obstacles to the realization of African American civil rights, there seemed to be no other solution than to compromise their power through intervention by the national government.[19] Once that threshold was crossed into state sovereignty, it made sense that the national government would also take the lead in the application of civil rights policy to other marginalized groups.[20] The question that remains is whether or not these acts by the national government did damage to the federal balance of power, or if it is an example of federalism functioning correctly. If the goal was to extend the American ideological commitment to individual rights to a belief that all citizens should be promised access to those rights, then the use of federalism in this regard would be perfectly appropriate and justified.[21] From this perspective, the power of the states was subordinated to the national government in the spirit of protecting minority rights against an oppressive majority, which is compatible with the principles of American democracy.[22] The persisting concern remains among some, however, that the inability or unwillingness of the states to act positively in the protection of African American civil rights does not necessarily signal an inability to act on behalf of any rights at any time. This is a significant shift from the founding era when it was expected the states would be the primary guardians of individual rights. This complicated relationship between federalism and civil rights can be better understood by reviewing some key developments and themes that inform them, including the relationship between federalism and rights before the Civil War, the role of the Reconstruction Amendments, and the dynamics between the national government and the states after the Civil War.

First, it is helpful to gain some understanding of the relationship between federalism and the protection of individual rights before the Civil War. Though perhaps the gravity of the situation could not have been appreciated at the time, the relationship between federalism and rights was a perfect storm brewing for decades before the war actually broke out. If we want to think of it as an equation: we can take "primacy of individual rights and the role of the states in protecting them" and add "slaveholding states' desire to maintain the institution of slavery" and we get both a reluctance on the part of the national government to intervene and a staunch belief on the part of the slaveholding states that their discretion on this matter was fully justified and protected by the U.S. Constitution. Of course, it would take a war to solve this problem.

For the first part of our equation, we have the "primacy of individual rights and the role of the states in protecting them." We are familiar with the concept of individual rights in early American political culture and the ways in which the Constitution was designed to protect them. Since the state governments were reserved the role of managing their internal affairs regarding the safety, wellness, and rights of the people residing in those states, the idea that the national government should or would be able to interfere in those matters runs contrary to that understanding of federalism.[23] For the next part of our equation, we have the "states' desire to maintain the institution of slavery." The preservation of states' rights became undeniably linked to the issue of slavery; a connection that would prove very difficult to break in later years. The preservation of slavery and the persistent discrimination against African Americans in the northern states prior to the Civil War occurred at the hands of state governments.[24] We would not go as far as to say that federalism was put into place to facilitate slavery and discriminatory behavior.[25] However, there is no doubt that this power structure allowed the founders to leave the matter for another day, as the states could take individual ownership of the decision without all of the states having to come to an agreement on the matter.[26]

That leaves us with our result: "the reluctance on the part of the national government to intervene and a staunch belief on the part of the slaveholding states that their discretion on this matter was fully justified and protected by the U.S. Constitution." The two components of this result were mutually reinforcing and stood in the way of any new understanding or implementation of rights' protection in the United States. Even those who believed in the legitimacy of national power were hesitant to advocate for this extension of power over the states to determine rights within each state.[27]

At the end of the Civil War, it was necessary to amend the Constitution to directly address the freedoms of African Americans. The Reconstruction Amendments were ratified in 1865, 1868, and 1870, and consist of the Thirteenth, Fourteenth, and Fifteenth Amendments to the Constitution, respectively. The Thirteenth Amendment prohibits both slavery and involuntary servitude within the United States' jurisdiction.[28] As the first amendment to formally place a limit on the states' authority over rights, the Thirteenth Amendment is also "the first to establish equality as an ideal in American life."[29] Though not given as much attention as the Fourteenth Amendment in future legal and political defenses against discrimination, it does also contain a provision granting authority to Congress for enforcement.[30]

The Fourteenth Amendment contains a citizenship clause, a due process clause, and the Equal Protection Clause, all of which are intended to protect all people against rights infringement.[31] The citizenship clause was significant because the original Constitution was silent on this matter, and that silence had historically deprived both free and enslaved African Americans of citizenship and the protected rights thereof.[32] Though the Equal Protection Clause did not automatically invalidate rights violations at the state level, it would go on to provide the constitutional basis for extending such rights through incorporation.[33] Additional provisions of the Fourteenth Amendment addressed such matters as prohibiting those who had "engaged in insurrection" from holding office and requiring states to extend the right to vote to all males aged twenty-one years or older in order to count their entire state population for purposes of representation.[34] The Fifteenth Amendment extends the right to vote without discrimination on the basis of race.[35] However, as with the Fourteenth Amendment, there is evidence that the Supreme Court did not initially read this amendment as a grant of suffrage but rather a prohibition against giving preference to one citizen over another on account of race.[36]

The purpose of amending the Constitution to include these protections stemmed directly from skepticism that the state governments of the former slaveholding states would extend and protect the rights of African

Americans.[37] This skepticism was rooted in the founding belief that rights violations would be more prevalent in smaller groups of people, thus the national government would be better equipped to deal with and prevent such violations than the state and local governments.[38]

Beyond understanding the purpose of the Reconstruction Amendments, there is the additional matter of the impact these amendments would have for American federalism and what the scope of that impact was intended to be. One perspective is that these amendments represented a drastic expansion of national power and a "death blow" to American federalism as it had been known.[39] The assumption here was that the states had suffered such a loss of sovereignty by way of these amendments that the federal system was not even truly federal anymore.[40] If one is inclined to view these amendments through such a lens, it is safe to say that they did alter the balance of federalism by taking the authority that had been reserved to the states over rights but that had not been used effectively to protect them.[41]

There is the competing perspective that these amendments represented a reasonable expansion of national power that altered the balance of power between the national government and the states but did so in a way that was legitimate and consistent with the principles of federalism. First, the amendments could only be as powerful as their implementation. As history would show, the American political system (at both levels) was a bit slow in applying some of the measures contained therein. In essence, federalism itself would temper the implementation and control the interpretation of these amendments.[42] Second, the proposal and ratification of these provisions as constitutional amendments, as opposed to only asserting congressional authority on other grounds, showed a willingness and desire to make changes to the political system within the confines of federalism.[43] Third, the assertion of national authority over the protection of rights was simply a demonstration of the "corrective" powers of federalism in which one level can intercede on behalf of a particular issue when the system as a whole seems to be moving in an undesirable direction.[44] The ability to create balance and to counter power with power is a foundational premise of federalism and was evident with the ratification of the Reconstruction Amendments. They did not serve to change the fundamental distribution or characterization of power, and, in fact, served to limit the reach of the national government by institutionalizing the government's intent with regard to rights. Through this lens, the connection between federalism and rights, specifically the use of federalism to advance the cause of rights, can be seen as quite complementary.[45]

The aftermath of the Civil War and its impact would take generations to address. The tension between the states and the national government and the civil rights movement that would grow to advance the cause at both levels would become a fixture of American politics and political culture. The tension between the levels of government grew, in part, from a desire to categorize both national power and state power in a dichotomous way, either good or bad. It was certainly observable that in the case of African American civil rights, the national government would likely need to spearhead the effort to protect rights.[46] That could be categorized as a demonstration of "goodness" by the national government, but it was certainly no guarantee that the entire national government was on board with such policies nor did it mean that those policies would be consistently and fairly implemented. The national government was viewed as the victor in the cause against slavery, but it did not mean that Americans should no longer be concerned with the issue of growing national power. Though some states had demonstrated opposition to implementing rights protections for all, many states had embraced their role in the protection of individual rights through state-level bills of rights.[47] State governments still had the potential to create new policies and programs and to address public issues using new and innovative methods by way of the sovereignty that federalism allows.[48]

Neither level of government was all good or all bad, not even on the topic of civil rights, but the desire to describe them in absolute terms created a lasting tension. Even though significant strides had been made toward protecting African American civil rights, the imperfection and incompleteness of those strides is evidenced in the development of the civil rights movement. This movement, like other social movements, represented and continues to represent a desire for the government to be more responsive to the people on civil rights issues and maximize protections for the individual. The relationship between federalism and civil rights is a complicated one but is foundational to the experience of American federalism. Beyond our basic understanding of this relationship and how it was impacted by the Civil War and the abolition of slavery, we can move forward to a discussion on federalism and civil rights policy development.

FEDERALISM AND CIVIL RIGHTS POLICY DEVELOPMENT

While this section should not be construed as a comprehensive discussion of civil rights policy, we can engage in a focused discussion about the developments that have been significant from the perspective of federalism. This will help build the foundation needed to assess whether federalism has helped or hindered the advancement of individual rights within the context of civil rights policy. It is also important to note that this discussion does not cover the role of citizen action in moving these policy objectives forward over time but rather focuses on governmental action that resulted in specific policy outcomes. It is acknowledged that this omission could overstate the significance of institutional action.[49] However, given the nature of the topic of federalism, this focus seems appropriate. There is a list of suggested readings at the end of this chapter for anyone interested in a more comprehensive coverage of the civil rights movement and civil rights policy development. Though this coverage must be limited, it is the intent to select a variety of impactful themes, legislative acts, and judicial decisions that adequately reflect the dynamic nature of civil rights policy after the Civil War.[50]

Themes of Civil Rights Policy Development

Before we move into a discussion of specific legislative acts and judicial decisions, we can reflect on a few broad themes that have arisen in the course of civil rights policy development and the determination if it should take place at the national or state level. These themes include issues of dual citizenship and the decision to use the Commerce Clause versus the Reconstruction Amendments to justify national civil rights policy.

First, there is the question of dual citizenship: Were individuals primarily citizens of the United States or the state in which they lived? The lack of a citizenship clause in the original text of the Constitution left the topic ambiguous, and this ambiguity was primarily used to deny rights to African Americans. Through the citizenship clause of the Fourteenth Amendment, the effort was made to establish and extend the concept of citizenship at the national level and incorporate African Americans along the way. However, the clause reads: "All persons born or naturalized in the United States and subject to the jurisdiction thereof, are citizens of the United States and of the State wherein they reside."[51] Was this clause written to indicate that the national government could directly protect individual rights from state infringement, or were the state governments still responsible for providing for specific rights and rights protection at the state level? Was the Fourteenth Amendment intended to—and could it, constitutionally—bypass the state to establish those direct rights protections on the basis of national citizenship? Could individual rights be nationalized and did the Fourteenth Amendment accomplish that?

A second recurring theme in the development of civil rights policy centers on how to best justify the role of the national government: through the Commerce Clause or using the Reconstruction Amendments? Though the intent of the Reconstruction Amendments has been debated, it would stand to reason that the Constitution was amended in order to provide constitutional grounding for national government action on matters of race and discrimination. However, for many years after their ratification, the courts were reluctant to read those amendments broadly and were more inclined to a narrow interpretation that would maximize state sovereignty on such matters. As a result, the Commerce Clause came into play as an expressed power that could be adapted to matters of race if those matters could be also connected to economic activity.[52] Of course, critics of that strategy have described it as an unjustified power grab by the national government, but it has been effective in arguing against discriminatory policies and for civil rights protections.[53]

Each of these themes represent complex challenges that would arise repeatedly over the years in civil rights policy development. We will see this pattern in our focused review. First, we will review select legislative actions and then significant court decisions that all served to shape the relationship between federalism and individual rights.

Select Legislative Action

The course of civil rights policy development involves a number of legislative acts that have been significant from the perspective of federalism. For each selected legislative act, we will focus on the purpose of the act and why it was a significant development for federalism. The first stop on this abbreviated legislative timeline is a series of laws known collectively as the Civil Rights Acts. We will then review state-level Jim Crow laws and the Civil Rights Act of 1964.

While Congress has passed a number of civil rights laws over the years, the first such laws were passed in rather quick succession in the years following the Civil War. These laws were deemed necessary both before and after the ratification of the Reconstruction Amendments as African Americans continued to face violence and discrimination.[54] These acts were the Civil Rights Acts of 1866, 1870, 1871, and 1875.[55] First, the Civil Rights Act of 1866 protected the rights of all citizens to enter into contracts and buy and sell property. This was the first civil rights legislation ever passed by Congress and was the result of the override of President Andrew Johnson's veto.[56] Though created for the general purpose of establishing and protecting specific economic rights, the bill was particularly significant for federalism due to the citizenship clause that it contained which asserted that everyone born in the United States was a citizen.[57] President Johnson objected to this bill, because he thought it overly empowered the national government and deprived the states of the ability to shape how the Thirteenth Amendment would be implemented.[58]

Next, the Civil Rights Acts of 1870 and 1871 (also known as the Enforcement Acts or the First and Second Ku Klux Klan Acts) were passed to address the blatant harassment, intimidation, and violence that was taking place at the state level to keep African Americans from voting. The 1870 Act was passed to prohibit racial discrimination in voter registration and to create penalties for anyone who would stop someone from voting on such grounds. The 1871 Act was then passed in February to give the federal government control over elections and was quickly followed by a third enforcement act that April which permitted the president to utilize the military, if needed, for enforcement of these laws.[59] The Civil Rights Act of 1875 prohibited racial discrimination in public places and specifically allowed African Americans to serve on juries. This law was passed as a direct response to the lackluster showing by state legislatures to protect civil rights on their own.[60] The purpose was to provide more specific guidance to what exactly the Thirteenth and Fourteenth Amendment were written to protect and to explicitly "outlaw racial discrimination in public accommodation, entertainment in transport, injuries, churches and publicly supported schools and charities."[61] Due to the provision of specific guidance for what activities would be protected, this law was viewed as a "challenge" to American federalism by both supporters and opponents.[62]

The significance of this series of laws for federalism is generally understood in terms of enhancing the power of the national government. These laws created a formal role for the national government to determine the treatment and rights for African Americans and their activities and to provide uniform protection for those rights regardless of the state they inhabited. These laws represented the establishment and expansion of national authority on matters of civil rights and a general shift in power toward the national government.[63] On the heels of the Civil War, this was an important move designed to override state decision making in order to create a more standard and consistent level of treatment and protection for African Americans in the United States.

Though these laws obviously had the support of the majority of lawmakers at the national level, they were quite contentious and a source of political conflict, even among those who were generally supportive of civil rights protections. Reasons for opposition included the legal burden the laws would ultimately create for African Americans, in that the protections granted by those laws would likely need lawsuits to trigger them; concerns of Republican lawmakers over electoral viability in the South; fears that these laws taken collectively built a foundation for a national police force; and lingering concerns over whether or not the Fourteenth Amendment truly represented the creation of a new expressed power for Congress in regulating civil rights.[64] These laws would be reviewed and interpreted by the courts in fairly short order.

Not all of the significant legislation for civil rights took place at the national level, and a brief treatment of state-level legislation on matters impacting civil rights help us to better understand the general tension and dynamic between the states and the national government on civil rights. Beginning at the end of the Civil War and expanding in 1877, when Reconstruction formally ended with the removal of federal troops from the South, the states began to pass and implement laws that were designed to discriminate against African Americans, limit their role in civil society, and keep them in a permanent underclass.[65] These laws were intended to keep African Americans segregated from and subordinated to white society.[66] These laws became known as "Jim Crow" laws after a minstrel show character, "a rural dancing fool in tattered clothing" created to mock and demean African Americans.[67]

One of the earliest forms of this type of legislation was the Black Codes, first enacted by Mississippi and South Carolina at the close of the Civil War.[68] The purpose of these laws was to create restrictions on the ability of African Americans to work and to monitor their activities through provisions requiring labor contracts, penalties for violating labor contracts, and penalties for not having stable employment.[69] Some of the penalties took the form of forced labor, which served to perpetuate the system of slavery that had been abolished.[70] These laws were strict in detailing "when, where, and how" African Americans could work.[71] Early on, Jim Crow law were more pervasive in rural areas, and African Americans could enjoy more freedom in southern cities.[72] As time progressed, however, efforts to spread these laws to the cities were successful, and African Americans became subject to racial segregation in public places, including phone booths and jails; barred from going to some public places entirely, including parks; and even prohibited from swearing on the same Bible as white people in Atlanta courts.[73]

These laws were significant for American federalism, because they represented an effective state-level effort to find ways to take power back from the national government. In many instances, these laws violated the spirit, but not necessarily the letter, of the law, as established by the Reconstruction Amendments. With the extremely limited application of federal civil rights statutes, the state governments found ways to assert racist policy, and the national government seemed unwilling or unable to counter these moves for quite some time.

Another significant legislative act took place at the national level in the form of the Civil Rights Act of 1964. It was the broadest and most significant piece of civil rights legislation passed since the Reconstruction Era. It was passed to provide the national government with a way to regulate how African Americans were treated in a wide variety of business exchanges. Its provisions, among others, included the desegregation of public accommodations and equal employment opportunities for African Americans.[74] It also required school districts to follow through with desegregation if they wished to be eligible to receive federal money.[75]

The constitutionality of this law was hotly debated as it slowly made its way through the House and Senate, having been stalled in the House for a period of time and then filibustered in the Senate.[76] This debate over constitutionality was with merit, as the language in the new legislation was quite similar to the earlier Civil Rights Acts that had not fared well under judicial scrutiny.[77] However, this time, instead of resting the argument for the legislation squarely on the language of the Thirteenth and Fourteenth Amendments, this law was connected to commerce. The Commerce Clause already allowed the national government to legislate on matters related to commerce, and racial discrimination in economic transactions could be shown to have an impact on commerce.[78] Therefore, the argument was made that national government had the constitutional authority to regulate matters of racial discrimination as they pertained to economic transactions. This shift to the Commerce Clause provided the Civil Rights Act of 1964 with constitutional footing for expanded national authority that was not and could not be achieved through reliance on the amendments.[79] The strengthening of the national government in this way was significant for American federalism, as it provided further limitations to the ways states had been allowing racial discrimination to persist for nearly one hundred years after the Civil War.

Select Judicial Decisions

The course of civil rights policy development has also been impacted by court decisions that have been significant from the perspective of federalism. For each selected court decision, we will briefly review the details of the case and why the decision was significant for federalism and civil rights policy development. There are instances where the court decisions discussed herein are directly linked to legislative acts reviewed above. Included in our review of court decisions are the *Slaughterhouse Cases* (1873), *Civil Rights Cases* (1883), *Plessy v. Ferguson* (1896), *Brown v. Board of Education* (1954), and *Heart of Atlanta Motel, Inc. v. United States* (1964. Due to shifts in thinking about civil rights, we can easily divide these cases into decisions that protected state sovereignty at the cost of civil rights and those that protected civil rights at the cost of state sovereignty.

State Sovereignty Over Civil Rights

It will come as no surprise that the first category, chronologically, deals with decisions that protected state sovereignty at the cost of civil rights protections. Here, we find the *Slaughterhouse Cases* (1873), *Civil Rights Cases* (1883), and *Plessy v. Ferguson* (1896). The *Slaughterhouse Cases* did not deal with issues of race, though the Thirteenth and Fourteenth Amendments were invoked to protect individuals in the state of Louisiana who believed that a state law combining all slaughterhouse businesses to one company was in violation of both amendments.[80] In addition to merging all slaughterhouse operations, the law also contained a clause prohibiting any local competition for an interval of twenty-five years. The local butchers affected by this law argued that "the monopoly created involuntary servitude" in violation of the Thirteenth Amendment, because they would not be able to work, and that the Privileges or Immunities, Equal Protection, and Due Process Clauses of the Fourteenth Amendment had all also been violated.[81]

The Court issued a 5-4 decision against the butchers, arguing that the Thirteenth and Fourteenth Amendment were only about formerly enslaved people, and were never meant to be broadened to include other issues.[82] Further, the majority opinion asserted that the Reconstruction Amendments were not intended to fundamentally change the nature of American federalism by allowing the encroachment of the national government into state matters such as this one.[83] Further, the Privileges or Immunities Clause was limited to "areas controlled by the federal government," including waterways, water safety, and eligibility requirements for federal offices.[84] The Fourteenth Amendment was not meant to protect any notion of "equal economic privileges" at the state level for anyone at all.[85]

This decision rejected the nationalization of individual rights and allowed the language of the Thirteenth Amendment to be more broadly interpreted.[86] It was significant for federalism, because it represented a significant reduction in national authority over civil rights. Though the case itself did not deal with race, the ruling and opinion is thought to be one of the most lasting and damaging blows to the usefulness of the Fourteenth Amendment in protecting civil rights.[87] At this critical time for the development of civil rights policy, the prevailing judicial understanding of American federalism favored preserving state sovereignty over expanding protections for civil rights.

The second group of cases in this category is known collectively as the *Civil Rights Cases* (1883), and they deal directly with the constitutionality of the Civil Rights Act of 1875. Though that Act protected equal access to transportation, lodging, and "places of public amusement," each of these cases features an incident wherein an African American was denied equal access to some such business on account of race.[88] The Court again applied a narrow interpretation of the Fourteenth Amendment, stating that there was a difference between state action and private action, and the national government had no authority to regulate discrimination by private individuals or groups.[89] The Court also believed that Congress had exceeded its authority in the Civil Rights Act of 1875 by way of the Thirteenth Amendment, in that the amendment only prohibited individuals from owning slaves and had no bearing or application to racial discrimination in other ways.[90]

This collective decision was significant for federalism, in that it greatly limited the application of the Thirteenth and Fourteenth Amendment as a constitutional basis for congressional action on matters of racial equality. The national government had taken positive action to grow its power and role in the protection of civil rights in light of the violations that were taking place at the state level, but the Court denied the constitutional legitimacy of those actions. In this decision, it was made clear that American federalism, as it was understood at that time, could not accommodate any efforts to establish or protect civil rights in the way that Congress had attempted with the Civil Rights Act of 1875.[91] Sections 1 and 2 of the Act were struck down as an unconstitutional extension of congressional authority.

Another important court decision that showed a prioritization of state sovereignty over the protection of civil rights was *Plessy v. Ferguson* (1896). This case involved a Louisiana state law entitled the "Separate Car Act" that mandated racial segregation on passenger rail cars. Based on the belief that the Fourteenth Amendment's Equal Protection Clause would invalidate any such law mandating segregation, Homer Plessy—a man who was one-eighth African American but qualified as black under state law—tested the law by taking a seat in a "whites only" car. He was arrested and his conviction was upheld at the state level.

When the Supreme Court heard this case, the determination was made that, while the Fourteenth Amendment was intended to create equal protection of the laws and before the law for African Americans, it was not intended to enforce any notion of social equality or engagement between the two races. The decision denied Congress of the ability to enforce the Fourteenth Amendment beyond a very limited interpretation of legal equality.[92] Further, it was determined that racial segregation alone did not constitute discrimination as long as the accommodations provided to each race were comparable. The Separate but Equal Doctrine was thus established and would stand until it was overturned in the case of *Brown v. Board of Education* (1954).

These cases are high profile and impactful examples of the Supreme Court ruling in ways that limited the application of the Reconstruction Amendments by challenging their intended meaning, invalidating congressional claims of enforcement, and upholding the preservation of state sovereignty even if that meant that African Americans would not get to experience full enjoyment of the civil liberties promised to citizens in the U.S. Constitution. In the latter category of cases, however, we see the Supreme Court reflect the changing times and begin to expand its view of congressional enforcement and prioritize the protection of civil rights, even at the cost of state sovereignty. These cases are equally impactful for the trajectory of federalism and civil rights policy development.

Civil Rights over State Sovereignty

The first such case that we will discuss is *Brown v. Board of Education* (1954).[93] This case was representative of several similar cases that had originated in multiple states contesting mandated racial segregation in the schools. The argument across the board against segregation was that racial segregation was in fact discriminatory and a violation of the Equal Protection Clause. The states had each argued that they were justified in their laws mandating segregation on the basis of the *Plessy* precedent that required them only to provide comparable facilities. The difference in American political culture from 1896 to 1954 proved to be quite different. By 1954, the Supreme Court was inclined to deliver a unanimous decision in favor of the protection of civil rights. The opinion of the Court was that racial segregation was discriminatory and created an insurmountable sense of inferiority in the African American children who were subjected to it.[94] Any state law that mandated racial segregation was thus struck down and invalid moving forward.

The impact of this decision has been debated, as the immediate impact was not as significant as the long-term impact. The long-term impact was that the *Brown* decision changed the tide of racism and discrimination in the United States and empowered the national government to prioritize civil rights over state sovereignty.[95] There is no doubt that the federal judiciary took the lead on civil rights protection and advancement at the end of a lengthy period of low executive and congressional action.[96] However, the reaction from the affected southern states was one of resistance, and the Supreme Court had to issue a second decision in 1955 compelling cooperation with the invalidation of state laws requiring segregation.[97] The argument that fueled that resistance, as expected, was the traditional states' rights argument driven by a particular understanding of American federalism.[98] Given this resistance and the limited ability of the courts to compel action, it has been argued that no significant movement forward occurred at the state and local level until executive and congressional interests caught up with the courts in the 1960s.[99] No matter which branch of the national government we credit with the advancement of civil rights in this era, it does seem reasonable to argue that the *Brown* decision set the stage for a number of significant legislative acts in the 1960s, including the Civil Rights Act of 1964.[100]

Regardless of where one falls regarding the impact of this case, and when it was truly realized, the decision is significant for federalism because it represented a drastic shift with regard to civil rights policy development. By invalidating the precedent set by *Plessy*, the door was reopened to considering matters of race by way of the Fourteenth Amendment. The limitations that were once read into it were entirely the product of the time in which it was read. American political culture was slow to adapt to changing ideas of race and freedom, and that was reflected in those earlier court decisions. Likewise, the inclusivity that was read into it in the *Brown* case was also a reflection of changing political culture, even if it was then a bit forward-thinking. The

Brown decision represents a shift toward expanding the authority of national government to protect civil rights at the cost of state sovereignty.

Another significant case in this category is *Heart of Atlanta Motel, Inc. v. United States* (1964).[101] This case involved a motel located near two major interstate highways that refused to serve African American guests. This policy was in direct conflict with Title II of the Civil Rights Act of 1964 that prohibited racial discrimination in places of public accommodation. The Supreme Court was asked to rule on the constitutionality of the prohibition. In a unanimous decision, the Court upheld the ability of the national government to prohibit racial discrimination in this matter, as there was evidence that the motel's operation did involve interstate commerce given the high number of out-of-state travelers that stayed there.[102]

The impact of this decision for federalism is clear, in that it further strengthened the role of the national government in protecting civil rights and inhibiting states from enforcing policies to the contrary. It is worth noting, however, that this is a case in which reliance on the Commerce Clause was not satisfactory to all supporters on the Court. Even after the *Brown* decision, the Court felt more comfortable justifying national authority using the Commerce Clause. Though the argument was effective, it still felt to some like a stretch from the original intent of the Commerce Clause.[103] Even so, it demonstrated the ability of the Constitution to be adapted to modern circumstances, though perhaps it was done in a way that did not please all sensibilities. The end result was a strengthened national position on matters of civil rights.

These court decisions illustrate the power of the judiciary in determining and maintaining the balance of power between the states and the national government over time. These decisions can be grouped into clear categories that line up with national sentiment on matters of racial discrimination, and the courts decided these matters according to emerging and prevailing norms at each point in time. During the earlier era, the priority was preserving state sovereignty, even at the cost of protecting civil rights. The belief was that the states alone were responsible for such matters and should be trusted to address them. During the later era, the courts no longer had the luxury of assuming that all states could and would manage that responsibility. Once it had become clear that civil rights would not enjoy consistent protection at the state level, the courts saw a changing role for the national government and supported the expansion of national power into this realm, even at the cost of state sovereignty.

The trends in civil rights policy development and federalism show an initial move toward national power at the time of the Civil War and shortly thereafter. For several decades, the shift was back to the states so as to allow them the opportunity to function as they had traditionally been expected to in the protection of individual rights. In the twentieth century, the tide changed, and pressure mounted on the national government to take the lead in this policy area due to an inadequate state response. By the end of the 1960s, the establishment and legitimacy of national authority on civil rights matters was largely complete. However, the United States continues to face conflict regarding matters of federalism and civil rights policy development.

FEDERALISM AND CIVIL RIGHTS TODAY

In large part, the remaining debate on civil rights policy looks a lot like the old debate: which level of government should be responsible for protecting access to individual rights? While the national government was ultimately shown to be the better protector, the national government really has only ever been as protective as American political culture would require.[104] When the country, as a whole, was more racist and less tolerant of government action on civil rights matters, the prevailing view was to allow the states to take the lead, without regard to whether or not rights would actually be protected. When the country became more concerned with making sure that all citizens had access to rights protections regardless of race, the national government was expected to intervene and ensure that this treatment was fair and consistent. The national government has only ever done what the American political culture would permit, and in the matter of civil rights, it was ultimately able to come through with protections that would create accountability at the state level.

The ongoing concern centers on how we reconcile the needs for rights protection with a notion of federalism that is truly balanced between the states and the national government. The United States has become more effective over time at protecting individual rights and providing for the consistent enjoyment of freedoms regardless of race, but this has required a uniformity in policy that can be viewed in tension with principles of federalism.[105] The protection of rights has arguably been prioritized over those federal concerns. In the context of racial politics, this prioritization is justified, but the question remains whether or not this particular matter should have carryover effects on all matters of rights protection. Specifically, would it be more beneficial for federalism to confine the handling of civil rights for African Americans to one category and allow other discussion of rights to take place in a separate context that might allow for meaningful state action?[106] There are several persistent civil rights policy matters that continue to feed this tension and debate over which level of government should oversee rights issues. One example of such a policy matter is criminal justice.

In order to get a sense of federalism and civil rights policy development today, we can review the core components of this issue, identify how each level of government is impacting this issue, and then finally what the status of current regulations are with regard to effectiveness in protecting individual rights. Once we conclude our review of federalism and civil rights policy-making in this section, we will be ready to assess whether or not American federalism has advanced or diminished the protection of individual rights in this policy area.

Criminal justice refers to the creation and enforcement of criminal law, the identification of which activities are legally permissible and which activities represent a societal threat. Beyond the creation of these standards is the decision regarding appropriate punishment. These decisions have historically been made at the state and local level, with national authority limited to specific matters of national concern such as smuggling.[107] Thus, the United States effectively has fifty-one total criminal justice systems, including the fifty states and the federal government, which creates many opportunities for inconsistencies in individual rights protections. The main areas of variance include the death penalty, which is used in some states and prohibited in others; the legality of marijuana, where some states allow it for medical and/or recreational use in opposition to the federal government which still classifies it as a controlled substance; and the length of incarceration for comparable crimes.[108] The trend has been toward more national involvement in matters of criminal justice, at least on paper. Congress has become more active in categorizing more activities as federal offenses, including carjacking and some gun and drug offenses.[109] However, due to the limited ability of the national government to enforce these laws, most criminal justice enforcement still takes place at the state and local level.[110]

The main issue with criminal justice and federalism is the incompatibility between how we understand civil rights and civil rights enforcement (the national level) and where criminal justice is primarily taking place (the state and local level). The specific concern involves the role of race in American thinking about crime, punishment, and victimization, and whether or not there are adequate protections at the state and local level to ensure that individuals are treated fairly and consistently in criminal justice matters with regard to race.[111] The argument is that there is disconnect between American understandings of civil rights and the practical implementation of criminal justice policy.

Federalism contributes to this problem because Congress is not empowered to do much at all to regulate criminal justice at the state and local level to prevent "racial inequalities in crime and punishment."[112] Further, matters of racial inequality have not historically been advanced through the use of the multiple legal venues that federalism provides, and they are not helped with regard to modern issues of criminal justice, either.[113] States have used this space to block reforms that would address racial inequalities, and the national government is fairly helpless to stop it.[114] Additionally, when Congress has had occasion to entertain topics of criminal justice, groups that represent racial minorities impacted by the criminal justice system do not typically have access to the lawmakers who are seeking information.[115]

Regarding effectiveness, we can argue that neither the national government nor the state governments are currently effective at protecting the individual's civil rights by way of the criminal justice system. The national government appears to be ineffective due to the lack of consistent jurisdiction over criminal justice matters and its reactionary pattern in dealing with these issues. The state government seems to be ineffective due to the numerous barriers that block effective citizen action to encourage criminal justice reform.

Those who view the national government as a logical player in criminal justice reform are not entirely misguided given the historical need for national action and leadership on other civil rights matters. Given the disproportionate number of African Americans in the criminal justice system, it would make sense that there would be a national strategy in addressing the inequities involved.[116] This view notwithstanding, the national government does not have solid constitutional footing with regard to criminal justice, as it has traditionally fallen under the police powers of the states.[117] The ability of the national government to weigh in on such matters has been largely dictated by the "broader social and political context" that is dominant at any given point in time, and when it does act, it does so more in the spirit of information gathering and sharing as opposed to finding concrete policy solutions.[118]

This ties directly to the second factor that fuels national ineffectiveness in dealing with criminal justice: the reactionary pattern of attention and action. In large part, national involvement in criminal justice matters has been a "selective endeavor."[119] The broader and significant socioeconomic implications of American criminal justice can easily be missed since Congress does not consistently have these policy issues on its agenda.[120] Over the last several decades, we have seen Congress respond to specific criminal justice issues when they have dominated national discussion and have received significant media attention, such as police brutality, prison conditions, and protest violence.[121] Unfortunately, this leaves Congress in a reactionary position to only respond to issues when they rise to the level of national awareness rather than assuming a more proactive position in dealing with what is truly a national issue that is playing out in countless localities.

The emphasis of state and local control over criminal justice matters might lead one to think that this level of government would then be the one most effective in addressing concerns and protections of individual rights. Unfortunately, the state level can be plagued with its own challenges in addressing such matters due to institutional barriers in place that reduce citizen influence and the neutralization of collective action efforts. First, the execution of any meaningful state-level criminal justice reform is daunting from the view of the criminal justice advocate. Applying pressure on state governments requires a highly complex and knowledgeable political organization that requires enough resources to maintain its presence and gain access to lawmakers. Unfortunately, many of these groups do not have adequate resources or the wherewithal to be able to navigate "fragmented lawmaking venues" nor can they maintain access and continuous pressure.[122] Traditional thinking about state-level governance has stressed its accessibility and responsiveness, but it has actually proven to be more cumbersome for citizens who wish to effect change in criminal justice policy. In this case, federalism seems to exacerbate the disadvantages of race and class in this country by setting up a highly decentralized criminal justice system that individuals are going to be hard-pressed to change or influence.[123]

This decentralized structure has the added impact of neutralizing the impact of collective action by forcing advocates to focus their efforts in multiple places and by impeding similar groups in the same location from working together.[124] Collective action mobilization and free rider issues are already significant issues for advocacy groups that wish to impact policy change on both the national level and the state level. Federalism makes this even more difficult for criminal justice advocates because they have to build a critical number of people from a smaller pool who would be directly impacted by the criminal justice policies of one state. It is difficult to get money and support from people in other states when they have similar issues to contend with in their own state.

Criminal justice is just one issue that continues to have implications for federalism and the protection of civil rights. Though there have been significant actions taken to impact the relationship between federalism and civil rights, the persistence of the tension in this current issue illustrates the fact that this is an ongoing matter, unresolved even today. If we look back over the last one hundred years, the preservation of states' rights in these matters became less of a priority to the American people, in general.[125] In large part, the prioritization of states' rights came at the great cost of civil rights protections, and over time that cost became far too much to bear.[126] The emphasis shifted to individual rights over states sovereignty and a need to ensure optimal enjoyment of individual liberties among all citizens, regardless of race.

FEDERALISM, CIVIL RIGHTS, AND INDIVIDUAL RIGHTS

The shift from state to national authority over civil rights matters served not only to diminish the role of the state but also served to establish a stronger relationship between individuals and the national government. In terms of dual citizenship, the direct support and relationship between the individual and the national government on civil rights policy served to prioritize that relationship and subordinate the relationship that individuals had with their respective state governments.[127] Particularly for African Americans living in southern states, the national government had far more to offer in terms of freedoms and protections, so this affinity was logical. For all of those sympathetic to the cause of civil rights, states had become, for a time, "vaguely sinister."[128]

Once national authority prevailed on civil rights policy, states could no longer persist in implementing and protecting discriminatory policies. A new generation of people was able to experience political socialization in a system that did not abide by the earlier application of federalism to civil rights that enabled so much discrimination. The negative connection between states' rights and the violation of civil rights began to fade into a distinct historical context that no longer applied. The diminishment of that negative connection was well-timed as public sentiment began to turn against expanded national authority in the 1970s. The main argument against state authority had been largely neutralized, and so trust in state-level governance could grow. The American federal system has empowered both the national government and the state governments to address civil rights policy development and implementation, and we can observe which level has the potential to do an effective job in the specific matter of criminal justice. However, we must now take the important next step of determining how well federalism has served the individual by way of civil rights policy. Has American federalism advanced or diminished the protection of individual rights in the realm of civil rights?

Three-Part Test

The first question of my three-part test is: Are individual rights in the realm of civil rights protected somewhere in the American political system? The answer is yes: civil rights are currently protected in the American political system at the national level, though there is the potential for growing protections at the state level through cooperative federalism and if state legislatures choose to pursue civil rights protections beyond what the national government provides. The protection of civil rights at the national level does represent an advancement for individual rights, as the states had an opportunity to enact such protections and did not in any meaningful way.

Second, is there reason to believe that this protection was enhanced through federalism, as demonstrated by issue mobility between levels of government to seek protections for individual rights? The answer is yes: there is reason to believe that the issue of civil rights was enhanced through federalism due to the issue mobility we can observe from one level of government to another. Since states' rights protections became synonymous with civil rights violations, it is easy to connect the dots between federalism and the allowance of civil rights violations by way of state sovereignty. The initial efforts of the national government at the end of the Civil War were thwarted for a time by the courts who wanted to preserve the tradition of rights protection at the state level, and did not believe that the Reconstruction Amendments should be interpreted in such a broad way as to allow national encroachment on state policy.

However, it is also federalism that allowed the national government to take corrective action when it was deemed necessary, and American political culture had also corrected to support such action. American federalism had established the initial responsibility of rights protection with the states, but it was shifted back to the national government once the issue of civil rights as a policy matter formalized at the end of Civil War. Successful federal mobility is a sign that federalism ultimately advanced the protection of individual rights. Had the national government not ultimately seized control of this policy area, then my conclusion on the effectiveness of federalism in providing for individual rights protections would be the opposite, as many states did not enact meaningful policy to protect civil rights.

Lastly, is there reason to believe that this rights protection will be lasting in a federal system, demonstrated by issue symmetry between the state and national level? This is a more difficult question to answer. I do believe that protections for the individual by way of civil rights policy are likely to be lasting at the national level; however, I also believe that there is a lack of symmetry in this policy area which will keep it a source of tension between the levels of government. Typically, the presence of issue asymmetry would make the policy area vulnerable to significant change, and we will see that unfold in later chapters. However, given the nature of the national action on civil rights (e.g., constitutional amendments), I do believe that the protections will be lasting. That being said, we are well aware of how pervasive racism and discriminatory policies are, and federalism is what allows for the vast amount of variance in individual experience at the state and local level. African Americans living across the country are impacted by state and local policies in varying ways, but current national regulation of civil rights matters has raised the floor on basic rights protections.

CONCLUSION

In the matter of civil rights policy, I conclude that American federalism has allowed for the protection of individual rights. Given that the states were able to violate individual rights for so long under this system, this was not an easy conclusion to arrive at. However, federalism allowed the issue to move from one level to another until both the culture and the political elite were supportive of using governmental authority to protect the individual's equal access to and enjoyment of the rights and liberties protected in the United States. In a unitary system, the national government would have set a uniform policy for all of the states, and given the actions of the Supreme Court in the decades after the end of the Civil War, those laws would have likely been less progressive than what the northern states would have preferred and on par with what the southern states preferred. Federalism allowed the northern states and southern states to pursue their own civil rights policies until such time as the political culture had shifted toward a more progressive and protective uniform national policy position. Perhaps federalism, though it did allow for individual rights violations to persist at the state level, also allowed for more progressive thought to develop and spread, leading to the more drastic culture shift of the mid-twentieth century.

The protection of individual rights in the context of African American civil rights still requires continued action as racist and discriminatory attitudes persist. Given the social and economic disadvantages that African Americans continue to face, the possibilities for discrimination are abundant in a federal system and not always so easy to immediately identify. The obvious path forward for greater individual protection in the realm of civil rights would be the passage of more progressive state-level laws to buttress national action, and this is a reasonable expectation of more progressive states. Policy areas ripe for this type of action include voting rights and material inequality. We will continue to see tensions exist at the state level regarding the role of the government and the protection of the individual with regard to civil rights. When these tensions boil over, they will rise to national attention, most likely by way of the Supreme Court. While this federal mobility can cause some anxiety for those in favor of protecting the individual in this realm, I do believe that federalism is what ultimately allowed the individual to be protected. Federalism has ultimately served to protect and promote individual rights in the context of civil rights policy.

NOTES

1. McConkie, "Civil Rights and Federalism Fights," 389.
2. Abraham, *Freedom and the Court*, 39.
3. Miller, *The Petitioners*, 24.
4. Ibid., 27.
5. Ibid.

6. Ibid., 21.

7. Miller, "The Invisible Black Victim," 806.

8. Ibid.

9. Ibid., 806–807.

10. Schapiro, *Polyphonic Federalism*, 7.

11. Ibid., 8.

12. Miller, *The Petitioners*, 22.

13. McConkie, "Civil Rights and Federalism Fights," 403.

14. Ibid.

15. Schapiro, *Polyphonic Federalism*, 52.

16. Ibid.

17. Yarbrough, "Federalism and Rights in the American Founding," 70.

18. Ibid.

19. Ibid.

20. Ibid.

21. McConkie, "Civil Rights and Federalism Fights," 403.

22. Ibid., 404–405.

23. Spackman, "American Federalism and the Civil Rights Act of 1875," 318.

24. Ibid.

25. McConkie, "Civil Rights and Federalism Fights," 390.

26. Miller, "The Invisible Black Victim," 810.

27. McConkie, "Civil Rights and Federalism Fights," 392.

28. U.S. Const. amend. XIII.

29. Rutherglen, "The Thirteenth Amendment, the Power of Congress, and the Shifting Sources of Civil Rights Law," 1552.

30. Ibid., 1554.

31. U.S. Const. amend. XIV, sec. 1.

32. Abraham, *Freedom and the Court*, 42.

33. Ibid., 41.

34. U.S. Const. amend. XIV, sec. 1.

35. U.S. Const. amend. XV, sec. 1.

36. Miller, *The Petitioners*, 148.

37. Tarr and Katz, "Introduction," xiii.

38. McConkie, "Civil Rights and Federalism Fights," 393.

39. Spackman, "American Federalism and the Civil Rights Act of 1875," 317.

40. Zuckert, "Toward a Theory of Corrective Federalism," 86.

41. McConkie, "Civil Rights and Federalism Fights," 393.

42. Rutherglen, "The Thirteenth Amendment, the Power of Congress, and the Shifting Sources of Civil Rights Law," 1551.

43. Zuckert, "Toward a Theory of Corrective Federalism," 87.

44. Ibid.

45. Elazar, "Federalism, Diversity, and Rights," 7.

46. McConkie, "Civil Rights and Federalism Fights," 403; Glazer, "Federalism and Ethnicity: The Experience of the United States," 84.

47. Glazer, "Federalism and Ethnicity," 85.

48. Ibid.

49. Francis, *Civil Rights and the Making of the Modern American State*, 15.

50. Gerstle, *Liberty and Coercion*, 280.

51. U.S. Const. amend. XIV, sec. 1.

52. Rutherglen, "The Thirteenth Amendment, the Power of Congress, and the Shifting Sources of Civil Rights Law," 1567.

53. Ibid.

54. Twagilimana, "Civil Rights Act of 1875," 81.

55. More information on these acts can be found on the United States House of Representatives "History, Art & Archives" webpage at: https://history.house.gov/Exhibitions-and-Publications/BAIC/Historical-Data/Constitutional-Amendments-and-Legislation. These may also be referenced as "civil rights bills."

56. "The Civil Rights Bill of 1866," *History, Art & Archives, United States House of Representatives*.

57. Miller, *The Petitioners*, 88; "The Civil Rights Bill of 1866," *History, Art & Archives, United States House of Representatives*.

58. "The Civil Rights Bill of 1866," *History, Art & Archives, United States House of Representatives*.

59. "Landmark Legislation: The Enforcement Acts of 1870 and 1871," *Art and History, United States Senate*.

60. Wyatt-Brown, "The Civil Rights Act of 1875," 764; Woodward, *The Strange Career of Jim Crow*, 33.

61. Spackman, "American Federalism and the Civil Rights Act of 1875," 313.

62. Ibid.

63. Ibid., 328.

64. Wyatt-Brown, "The Civil Rights Act of 1875," 764, 766, 768.

65. Woodward, *The Strange Career of Jim Crow*, 25.

66. Ibid., 7.

67. "Jim Crow Laws," *History*; "How the History of Blackface is Rooted in Racism," *History*.

68. Woodward, The Strange Career of Jim Crow, 23; "Black Codes," *Black History, History*.

69. "Black Codes," Black History, History.

70. Ibid.

71. "Jim Crow Laws," *History*.

72. Ibid.

73. Ibid.

74. Van Der Silk, "Civil Rights Act of 1964," 81.

75. Schapiro, *Polyphonic Federalism*, 45.

76. Van Der Silk, "Civil Rights Act of 1964," 81–82.

77. Rutherglen, "The Thirteenth Amendment, the Power of Congress, and the Shifting Sources of Civil Rights Law," 1560.

78. Ibid., 1559.

79. Ibid., 1561.

80. *Slaughterhouse Cases*, 83 U.S. 36 (1873).

81. *Slaughterhouse Cases*, 83 U.S. 36 (1873).
82. *Slaughterhouse Cases*, 83 U.S. 36 (1873).
83. Spackman, "American Federalism and the Civil Rights Act of 1875," 319.
84. *Slaughterhouse Cases*, 83 U.S. 36 (1873).
85. *Slaughterhouse Cases*, 83 U.S. 36 (1873).
86. Spackman, "American Federalism and the Civil Rights Act of 1875," 319.
87. Gerstle, *Liberty and Coercion*, 280.
88. *Civil Rights Cases*, 109 U.S. 3 (1883).
89. Ibid.; Rutherglen, "The Thirteenth Amendment, the Power of Congress, and the Shifting Sources of Civil Rights Law," 1552.
90. *Civil Rights Cases*, 109 U.S. 3 (1883).
91. Spackman, "American Federalism and the Civil Rights Act of 1875," 328.
92. Rutherglen, "The Thirteenth Amendment, the Power of Congress, and the Shifting Sources of Civil Rights Law," 1552.
93. *Brown v. Board of Education*, 347 U.S. 483 (1954).
94. Ibid.
95. Somin, "The Supreme Court of the United States: Promoting Centralization More Than State Autonomy," 470.
96. Ibid.
97. *Brown v. Board of Education*, 349 U.S. 294 (1955). There is the criticism that this action did not do enough to compel action, however, with the phrase "all deliberate speed." It has been described as too vague and gave the states too much latitude to implement desegregation at a slower pace.
98. McConkie, "Civil Rights and Federalism Fights," 398.
99. Somin, "The Supreme Court of the United States: Promoting Centralization More Than State Autonomy," 470.
100. McConkie, "Civil Rights and Federalism Fights," 398.
101. *Heart of Atlanta Motel, Inc. v. United States*, 379 U.S. 241 (1964).
102. Ibid.
103. Gerstle, *Liberty and Coercion*, 324.
104. Spackman, "American Federalism and the Civil Rights Act of 1875," 328.
105. Elazar, "Federalism, Diversity, and Rights," 8.
106. Yarbrough, "Federalism and Rights in the American Founding," 70–71.
107. Miller, "Criminal Justice," 139.
108. Ibid.
109. Ibid.
110. Ibid.
111. Miller, "The Invisible Black Victim," 809.
112. Ibid., 811.
113. Ibid., 812.
114. Ibid., 812–813.
115. Ibid., 825.
116. Ibid., 826.
117. Ibid., 812.
118. Ibid., 813, 815.

119. Ibid., 813.
120. Ibid., 814.
121. Ibid., 815.
122. Ibid., 806–807, 812.
123. Ibid., 835.
124. Ibid., 807.
125. Nagel, "On the Decline of Federalism," 127.
126. Ibid.
127. Ibid., 129.
128. Ibid.

SUGGESTED READINGS

Abraham, Henry J. *Freedom and the Court: Civil Rights and Liberties in the United States*. New York and Oxford: Oxford University Press, 1988.

Francis, Megan Ming. *Civil Rights and the Making of the Modern American State*. New York, NY: Cambridge University Press, 2014.

Miller, Loren. *The Petitioners: The Story of the United States Supreme Court and the Negro*. Cleveland and New York: Meridian Books/The World Publishing Company, 1966.

Rutherglen, George. "The Thirteenth Amendment, the Power of Congress, and the Shifting Sources of Civil Rights Law." *Columbia Law Review* 112, no. 7 (2012): 1551–1584.

Woodward, C. Vann. *The Strange Career of Jim Crow*. New York: Oxford University Press, 1974.

Chapter 5

Federalism and Education

Our next public policy topic for consideration is education. Like civil rights, education policy has a long history in the United States, has been significantly impacted by federalism, and has also dealt with issues of equality and access. Generally speaking, education has always been important to Americans.[1] Beyond the merit of having an education, however, Americans have also viewed education as an integral part of the American experience and as a tool that facilitates upward mobility and equality.[2] The long-standing value placed on education can be observed not only through the early colonial establishment of schools but also through the increasing role of the government in maintaining and standardizing education over time.[3] Unfortunately, there are also long-standing issues with access to education and quality of education. The matter of providing life-shaping information to the youth of each community draws strong responses on all levels, from the local community to the national government. The topic of education becomes significant for federalism when these levels of government disagree on the best course of action forward for the youth of this country. There has been a general concern over time that the American educational system does not serve all of its students equally, and that students in one place may not have access to the best and most useful resources while students in another enjoy many advantages. This idea that the education system is not adequately serving all students is the primary cause for the reform movement.[4] We will review a few components of that movement as we develop our understanding of federalism and education in this chapter. Our primary interest lies in determining how well the rights of the individual have been served with regard to federalism in the area of education policy. Has federalism in education policy advanced or diminished individual rights? Education and the access to information and intellectual skills it facilitates lead to important consequences, including the wellness of a democratic political system and the "well-being of individuals and communities" with regard to their economic and social functions.[5] In developing a foundational understanding of the role of education, we can begin by reviewing the benefits of education in the United States along with a few normative theories regarding education.

EDUCATION

There are a number of important benefits that are derived from having an education. First, education is a tool that facilitates access to economic, social, and political activity.[6] A significant part of the American experience is the ability to engage in all parts of public life. Any political system that is grounded in classical liberal political thought will value the contributions of the individual and believe that all individuals have the right to meaningfully participate in public life. That engagement is supported by the free flow of information, self-expression, and the ability to think critically and sort out fact from fiction in order to make good decisions at both the individual and societal level. Engagement in economic, social, and political matters requires knowledge that an education can provide, so that actions taken on these matters can be based on evidence and logic and be as reasonable and rational as possible. This is again consistent with classical liberal expectations of the individual.

Second, and more specifically, education allows the individual to develop the skills necessary for the maintenance of a democratic system, to the extent that education facilitates freedom for the individual and gives increased meaning to the government resting upon the will of the people.[7] The connection between education and democratic sustainability was promoted by significant figures of the founding era including Thomas Jefferson.[8] While there were educational opportunities for children during the colonial era, the responsibility for education was concentrated in private hands and the education provided likely had a religious influence. Jefferson valued public education, in particular, with a focus on preparing individuals for responsible and engaged citizenship.[9] A political system that includes democratic principles requires an informed citizenry that is able to communicate meaningful ideas and preferences to those with political power. In order to generate meaningful ideas and preferences, these individuals should be educated.[10] Arguably, this is a national concern, which is where the idea of public education gained traction. When we consider the viability of democratic governance, the relevance of the topic from a public and large-scale perspective is clear. Education can be a tool for determining a common vision for democracy, while leaving plenty of room for competing policy ideas and solutions to public problems, of course. In this regard, the education of children can be viewed as a responsibility that goes beyond what their respective parents can provide and becomes the concern of the larger society.[11] In the context of federalism, however, the question becomes: when we consider the role of the public in determining educational standards and regulation, which level of governance should be more influential? In the case of American public education, the choices are the local level, the state level, the national level, or some combination thereof.

In his article "Seeking Civic Virtue: Two Views of the Philosophy and History of Federalism in U.S. Education," philosophy professor Dustin Hornbeck provides an explanation of the various theories that have informed the debate over who should control education.[12] Such theories include both conservative and liberal theory.[13] The conservative theory of education control develops from the belief that a child's education should be in line with their parents' beliefs and preferences.[14] While this theory may seem to align with a preference for home schooling, it can also be understood to support local control of education based on the assumption that the values of the community will most closely align with the values of its individual members.[15] The liberal theory of education control is more focused on the interests of the children through the provision of quality education to all, rather than focusing on parental autonomy under the conservative theory.[16] This focus aligns with placing control over education policy in a centralized location so that education can be consistent and of comparable quality for all students.[17] Both theories can be construed to be in favor of advancing individual rights via educational opportunities, but they differ in whose individual rights are advanced and how they are advanced. From the conservative perspective, rights are enhanced by allowing parents to maximize their control and influence over the education of children, while liberal theory seeks to enhance individual rights through the provision of consistent quality education for all children.

Education and Individual Rights

With regard to individual liberty, what does it mean for the individual to be protected with regard to education policy? Given the nature of education and our operational understanding, it seems that liberty can exist here in a positive or a negative sense. This tension between positive and negative liberty has led to the ongoing struggle to agree upon an ideal balance among the various levels of government and the roles they should play. Remembering that individual liberty can mean both freedom from (negative) and freedom to (positive), we can sort out these views as they pertain to education policy.[18] Arguably, the goal of education policy has always been based on some idea of providing more access to educational opportunities.

The earliest conceptions of that goal were negative in nature: allowing individuals the freedom from governmental intervention to privately determine how to provide education. However, over time it became apparent to some that the freedom that local autonomy provided led to an overall inequality of opportunity for individual students. What meant freedom for one group of actors actually limited freedom for another, namely the students. National action on education policy dates back to the founding era.[19] However, it was not until the mid-1900s that the political and cultural environment changed to give positive liberty equal footing with negative liberty in education policy.[20] This shift would create the backdrop against which greater national authority and action in education policy could develop.[21] The connection that grew between the development of education policy and positive liberty was based on the idea of education as a path to living an intentional life with meaningful choices.[22] This perspective asserts that without centralized affirmative governmental action, the access to this necessary education could be limited for some, and this lines up with the development of civil rights as a politically salient topic. Building on the changing interpretation of rights protections via civil rights court decisions, access to education was enhanced as a fundamental right protected by the Constitution, though the Constitution itself is silent on the matter.[23]

As with civil rights, however, the prevailing perspectives on education and individual rights and the role of the government have vacillated over time, and the current political trend at the national level is toward a negative conception of liberty and individual rights. From this perspective, the focus shifts from allowing more governmental intervention to promote equal access to education to diminishing governmental intervention to allow greater discretion at the state level at the cost of unequal outcomes.[24] Matters of educational opportunity and equitable access are increasingly left to market forces instead of governmental intervention.[25] Given this country's history of explicit and implicit discriminatory practices, there is reason to be skeptical of this approach. The question remains, then, of how best to promote individual rights in the context of education policy. What does it mean for the individual to be free with regard to the government's role in education? Even though the Constitution does not explicitly mention education, that does not change the value that the founders placed on it and the role that it plays in a democracy. Also, in light of this country's history of requiring affirmative government action to guarantee access and equal opportunity, an increased role for centralized action on education policy is justified. Thus, I am inclined to define individual liberty in the context of education policy in positive terms. The national government has a role to play to ensure consistent access to quality educational opportunities given that an education is necessary to facilitate engaged citizenship and to live a meaningful life.

Education and Federalism

In the context of federalism, we must have a sense of what guidance, if any, we can draw from the founding era and the Constitution to determine where best to situate education policy. There was some early interest in creating a national administration of higher education, as James Madison proposed a national university during the constitutional convention.[26] There are no records, however, of primary or secondary education being discussed as a matter of national policy or constitutional relevance.[27] At the time, the conservative view that education should be under the purview of the local community could have been far too pervasive to justify national intrusion.[28] As a result, there is nothing conclusive from this era to tell us unequivocally which level of government should control education, nor can we draw any guidance about how that authority could be shared.[29] The absence of direct delegation of power over education to the national government could invoke the Tenth Amendment, thereby reserving it to the states.[30] Prior to the Constitutional Convention, however, the first national action on public education occurred by way of the Land Ordinance of 1785 under the Articles of Confederation. It mandated that each township in the Northwest Territory have land set aside for educational purposes.[31]

In attempting to determine founding intent with regard to education policy, we also have the benefit of hindsight to know how the Constitution has been interpreted to allow for federal intervention. References to providing for the "general welfare of the United States" and the ability to tax and spend for the provision thereof has allowed such power to develop.[32] Whether such language was intended to cover the issue of education is debatable, but it has been upheld. In a manner consistent with federalism, the Constitution can be understood in different ways to support varying levels of governmental control. This flexibility has allowed the management of education policy to enjoy a degree of "fluidity" over time.[33] Over the course of American history, we can observe the tradition and influence of local control, the transfer of authority and influence to state government, and the centralization of policy at the national level. What makes the relationship between federalism and education particularly complicated is that the fluidity of these shifts has not been conducive to maintaining clear divisions of authority. The roles that level of government play have all come to coexist in a somewhat confusing and convoluted way.

The tradition of education in the United States is strongly rooted in the local community, dating back to a time when school operating costs were typically and almost exclusively paid by the local community.[34] The role and significance of local control has been called the "hallmark of American public education."[35] The education system developed on two tracks, one for families with resources and one for families without, and both originated out of local initiatives. For families with resources, education was a private matter in which the family could choose to use their own funds to utilize tutors, private schools, or opportunities to study abroad.[36] However, concern for poor families without adequate education resources prompted an interest in public education under local control, first in Massachusetts and then throughout New England.[37] The idea of public education came to be viewed more broadly as a viable and desirable option for all students in New England, though the rest of the colonies continued to see public education as an option best suited for the poor.[38] The first state governmental action regarding education policy took place when the Massachusetts General Court mandated that local governments provide public education.[39] However, it did not detail any transfer of money from the state level to provide that education.[40] The persistence of local control was further supported by the nature of the country's expansion westward in small isolated communities.[41] The local creation, administration, and funding of schools was "the norm" at the founding and into the United States' early years.[42] Even so, the need for centralization and the resulting growth of state control would also find its roots in this era and become the new norm moving forward through the nineteenth century.

There have been a number of educational objectives that have led to the centralization of policy, and I have already mentioned one of the earliest: the desire to provide education to the poor. Pennsylvania and New York were two of the first states to require a public education plan for poor children.[43] The "common school movement," in which public schools became more desirable and viewed as socially necessary, grew over the course of the 1800s.[44] This movement was established to create standard and consistent access to quality education.[45] Other policy developments that justified a growing role for the state included compulsory attendance laws and changing professional standards for educators. Compulsory attendance laws served to dramatically increase school attendance and became universal in the 1900s.[46] These laws created a larger role for the state governments in the provision of education.[47] If a state were to make it mandatory for students below a certain age to attend school, then that state would also now bear some obligation to make sure that an adequate number of schools would be available to accommodate this growing student population. As such, the state governments grew in their capacity to determine matters such as financing the construction and maintenance of school buildings and some manner of effective school governance.[48] Changing standards for educator professionalization also influenced the centralization of control over education. As professional standards developed, the variations in qualifications that were allowed to exist at the local level were no longer acceptable. If some teachers were expected to have a certain level of education and training and others were not, then the inconsistent quality of education available to students could come into conflict with state constitutions' obligation to provide quality public education. To ensure that the quality of education would be consistent, the adoption of state and national standards became the norm.[49]

There were a few key developments that illustrate the institutionalization of governmental authority over education at both the state and national level. First, there was the expanded use of state constitutions. Over time, more states began adding language to their constitutions requiring the state government to provide public education until eventually all states had some constitutional provision.[50] That is not to suggest that all states interpreted the duty in the same way; however, they all had some acknowledgment that the state was bound to provide for public education of all students. Much like other developments in the creation and development of public education, early milestones in the development of education administration began in New England. The first state board of education was founded in Massachusetts in 1837.[51] Even as state-level administration grew, the importance of local authority and decision-making autonomy remained important. These local school boards would be the precursors to today's school boards and were intended from the beginning to function in an independent and nonpartisan way.[52]

Second, the use of congressional legislative action demonstrated the growing national interest in education policy. One example of such action is the Morrill Act of 1862. This law was passed in order to designate public land in each state for the establishment of "land-grant" colleges specifically focused on agriculture.[53] A few years later in 1867, the U.S. Office of Education (OE) was created in order to collect and archive information about education.[54] This was not a cabinet-level position nor did this office have much direct impact on the delivery of education. A second piece of legislation worth mentioning in this context is the Smith–Hughes Act of 1917, which was passed during World War I. The law was specifically written to provide federal funding for vocational training as a part of secondary education.[55] There are other laws that have important implications for the relationship between federalism and education policy, and we will discuss those further in the section on federalism and education policy development.

Speaking generally about the more recent interest of the national government in education policy, there are some data available for the last half of the twentieth century.[56] While we can identify some specific subtopics in education that have drawn consistent interest, it is difficult to detect any persistent trends in levels of national interest. Congressional legislators have been consistently interested in topics of violence and drug use among students, while other topics, such as breakfast and lunch programs, have drawn more limited or sporadic interest.[57] More recent topics of interest

involve matters of accountability and school choice.[58] While the number of
congressional hearings on educational matters has not always increased at a
steady rate, it is observable overall that national political figures, including
members of Congress, presidents, and presidential candidates, had grown
increasingly concerned about education policy issues over the second half
of the 1900s.[59]

In terms of building a general understanding of federalism and education
policy, there are a few persisting issues that complicate this dynamic: the
limits on national authority, the need for education reform, and the lack of
organizational flexibility. First, there are many issues with the creation and
implementation of education policy that the national government is simply
not empowered to solve.[60] As we will see, that has not stopped the national
government from trying. Second, the relationship has been complicated by
past and present needs for education reform with regard to issues, such as
racial segregation, school finance, accountability, and standards creation.[61]
Federalism has created obstacles to reform efforts, particularly with regard
to providing equal education opportunity.[62] Federalism has also been cited
as a problematic issue when dealing with new technologies such as digital
learning that do not keep to strict geographic areas.[63] It is unclear which level
of government should be responsible for regulation to ensure that access to
learning is consistent and equitable in this environment.[64] Third, federalism
in education policy lacks organizational flexibility and coherence to allow
work to be done. The tradition of local control over school districts has
made people comfortable with school district administration autonomy and
authority, but that local control can be both too powerful and too weak. It
is too powerful in constraining the professional judgment of the educators
actually working in the schools, yet too weak to serve as an advocate for
local interests at the state or national level.[65] It is not consistently clear what
national action could alleviate these matters, and there is a continuing debate
on that question.[66] There is enough evidence to support the view, however,
that federalism and education policy make an uneasy pairing that does not
often lead to consistent or timely responses to the needs of the students, and
thus raises doubts regarding the ultimate protection of individual rights in this
policy area. Many eras of reform and innovation have come and gone. The
failures have been blamed on a "flawed" system that has not met the needs of
a changing educational landscape due to the multiple levels of regulation and
decision-making that federalism allows.[67]

The relationship between federalism and education is involved and has
clear connections to civil rights policy as well. Beyond our basic understanding of this relationship and how it was impacted by the tradition of local control, the need for centralization, and the growth of national interest, we can
move next to a discussion of federalism and education policy development.

FEDERALISM AND EDUCATION
POLICY DEVELOPMENT

Much like civil rights policy, the development of education policy has long since been fraught with tension between wanting to rely on the states to best provide for the citizens and fearing that the states are not quite up to the task. Particularly over the last several decades, the federal government seems to cycle between more intervention and less, depending on the political mood of the country at each point in time.[68] Interestingly, the ongoing back-and-forth between the states and the national government is not necessarily the worst-case scenario, though it does lead to a level of instability. The worst-case scenario would be if neither level of government was willing to be proactive and responsive to the challenges of delivering quality public education. For instance, in the matter of school funding, the federal government has deferred to the states, yet many states have been reluctant to engage in any meaningful policy changes to address structural reforms that could make education funding more equitable within each state.[69] If no one is willing to act, then the quality of public education could be compromised.[70] As we will see by the end of this chapter, public education is facing a number of threats, and the ambiguity federalism creates for education policy could be a threat as well.

Themes of Education Policy Development

Debates over education policy have centered on issues of responsibility, accountability, and funding for quite a while with no lasting solution.[71] However, the process of education policy development is a cumulative one, and all of the features of education policy today as it relates to federalism are the products of past legislative reform and court decisions.[72] In our focused review of the actions that have been particularly significant for federalism, there are a few recurring themes, including equality and accountability. First, these actions, in many instances, have been focused on creating some level of educational equality and uniformity so as to better protect vulnerable students. Federalism has allowed education policymaking the mobility it has needed to actively mediate the debate between negative and positive liberty so as to best protect individual rights in this policy area.[73] Politicians on both the state level and national level have been called on time and again to find that middle ground that allows for both liberty and equality. Unfortunately, issues with both quality and inequality in education are persistent, and that fact can be observed through the many attempts over time to address them.[74]

A second recurring theme in education policy development is accountability, and it comes up repeatedly in terms of performance standards, professional qualifications, and funding schemes. Federalism makes the creation of an understandable division of labor challenging, and so it follows that establishing accountability can be very difficult as well. When the national government has asserted itself in these matters, there has been pushback from the states. Even in the course of attempting to take the upper hand in creating standards and establishing accountability, the national government has found itself in the position of needing the cooperation of the states. When the federal government has engaged in more benevolent practices by creating latitude for the states to act, the end result has not always lined up with the initial intent of the legislation. Stricter standards and accountability can cut in multiple directions, and so even when all parties are arguably working to advance the cause of students and their education, there are a number of complicating factors that keep everyone from rowing in the same direction. Our review of select legislative, judicial, and executive actions will shed light on these themes. We will begin with a focused review of select pieces of education legislation that have been significant for American federalism.

Select Legislative Acts

There are a few ways to determine national interest in education policymaking, but one reliable method is through evaluating legislative trends to see how exactly the national government has utilized its lawmaking power to impact this policy area.[75] To this end, we will review a few pieces of federal legislation that were specifically created to shape public education. However, it should be noted that such a review does not include educational provisions that are embedded in other "catch-all laws" that are not written for an express educational purpose.[76] I do believe, though, that we can glean enough from the legislation that is substantively oriented on the topic of education to see how the relationship between federalism and education policy development has functioned over the years. We will review the National Defense Education Act of 1958 (NDEA), the Elementary and Secondary Education Act of 1965 (ESEA), the No Child Left Behind Act of 2001 (NCLB), and the Every Student Succeeds Act of 2015 (ESSA). The last two laws are renewals of the ESEA and are especially useful in showing the changes that federalism has facilitated with regard to the creation and implementation of education policy.

When the NDEA was passed in 1958, the decision in *Brown v. Board of Education* (1954) had already set the stage for increased national action on education policy. The NDEA was the first of this era to assert that role, and in this case, the purpose was to regulate academic standards. The law was passed out of concern that American students were falling behind their international counterparts in the academic disciplines of math, science, and foreign language.[77] The Soviet Union had successful launched the satellite

Sputnik in 1957, and this had caused fear and concern among American politicians that the government was not doing enough to support math and science education.[78] Recognized as the first comprehensive piece of education legislation, the NDEA allowed for one billion dollars to be appropriated over seven years in order to support the advancement of American students in those relevant disciplines.[79] The NDEA was significant for federalism because it represented an unprecedented assertion of national authority in the area of education policy. Rather than relying on the states to recognize the need for expanded emphasis in those disciplines closely related to security and national defense, both President Dwight Eisenhower and Congress felt it was appropriate for the national government to act in support of education initiatives that advanced the national interest. This move harkened back to the theoretical idea that the education of American children produces a societal and national benefit that we have a collective interest in, thus justifying this expansion of national authority.

National interest in education would continue into the 1960s. As part of President Lyndon Johnson's Great Society program, he wished to create a task force on education that would report back to him with recommendations, and John Gardner, the president of the Carnegie Corporation, was named the chairperson.[80] Of the roughly sixteen members of the task force, there was but one state official and two local officials, which was thought to indicate the low level of enthusiasm that President Johnson's administration had for state and local feedback.[81] It would not be a surprise when this group then returned recommendations for an unprecedented role for the national government in education. Consistent with the goals of the Great Society legislative program, the Gardner Education Task Force submitted a memo to the president that had an antipoverty focus and sought to support vulnerable students in a variety of ways and ranging from primary to higher education.[82] The proposal did contain a recommendation to create a federal education department, though that would not happen until late in the Carter administration.[83] The task force's final report would ultimately shape the language of the ESEA.[84]

This legislation was significant for American federalism in education policy development because it truly "changed the role of the federal government in the world of K-12 education."[85] The focus was on creating equal access to quality education for all students, especially the most vulnerable, and creating a centralized role for the national government in accomplishment of this goal.[86] Of particular note is Title I of the ESEA, which directly addressed the need for and provision of federal funds for local school districts who have particular needs regarding student poverty.[87] The ESEA also contained language requiring periodic reauthorization, which would allow for future policy modifications and significant shifts in the roles for the national and state governments. Federalism allowed the national government to take the opportunity to assert itself in this arena, and federalism would also allow for policy preferences to shift in meaningful ways over time.[88]

The ESEA was reauthorized over the years with some incremental changes made in one direction or another. The most significant modifications to the ESEA began with the passage of the 2001 reauthorization, the No Child Left Behind Act, which represented the most expansive role the national government had ever had in education policy.[89] The purpose of the legislation was to advance both equitable access to education for all students and promote high educational standards.[90] Like the original ESEA, NCLB was created out of concern that there was not enough meaningful action happening at the state level by way of the state constitutional provisions to ensure that all students were accessing quality education in an equitable way.[91] Whereas the states had been engaging in a larger role in academic achievement since the 1980s, the national government had not been directly involved with the oversight of such standards until this time.[92] The law contained both curricular and accountability requirements that delineated the need for both scientifically based and verified academic programming[93] and the provision of a "highly qualified" teaching workforce that would meet specific standards.[94] Despite these claims of national power, NCLB did remain a program cognizant of the limits of federalism as it stopped short of establishing a national educational curriculum or means of assessment.[95] The law also required the states to set specific academic and teacher hiring standards.[96]

The NCLB was significant for federalism in the area of education policy development for a number of reasons. First, the federal government had never enacted a law that so empowered it to regulate education, and this was coming after a short era of devolution in which state autonomy had grown preferable to national authority in other policy areas. NCLB raised a perennial issue of federalism: the connection between policy authority and funding responsibility.[97] Second, called a coercive policy by its critics, the NCLB represented the desire of the national government to influence policy in a way that exceeded its willingness to provide funding.[98] When the national government sets out to establish policy objectives for the state governments, these can turn into "unfunded mandates" wherein the states must comply with national policy on their own dime to avoid the penalties set by the national government. Critics of NCLB called it an unfunded mandate.[99] Third, the goals of the legislation were viewed as "unrealistically rigid."[100] The legislation did a better job of creating provisions for standard-setting and accountability than laying out exactly how these provisions would be enforced by the national government.[101] Lastly, the flexibility the law did provide the states in setting both specific student academic standards and teacher hiring standards led to many states lowering standards to a level easier to meet.[102] The controversial reception of NCLB led to a protracted reauthorization process that would not culminate in new legislation until 2015, far missing the preset 2007 reauthorization date. During this interval, Congress would debate such matters as school choice, state use of federal money, and teacher accountability.[103]

The next and final legislative act for our review is the ESSA, the most recent reauthorization of the ESEA. Generally thought to shift some power back to the states, ESSA was also designed to maintain some national oversight as well.[104] There are several significant components of this law and ways that it departs from NCLB, including the enhancement of state authority to "develop, test, and measure academic metrics and standards."[105] The federal government's authority to monitor for compliance was greatly reduced as states were given more authority over the creation and implementation of their accountability and remediation plans.[106] The ESSA imposes strict limits on how the federal government can impact any state's plans for remediating underperforming students, teachers, or schools.[107] The states are still required to submit their accountability plans to the federal government, but they have increased freedom to choose their desired academic goals.[108]

The passage of the ESSA was significant for federalism and education policy development, in that it "repositioned" the authority the NCLB gave the national government back to the states.[109] The ESSA actually reinstated state control to a level beyond where it was when NCLB was first passed.[110] It is notable in the context of federalism that the reforms contained in the ESSA are about restoring state authority, and do not go so far as to return any significant authority to the local level.[111] There are persisting concerns that this shuffling and shifting of educational authority has not necessarily served to advance education policy but has rather diminished accountability by imparting instability into this policymaking process.[112] The policies have changed so dramatically and the responsibility has been repeatedly shifted so that we do not have a good sense of which policies have worked where and who should be held responsible for those outcomes. In the legislative environment that produced ESSA, it seems the balance between liberty and equality has once again tipped toward liberty and a negative conception at that. The changing and diminishing role of the national government could be linked to a diminished recognition of and concern for educational inequities.[113] It is uncertain at this juncture what results the increased state authority over education policy will yield, but we do know that in issues where federalism permits greater state and local authority, the results will be wide-ranging in both approach and effectiveness.[114]

Select Judicial Decisions

Our review of federalism and education policy development also includes a few select court decisions. The courts are empowered to use their authority to bring attention and provide guidance to specific educational matters, and have done so on a number of occasions.[115] In order to better understand the role of the courts in education policy development, we will engage in a focused review of *Cumming v. Richmond County Board of Education* (1899), *Brown v. Board of Education* (1954), and *San Antonio ISD v. Rodriguez* (1973).

As with civil rights policy, we can find historical court cases dealing with education policy that demonstrated an initial reluctance of the Supreme Court to insert itself in state affairs. In the case of *Cumming v. Richmond County Board of Education* (1899), a lawsuit was filed when a high school for African American students was closed in order to provide money to open and operate four elementary schools for African American students.[116] The petitioners contended that their rights by way of the Fourteenth Amendment had been violated, in that they were taxed to pay for schools and yet there was no public high school provided for African American students.[117] When the case came before the Supreme Court, the court determined that it did not have jurisdiction in this case, as the state's Constitution adequately described its obligation to provide public education and there had not been a clear violation of rights that would justify federal intervention.[118] The states could be left to determine who would be educated and how, with the federal government only engaging in egregious cases of rights violations, the likes of which racial segregation did not yet qualify. This case was significant for federalism and education policy development because the Supreme Court decided to forego an opportunity to assert national authority into a matter of racial segregation in education, thus empowering the state of Georgia to manage its own education policy with regard to who would be educated and where.

A second court decision significant for federalism and education policy development is the previously discussed case of *Brown v. Board of Education* (1954). This decision overturned the precedents set by both *Cumming* and *Plessy* in determining that de jure segregation in public education was unconstitutional.[119] Without reiterating the points of this case, suffice it to say that its significance for federalism lay in its acknowledgment of a strong role for the national government in eliminating race as a factor that could be used to determine how and when education would be provided. The states would no longer have the latitude to make such determinations and racial segregation would henceforth be recognized as a discriminatory practice.

A final case for our review is *San Antonio ISD v. Rodriguez* (1973).[120] In this case, the Texas public school funding scheme was challenged for its reliance on local property taxes to generate revenue for public education, as this method yielded unequal and constitutionally unfair educational experiences for students living in poorer areas.[121] In this case, the Supreme Court found that the Equal Protection Clause of the Fourteenth Amendment had not been violated because there was not a suspect class that had been identified or clearly impacted by the policy, and at no point were any students denied access to education.[122] This decision was significant for federalism and education policy development for a few reasons. First, it established that access to education—absent any clear reference to race—was not a constitutionally protected right that the federal courts would be willing to recognize.[123] Second, it set a precedent that would limit the role of the federal government to intervene on matters of funding and other conditions of education delivery, including potential for achievement, for years to come.[124] Third, it would elevate the role of the states and the determinations of state courts in determining the conditions of education in each state.[125] This decision would usher in the second and third phases of school finance reform legislation, both of which limited petitioners to relief only under their state constitutions and by way of their state court systems.[126]

These select court decisions were significant in shaping the capacity of the state governments and national government, respectively, to control the conditions of education delivery. While we can observe the assertion of national authority with regard to racial discrimination, the tension between the states and the national government was ultimately resolved in favor of the states with regard to school finance.

Select Executive Actions

In building an understanding of the relationship between federalism and education, we also have the opportunity to review a few select executive actions that proved to be quite impactful. Specifically, we have recent examples from the Barack Obama and Donald Trump administrations. In these examples, we find instances of presidents using executive action to expand national authority and to limit national authority.

One example of an executive action that impacted federalism and education policy development is President Barack Obama's Race to the Top (RTTT) initiative. This initiative developed after the date for ESEA reauthorization had come and gone and congressional gridlock made passage of a bill elusive.[127] President Obama's views on education policy overlapped with his predecessor, President George W. Bush, on a few items including the role of the federal government in encouraging policy change and experimentation and the importance of school and teacher accountability in improving student achievement.[128] The RTTT was a competitive grant program in which states could vie for a share of over four billion dollars.[129] Successful states would be able to demonstrate efforts to maintain teacher and school accountability and create school choice for the students, among other provisions.[130] Though Obama's RTTT program did not have full support of the Democratic Party, these efforts did succeed in pressuring many states to reform their policies.[131] However, the Government Accounting Office (GAO) reported in 2011 that there were several states who may have overpromised in their grant applications, and were actually struggling to meet deadlines set for reform implementation.[132]

The RTTT initiative was significant for federalism and education policy development for a few reasons. First, it represented a bold if not unprecedented use of executive authority to advance education policy. This aggressive move drew the attention of the states who were interested in accessing those grant funds, but the program drew criticism for encouraging states to move too quickly with too many reforms in order to be competitive.[133] Second, this move for sustained or increased national power has been blamed or credited, depending on the perspective, with a political backlash that led to the ESSA passing and significantly shifting authority over education policy back to the states.[134] While President Obama was able to achieve the initial goal of creating a new role for the federal government in the influence of education policy, his choices may have actually led to the opposite outcome he desired.

Other instances of impactful executive actions come from the Trump administration. One such action was the withdrawal of an Obama-era *Dear Colleague* letter that had given guidance on Title IX implementation. Title IX refers to a section of the Education Amendments of 1972 that directly prohibits discrimination on the basis of sex in educational programs that receive federal funding.[135] In May 2016, the Obama administration issued guidance to affected institutions that gender identity should be broadly read into protections extended on the basis of sex.[136] This letter was not binding but intended to provide guidance as to the expectations of the federal government regarding Title IX implementation.[137] This guidance was specifically intended to allow students to use the bathroom that aligned with their gender identity, and in February 2017, the Trump administration revoked the letter.[138] The revocation of the *Dear Colleague* letter in this instance has a few implications for federalism and education policy development and individual rights. Clearly, the intent of this action was to diminish the role of the national government with regard to Title IX application and shift more responsibility to the states regarding to what extent they wish to protect students on the basis of gender identity. This action has further implications for individual rights, because arguably the *Dear Colleague* letter had been written with the intent to use the influence of the national government to create a new standard of protection regarding gender identity. The revocation of that protection has been met with concern for transgender students.[139] There has also been litigation specifically challenging the withdrawal of the guidance.[140] This move represents a decrease in individual rights protections.

Another example is the use of executive orders. Like President Obama, President Trump has engaged in executive action on education policy matters despite enjoying unified government for the first two years of his term.[141] An example is the Presidential Executive Order on Enforcing Statutory Prohibitions on Federal Control of Education, signed on April 26, 2017.[142] The purpose of the executive order was to establish a new executive branch policy that protects state and local control over education.[143] The executive order contains prohibitions against federal encroachment on any matters involving curriculum, school personnel, library resources, textbooks, and other instructional materials.[144] The impact of this executive order on federalism and education policy development is that it breaks cleanly with any remaining notions of national control over education policy for the time being.

The trajectory of education policy development has been very uneven and reactive, due in part to the role federalism has played in it. Through a review of select legislative, judicial, and executive actions, we can observe moments in time when the national government enjoyed clear dominance over this policy area and times when the states have been permitted to exert more control. With the exception of school finance reform, the national government has been largely constitutionally supported when it has wanted more power. The ebbs and flows of public sentiment and dominant party views seem to be more impactful in determining what the balance of power is going to be between the national government and the states. This may go a long way toward explaining the persistent issues that are present in education policy debates today.

FEDERALISM AND EDUCATION TODAY

The ongoing concern in the subject area of federalism and education is how to balance the need for educational equity and access with a balance of power between the states and the national government. Unfortunately, we still have plenty of evidence that the public education system continues to foster social inequalities that stem from inconsistent educational quality and financing.[145] The more recent actions of the national government to address educational inequities were NCLB and RTTT, and both of those programs have been largely dismantled.[146] This has left many to wonder what the future holds for individual rights in the realm of education policy. It is worth noting, however, that there is evidence that these measures did not work fully as intended, and the expanded role of the national government actually served to inhibit progress and meaningful change.[147] Certainly, it could be the case that education policy cannot truly correct the causes of the educational inequities: poverty and racial discrimination.[148] It could be that any efforts to address educational inequities that do not directly address generational poverty and racism are misguided, but if that is the case, then what is to be done and who is to do it? At the present time, the prevailing view of the national government is to keep education policy at the state level. The passage of the ESSA and the executive actions of President Trump have established that state-level control is the clear preference. There are number of persistent issues in the realm of education policy, however, that will continue to test the limits and expectations of federalism, including setting standards for both student achievement and educator accountability.

The underlying issue here has always been a concern that children across the country are not all receiving a high-quality education. Federalism allows for policy variation that can both serve local needs and preferences and also create a path to undesirable conditions for some members of the community. Depending on the resources available and the objectives and priorities of state and local school boards, it is possible that students who are educated at the same time but in different locations are having quite disparate experiences. Given the importance of education to the pursuit of life goals and realizing a high quality of life, this variation is problematic. Without some way to establish a minimum standard and hold people accountable for education outcomes, students will have a portion of their future predetermined by the education they can access. The problem lies in establishing such standards without infringing on the autonomy of the states and local school districts. How do we establish minimum standards for student achievement and teacher and school accountability in a way that is effective and reasonable to implement? These issues have been addressed, and yet we have not found a stable resolution.

One of the ongoing challenges has been aligning the goals of the national government and the states regarding the establishment of standards. NCLB and RTTT, in particular, prioritized the establishment and enforcement of standards, though both programs had their flaws and strategic challenges, namely, how to get states to cooperate consistently. While the federal government was clear on its position that quality of teaching and student achievement outcomes could be enhanced by measuring performance and adhering to standards, state policies have not consistently reflected that same commitment.[149] Some states have developed penalties for substandard work, while others have granted permanent contracts to teachers who have not demonstrated any level of teaching effectiveness.[150]

One of the most noteworthy and controversial efforts to standardize education was the implementation of Common Core standards by the states.[151] Common Core represented an effort by the National Governors Association Center for Best Practices and the Council of Chief State School Officers to create objectives and guidelines to better prepare K-12 students for college and careers.[152] Common Core is an interesting example of a cooperative attempt at the state level to agree upon a standard of education that could benefit students across the country and to help those states and districts whose students were not graduating as prepared for college and career as they needed to be.[153] However, even though the genesis of this idea was at the state level, many teachers and parents still felt like it was a top-down attempt to micromanage education and take control away from local interests who believed that they knew better what would be effective for their students.

The issue of creating a minimum standard for student achievement and teacher and school accountability concerns federalism for several reasons. First, these concepts are not compatible. Streamlined uniform policy implementation in a decentralized organizational structure is a very difficult task. The matter of teacher preparation and hiring standards illustrate this difficulty. Under NCLB, an attempt was made to create a "highly qualified" teacher standard to elevate the quality of teaching in the K-12 classroom. In this model, the national government was imposing a hiring standard that layered on top of a state-level certification system that then layered on top of the district and school-level hiring policies.[154] While certainly everyone would agree that highly qualified teachers are desirable, ESSA's termination of this requirement was not entirely surprising to those interested in education policy and aware of the ongoing tension that federalism presents here. Federalism has been considered to be a direct obstacle to many reform efforts over the last few decades, and especially for the implementation of minimum standards and accountability.[155] Federalism allows for policy mobility and sharing of responsibility, and this applies to accountability as well. If policy implementation goes awry in a federal structure, the process for holding anyone accountable is instantly more challenging.[156]

Second, it is difficult to develop one standard when you have fifty states and infinitely more school districts. The main challenge is agreeing upon what a reasonable standard is. How well can any one student be expected to perform? If they do not perform to a certain standard, to what extent is the teacher and/or school responsible? How does one know who is ultimately responsible for academic achievement and what constitutes a realistic outcome? Who gets to decide the answers to all of these questions? Historically, the development of most academic standards, accountability plans, and teacher preparation requirements has come from the top down rather than originating with teachers or local boards of education.[157] This process will most likely always cause issues with credibility and buy-in among those who are charged with implementation.

Additionally, teachers' advocates are very skeptical of performance measures that will pose an unreasonable risk to teachers' job security. For example, teachers' unions are in place to bargain for good work conditions and job security, and will be likely to push back against accountability standards that are thought to place too much accountability on the teachers as that could jeopardize their career.[158] Conversely, districts with weaker unions may not be able to advocate for their teachers as well, and thus the teachers may face more stringent accountability requirements for student achievement. Without weighing in strongly on the substantive matter of teacher accountability, the variation in standards in an environment that is working toward a uniform standard is problematic for educational quality and consistency for both students and teachers. Again, it is not terribly surprising that attempts at this type of reform have ended with a pullback.

Third, the carrot-and-stick approach of federal policy to compel cooperation does not seem to work consistently enough. President Obama's RTTT initiative, which allowed access to generous grant funding under a competitive application process, did not yield the level of compliance that one would hope for. The states were willing to promise a great deal of reform to get the grant money, but fewer than half of the states met the deadlines and goals that they had set.[159] If the marks set by this policy were missed, the grant recipients were threatened with the loss of federal funding, though there is no evidence of this happening.[160] If offering carrots and sticks is only method the federal government has to work cooperatively with the states, and the federal government is not willing to use the stick, then that plan will not work. It is also possible that using the stick would not work either. The strategy of depriving an already struggling district of funds that it arguably needs more than other districts does not make much sense. The implementation of that type approach could create a race to the bottom, not the top. This would directly diminish the students' education and enjoyment of individual rights.

Everyone involved in education as a student, parent, teacher, or administrator understands the need for standards and accountability. This is why we utilize grades, prohibit cheating, and establish expectations for the work that everyone is doing to contribute to the educational process. However, that agreement does not go far enough to smooth the way to uniform standards and expectations. The setting of standards for student performance and educator accountability is a persistent issue that continues to have implications for federalism and the protection of the individual with regard to education. We have reviewed several legislative, judicial, and executive actions that have impacted the relationship between federalism and education, but this persisting issue demonstrates that there is still much to resolve in order to advance individual interests. The discussion of education as a matter of federalism seems to have become one entirely focused on states' rights, and the individual has been lost in the shuffle as education policy has been volleyed back and forth between the national government and the states.

FEDERALISM, EDUCATION, AND INDIVIDUAL RIGHTS

The value of education in the United States is beyond measure given how vital education is to one's ability to contribute in a meaningful way to American politics and society. It seems that the relationship between the individual and the national government should be foremost in equipping the people with the skills they need to contribute and be heard. While it is understandable why education would fall to the states given the treatment of the topic in the U.S. Constitution, the experience of policymaking and implementation at the state level does not appear to be adequate from the perspective of individual rights. There is not yet an ideal solution at the national level, but in each instance the national government has encountered implementation issues, the reaction has been to give the power back to the states. This pattern does not seem to benefit the students, the individuals we are most concerned with in this scenario.

Three-Part Test

The first question of my three-part test is: Are individual rights in education policy protected somewhere in our political system? The answer is yes: individual access to education is currently protected in the American political system at the national level, though that applies specifically to the prohibition of racial segregation and overtly discriminatory practices. Individual access to education is also protected at the state level. All fifty states have educational clauses written into their state constitutions identifying education as a state-level obligation and right. However, it should be noted that the constitutional language is not uniform, and a recent study revealed at least eight different key levels of protection the states have utilized.[161] Only two states (Oregon and Virginia) require the state government to identify academic standards, and only seven reference "equal rights."[162] There is the potential for growing protections at the state level. This growth could occur if state legislatures choose to pursue enhanced individual access to quality education beyond what they are required to do under any national policy or in the absence of national guidance. There is also the possibility for an expanded role for the national government should the political tides turn once again toward such an arrangement, though better strategies for implementation and cooperation would be necessary.

Second, is there reason to believe that the protection of individual rights in education policy was enhanced through federalism, as demonstrated by issue mobility between levels of government to seek protections for individual rights? The answer is mixed, both yes and no. With regard to race, the ability of the national government to insert itself into state matters and to prohibit racial segregation in the schools absolutely enhanced the protection of individual rights regarding education. With regard to poverty, the national government has also effectively used its authority to create access through national legislation such as Title I of the ESEA and its reauthorizations. However, it does seem that the mobility of this issue between levels of government has ultimately rendered it unsuccessful in facilitating equitable access to quality education for all students. Even when the national government has taken a more aggressive stance on education policy, it has largely been dependent on state willingness to effectively implement the policy.

Over the past few decades, the level of government responsible for overseeing the creation and implementation of education policy has changed repeatedly, with preferences not always aligning neatly along party lines. We have had both Democratic and Republican politicians advocate for national control and state control at various points in time. Of course, the politics of public opinion have been a driver as well, and education policy has become quite reactive and unpredictable as a result. We have current students who have been educated in both an NCLB and ESSA environment, and that shift is significant. Education and federalism have proven to be a volatile match because of the challenges and complications of education delivery. While civil rights and federalism clearly presented with unique issues, the matter was ultimately clear-cut. We have not societally or culturally arrived at that point with education, even though it has been felt that way at certain points in time. Until we can land on a decision about where and how education policy should be determined, we will continue in this loop with the children paying the price for our indecision. The ultimate battle here is on the issues of liberty and equality, and the varying interpretations of these terms pose challenges for many other issues as well.

The founders were well aware of the issues surrounding federalism and education. The wording of the Constitution arguably reserved education policy to the state and local authorities, and there are many reasons why this made sense then and now.[163] But there is also a role for the national government to play with regard to instilling common ideals and the foundational knowledge for effective citizenship.[164] Determining the solution to most effectively balance these interests and advance the rights of the individual with regard to education has been elusive. Most of the arguments against national control seem to rest on the history of local control and concerns of the national government infringing on state sovereignty.[165] The other primary argument for state control has to do with simplifying processes and eliminating the confusion that can result from having "too many cooks in the education kitchen."[166] The current Secretary of Education, Betsy DeVos, has been quoted as saying that the Department of Education should be abolished, and her position alone is significant for setting the tone of the current debate.[167] Most of the arguments for national control rest on the recognition of a national interest in education,[168] the evidence that the national government has historically been more effective at protecting individual rights,[169] the argument that the national government is better suited for reform,[170] and the ability of the national government to use resources and authority to enforce policy in a unified way.[171]

Lastly, is there reason to believe that this protection will be lasting in a federal system, demonstrated by issue symmetry between the state and national level? The answer to this question is also mixed. I do believe that protections for the individual by way of education policy are likely to be lasting at the national level with regard to racial discrimination and measures to deal with poverty. However, I also believe that there is a lack of symmetry in this policy area which will keep tensions high between the levels of government. There is evidence of significant policy variations and differences in policy priority from state to state and between the states and the national government. At present, the national government is working to distance itself as far from education policy as federal law will allow. Based on past experience with education policy, there is no reason to believe that this will forever be the position of the federal government. It is likely that control over education policy will continue to pass from the national government to the state government and back again. Due to the asymmetry on this issue, I do not believe that individual rights in education policy are likely to be protected over time.

CONCLUSION

In the matter of education policy, I conclude that American federalism has not allowed for the long-term protection of individual rights, despite the success in protecting rights with regard to race. While the federal government is presently comfortable with allowing states to take the lead on education policy, thus heightening the amount of variability and diminishing standardization, individual rights regarding education are likely to be compromised. In theory, the states are just as capable of creating and implementing policies that establish standards and maintain equitable access to quality education, but there is simply not a great deal of evidence that states have embraced this power. Until the political culture shifts firmly in one way or another regarding the tension between liberty and equality in education policy, control is likely to continue volleying back and forth depending on who is in charge. If at some point, the culture shifts in favor of positive liberty in education policy in which students are free to access quality education in an equitable way rather than states being free from national engagement in this policy area, then individual rights in education policy would be maximized.

There remains a great deal of potential in the relationship between federalism and education, but overall federalism has done more to hurt educational reform than help it. Education is important to the United States, not just to individual states. The ability of American citizens to participate in political life as engaged citizens is a national concern and not one that should be compromised by local funding, values, and priorities. Further, my conclusion is based on identifying the student as the individual of primary concern. In debates over education policy, the focus has centered on the tension between the states and the national government, with little attention paid to the individual. This policy debate should not be about the freedom of the states to determine education policy within their state but rather the freedom of the individual student to access a quality education in the same way that student in other states can. The national government is positioned to best oversee that if the complications of federalism could somehow be addressed or reduced in this matter. The relationship between the individual citizen and the national government is a feature of federalism as the founders understood it, and it is a valuable tool in understanding how best to move forward with education policy in the context of a federal system so as to maximize individual rights.

NOTES

1. Williams, "American Education and Federalism," 1.
2. Ibid.
3. Ibid., 2.
4. Kramer, "Achieving Equitable Education through the Courts," 3.
5. Vergari, "Safeguarding Federalism in Education Policy in Canada and the United States," 534.
6. Heise, "From No Child Left Behind to Every Student Succeeds," 895.
7. Kramer, "Achieving Equitable Education through the Courts," 1.
8. Ibid.
9. Hornbeck, "Seeking Civic Virtue," 62.
10. Ibid., 56.
11. Ibid., 58.
12. Ibid., 57.
13. Ibid.
14. Ibid.
15. Ibid.
16. Ibid.
17. Ibid.
18. Bowman, "The Failure of Education Federalism," 12.
19. Ibid., 17.
20. Sundquist, "Positive Education Federalism," 365.
21. Ibid.

22. Bowman, "The Failure of Education Federalism," 12.
23. Ibid.
24. Ibid.
25. Heise, "From No Child Left Behind to Every Student Succeeds," 1859.
26. Hornbeck, "Seeking Civic Virtue," 60.
27. Ibid.
28. Ibid.
29. Heise, "The Political Economy of Education Federalism," 129.
30. Williams, "American Education and Federalism," 5.
31. Ibid.
32. Vergari 2007 313; Williams, "American Education and Federalism," 5.
33. Heise, "From No Child Left Behind to Every Student Succeeds," 1864.
34. Finn and Petrilli, "The Failures of US Education Governance Today," 23.
35. Williams, "American Education and Federalism," 2.
36. Ibid., 4.
37. Ibid.
38. Ibid.
39. Ibid.
40. Ibid.
41. Ibid., 6.
42. Hornbeck, "Seeking Civic Virtue," 61.
43. Ibid.
44. Ibid., 62.
45. Williams, "American Education and Federalism," 6.
46. Ibid., 5.
47. Hornbeck, "Seeking Civic Virtue," 62.
48. Finn and Petrilli, "The Failures of US Education Governance Today," 23; National Center for Education Statistics, *Digest of Education Statistics, 2003* (U.S. Department of Education, 2004).
49. Williams, "American Education and Federalism," 6.
50. Bowman, "The Failure of Education Federalism," 10; Williams, "American Education and Federalism," 5.
51. Williams, "American Education and Federalism," 5.
52. Hornbeck, "Seeking Civic Virtue," 62; Finn and Petrilli, "The Failures of US Education Governance Today," 23.
53. Williams, "American Education and Federalism," 5.
54. Ibid., 6.
55. Hornbeck, "Seeking Civic Virtue," 63.
56. Manna, *School's In*.
57. Manna, *School's In*, 48–49.
58. Ibid., 49.
59. Ibid., 48.
60. Bowman, "The Failure of Education Federalism," 1.
61. Robinson, "The High Cost of Education Federalism," 290.
62. Ibid.

63. Finn and Petrilli, "The Failures of US Education Governance Today," 26.
64. Ibid.
65. Ibid., 32.
66. Bowman, "The Failure of Education Federalism," 7.
67. Ibid.
68. McGuinn, "From No Child Left Behind to the Every Student Succeeds Act," 408.
69. Bowman, "The Failure of Education Federalism," 1.
70. Ibid.
71. Ibid., 2.
72. Pinder, "Federal Demand and Local Choice," 3.
73. Sundquist, "Positive Education Federalism," 372.
74. Bowman, "The Failure of Education Federalism," 25.
75. Manna, *School's In*, 69.
76. Ibid., 70.
77. "National Defense Education Act," *History, Art & Archives, United States House of Representatives*; Pinder, "Federal Demand and Local Choice," 3.
78. "National Defense Education Act," *History, Art & Archives, United States House of Representatives*.
79. Ibid.
80. Manna, *School's In*, 76.
81. Ibid.
82. Ibid., 77.
83. Ibid.
84. Ibid.
85. Hornbeck, "Seeking Civic Virtue," 63.
86. Ibid.
87. Ibid., 64.
88. Ibid.
89. Heise, "The Political Economy of Education Federalism," 125.
90. Robinson, "The High Cost of Education Federalism," 322–323.
91. Pinder, "Federal Demand and Local Choice," 13.
92. Ibid., 14.
93. Ibid., 16.
94. Robinson, "The High Cost of Education Federalism," 327.
95. Ibid., 329.
96. Ibid.
97. Heise, "The Political Economy of Education Federalism," 129.
98. Ibid.
99. Ibid., 125.
100. Rivlin, "Rethinking Federalism for More Effective Governance," 396.
101. Pinder, "Federal Demand and Local Choice," 15.
102. Robinson, "The High Cost of Education Federalism," 325.
103. Bowling and Pickerill, "Fragmented Federalism," 326.
104. Hornbeck, "Seeking Civic Virtue," 64.

105. Heise, "From No Child Left Behind to Every Student Succeeds," 1872.

106. McGuinn, "From No Child Left Behind to the Every Student Succeeds Act," 406.

107. Heise, "From No Child Left Behind to Every Student Succeeds," 1873.

108. McGuinn, "From No Child Left Behind to the Every Student Succeeds Act," 405.

109. Heise, "From No Child Left Behind to Every Student Succeeds," 1859.

110. Ibid.

111. McGuinn, "From No Child Left Behind to the Every Student Succeeds Act," 409.

112. Sundquist, "Positive Education Federalism," 353.

113. Ibid., 376.

114. McGuinn, "From No Child Left Behind to the Every Student Succeeds Act," 409; Weiss and McGuinn, "From No Child Left Behind to the Every Student Succeeds Act," 2016.

115. Kramer, "Achieving Equitable Education through the Courts: A Comparative Analysis of Three States," 51.

116. *Cumming v. Richmond County Board of Education*, 175 U.S. 528 (1899).

117. Ibid.

118. Mahon, "Cumming v. Board of Education of Richmond County," *Encyclopaedia Britannica*.

119. Sundquist, "Positive Education Federalism," 368.

120. *San Antonio Independent School District v. Rodriguez*, 411 U.S. 1 (1973).

121. Ibid.

122. Bowman, "The Failure of Education Federalism," 22.

123. Ibid.; Pinder, "Federal Demand and Local Choice," 4.

124. Pinder, "Federal Demand and Local Choice," 4.

125. Ibid.

126. Ibid.

127. McGuinn, "From No Child Left Behind to the Every Student Succeeds Act," 392.

128. Ibid., 393.

129. Patrick, "Fiscal Federalism, Performance Policies, and Education Reforms," 598.

130. Ibid.

131. McGuinn, "From No Child Left Behind to the Every Student Succeeds Act," 396–397.

132. Ibid., 398.

133. Ibid., 398–399.

134. Ibid., 392.

135. Rose and Goelzhauser, "The State of American Federalism 2017–2018," 331.

136. Heise, "From No Child Left Behind to Every Student Succeeds," 1876.

137. Ibid.

138. Rose and Goelzhauser, "The State of American Federalism 2017–2018," 331.

139. Ibid.

140. Heise, "From No Child Left Behind to Every Student Succeeds," 1877.
141. Rose and Goelzhauser, "The State of American Federalism 2017–2018," 319.
142. "Presidential Executive Order on Enforcing Statutory Prohibitions on Federal Control of Education," *White House.*
143. Ibid.
144. Ibid.
145. Sundquist, "Positive Education Federalism," 351.
146. Ibid., 352.
147. Ibid.
148. Ibid.
149. Patrick, "Fiscal Federalism, Performance Policies, and Education Reforms," 594.
150. Ibid.
151. Bowling and Pickerill, "Fragmented Federalism," 327.
152. Ibid.
153. Ibid., 328.
154. Finn and Petrilli, "The Failures of US Education Governance Today," 26.
155. Ibid., 28.
156. Ibid.
157. Ibid.
158. Patrick, "Fiscal Federalism, Performance Policies, and Education Reforms," 617.
159. Ibid.,596.
160. Ibid.
161. Dallman and Nath, "Education Clauses in State Constitutions Across the United States," 2.
162. Ibid.
163. Hornbeck, "Seeking Civic Virtue," 59.
164. Ibid., 65.
165. McGovern, "A New Model for States as Laboratories for Reform," 1528–1529.
166. Finn and Petrilli, "The Failures of US Education Governance Today," 21.
167. Camera, "DeVos: I'd be fine ditching the education department," *US News*; ,Hornbeck, "Seeking Civic Virtue," 66.
168. Bowman, "The Failure of Education Federalism," 53.
169. Rivlin, "Rethinking Federalism for More Effective Governance," 396, Hornbeck, "Seeking Civic Virtue," 58, Robinson, "The High Cost of Education Federalism," 304.
170. McGovern, "A New Model for States as Laboratories for Reform," 1521.
171. Vergari, "Safeguarding Federalism in Education Policy in Canada and the United States," 534.

SUGGESTED READINGS

Finn, Chester E., Jr. and Michael J. Petrilli. "The Failures of US Education Governance Today." In *Education Governance for the Twenty-First Century: Overcoming the*

Structural Barriers to School Reform, edited by Paul Manna and Patrick McGuinn, 21–35. Washington, DC: Brookings Institution Press, 2013.

Hornbeck, Dustin. "Seeking Civic Virtue: Two Views of the Philosophy and History of Federalism in U.S. Education." *Journal of Thought* 51, no. 3–4 (2017): 52–68.

Kramer, Liz. "Achieving Equitable Education through the Courts: A Comparative Analysis of Three States." *Journal of Law & Education* 31, no. 1 (2002): 1–51.

Manna, Paul. *School's In: Federalism and the National Education Agenda*. Washington: Georgetown University Press, 2006.

Sundquist, Christian B. "Positive Education Federalism: The Promise of Equality after the Every Student Succeeds Act." *Mercer Law Review* 68, no. 2 (2017): 351–387.

Chapter 6

Federalism and Same-Sex Marriage

The development of same-sex marriage (SSM) policy in the United States provides yet another opportunity to explore the utility of federalism in the protection of individual rights. While both civil rights policy and education policy have been controversial at times with regard to federalism and the division of power regarding those matters, SSM is a bit more complicated due to its connections to religion and religious freedom. The introduction of religion to our discussion of federalism brings in another element of individual rights protection, specifically by way of the First Amendment. Teasing out which policy actions facilitated by federalism advance individual rights and which inhibit them becomes more challenging in this scenario. Following the format of the previous chapters, however, we will work through some foundational information regarding marriage, SSM, and federalism, review some key legislative and judicial actions on SSM that have been significant for federalism, and then finally evaluate how federalism has functioned in this policy area to enhance or diminish the protection of individual rights.

One of the challenges in understanding marriage generally and SSM in particular is how personal the topic is from a religious, social, and emotional standpoint. Many people are inclined to think that their personal experiences are indicative of the collective experience at that point in time and across time, and may not readily appreciate that others may have different perspectives on and experiences with marriage and family.[1] Even the most abbreviated study of SSM takes one through historical, philosophical, legal, and political literature, all which illustrate how complex the matter is. As recently as 2013, Supreme Court Justice Samuel Alito called SSM "newer than cell phones" and others have contended that nowhere in American history or beyond have we seen an acknowledgment or legitimation of SSM.[2] At the same time, there are personal recollections and historical documentation

147

that contradict those assertions and contend that the topic is actually quite older than cell phones.[3] Even the idea that marriage between one man and one woman has not been challenged runs afoul with the historical record when we look to past controversy over polygamy and pronounced conflict between the national government and Mormons in the state of Utah.[4] That controversy also focused on religious conflict, and the national government took a decidedly limited view as to the extent religious views could challenge prevailing notions about marriage at that time. Regardless of one's views on the particular topic of polygamy, I mention it only to say that debates and discussions of marriage are not new, and people are inclined to think their perspective and experience is a legitimizing force on the topic of marriage.

Depending on one's perspective, the topic of SSM can link quite seamlessly to matters of civil rights. The gay rights movement, generally speaking, developed to address many of the same types of prejudices and indignities that have plagued racial minorities.[5] Further, the women's rights movement developed and progressed through the use of a social movement, court action, and legislation at the state and national level, which also served as a "template" for the gay rights movement to use.[6] The women's rights movement's focus on gender provided an even clearer entryway for sexuality to become a politically salient issue.[7]

This chapter provides us with an opportunity to extend our evaluation of federalism to a topic that may not be historically new, but it is newer with regard to saliency in American politics. In order to develop a broader understanding of the history of SSM and its relationship with federalism, we will begin with an abbreviated review of marriage in the United States.

MARRIAGE

As with many American legal and religious traditions, colonial and early American marriage trends were shaped by their British heritage.[8] While many colonies were established on the basis of religious dissent, the marriage tradition was at the time of a religious nature and governed by British ecclesiastical courts.[9] As a result, this tradition served as the foundation of colonial American marriage, though marriage in the United States would eventually develop into a civil law arrangement with concurrent and privately managed religious involvement.[10] However, the civil law did not immediately shed its religious foundations. Marriage was considered a permanent union of one man and one woman, and that union legally subordinated the woman to the man, a status known as coverture.[11] It was not until 1839 that state-level legislation known as the Married Women's Property Acts began progressing through the states to eliminate the legal restrictions placed upon married women.[12] Over time, the states also moved away from the idea of marriage as a "divine institution," and began to allow for the legal creation of informal marriage and the legal process of divorce to end a marriage.[13]The further development of no-fault marriage in the 1900s allowed for divorce even if no one had committed any grievance, thus significantly shifting marriage from a social institution to an individual preference.[14]

This shift from marriage as an institution to support the birthing and raising of children for the benefit of society to marriage as a path to individual happiness and fulfillment opened the door for increased consideration of marriage in same-sex relationships.[15] If marriage was about happiness and life partnership with a soul mate, then perhaps it could be extended to relationships that might not necessarily produce offspring. These developments led to a changing view of marriage in the United States, and those changes played a role in the emergence of SSM as a politically salient topic.

SAME-SEX MARRIAGE

There is evidence dating back to the 1800s of urban communities of homosexual people that were visible in ways that had not previously been viable due to limitations of law and social acceptance.[16] We also know of same-sex couples living together as if they were married without any legal or religious sanctioning.[17] Known as "Boston Marriages," female couples cohabitated in New England in the 1800s.[18] As the profile of homosexual people and same-sex relationships began to increase, however, so did opposition and the desire to use laws to prohibit same-sex sexual activity.[19] Taken a step further, the Lavender Scare of the 1950s resulted in a large-scale removal of suspected homosexual people from government jobs.[20] The fear of homosexual people grew from a notion that homosexuality was a deviant behavior that created a risk for American morality.[21]

Though the opposition to homosexuality and same-sex relationships would continue to grow as a formal movement during the 1900s, the creation of lesbian and gay communities also took a step forward due to the physical and social mobility generated by World War II.[22] Many homosexual people had not met other homosexuals prior to the war, and after the war, not all of these individuals wanted to return to their hometowns where they might not have the opportunity to live openly as homosexual individuals. Rather, some people chose to move to places like San Francisco, New York, and Washington DC, where they could live in more diverse and supportive communities.[23]

There is evidence that the desire or demand for SSM at this point was not wide-ranging as many homosexual people still shared heteronormative views of marriage and in many ways simply wanted to be left alone in their private affairs.[24] It would not be until the 1970s that same-sex couples would begin actively trying to obtain marriage licenses. The most active phase of the SSM political movement would begin decades after that as a reactionary measure to state and national efforts to limit same-sex relationships and prohibit SSM.[25]

A recurring question from those opposed to SSM has focused on the purpose of SSM and the need for the SSM movement, namely, Why do same-sex couples wish to be married? What would it accomplish? It is helpful to review the theoretical questions regarding the necessity of SSM policy. Regarding the necessity, marriage offers a way to establish legal commitment to another person, and many people in same-sex relationships want the same opportunity as those in heterosexual relationships to demonstrate that commitment and gain public acceptance.[26] Additionally, there are estimated to be over 1,000 federal rights and protections—ranging from matters of real estate to taxation—that are available only to married couples.[27] These marriage benefits notwithstanding, there have also been debates within the LGBT movement as to whether or not marriage equality should be a policy priority when there were so many other ways members of this community were struggling to function as equals in American society.[28] Despite resistance to SSM from inside and outside the movement, the issue continued to develop saliency, due in part to the progression of the women's movement and development of gender-based rights protections.[29] The timing of the marriage equality movement was ultimately reactive to fears of SSM and efforts to stop it, including the proposal of an amendment to the U.S. Constitution.[30]

Though the main purpose of this chapter is not to flesh out the full debate over SSM, it can be useful to have a general sense of the various schools of thought in order to better understand the way SSM policy has developed. In his book *Same-Sex Marriage in the United States*, political scientist Jason Pierceson spells out the three main positions on SSM, including the natural law perspective, the liberal constitutionalist perspective, and the radical social critique that emanates from feminist and queer theory.[31] First, the natural law perspective opposes SSM on the grounds that marriage is based on the need for human procreation and the ability of male and female pairings to accomplish this goal.[32] The natural law perspective is religiously derived and has strong Christian influences.[33] Second, the liberal constitutionalist view is in favor of SSM. The support for SSM is rooted in the liberal constitutionalist preference for preserving equality for all and the protection of individual rights for all.[34] These rights and freedoms are thought to be protected by the Constitution and supported by the ideological foundation of classical liberalism.[35] Third, the radical social critique is against SSM on the grounds that marriage is an oppressive patriarchal institution that is not good for anyone, homosexual or heterosexual.[36] In this case, wanting what other people have actually represents wanting something that will harm the human condition rather than enhance it. This brief snapshot of the conflicting views gives us a little more knowledge upon which we can grow our understanding of the relationship between federalism and SSM.

Same-Sex Marriage and the Individual

With regard to individual liberty, it is of particular importance to establish what it means for the individual to be protected with regard to SSM policy. It is challenging to make this determination without consulting one's own views of SSM and religion. If one is of the opinion that religious liberty should supersede marriage liberty and equal protection, then they are primarily concerned with the rights of individuals who oppose SSM on religious grounds. If one is more inclined to think that liberty in marriage and equal protection is either more important than religious liberty or is of the opinion that the protection of SSM is not in conflict with religious liberty, then they would prioritize the rights of individuals who are in favor of SSM. This chapter cannot hope to sort out the issues between these two perspectives; however, I do think there is some agreement with the type of liberty at play here. It seems that both perspectives are defining liberty in positive terms, meaning that they each see a role for the government in protecting the freedom to do something. For advocates, they are looking for the government to protect their right to marry a same-sex partner. For opponents, they are looking for the government to protect their right to not provide public services that support SSM. I do think there was a time that negative liberty was a possibility, and it would have taken the shape of allowing same-sex couples to apply for marriage licenses and wed in civil ceremonies. These couples would have technically been "left alone" and free from intervention. However, dating back to when the first marriage licenses were formally denied in the early 1970s, the role of the government was then foretold to be a part of this process in some way.

The tendency is to think of American liberty in negative terms, and this derives from the strong individualistic ideals that have been pervasive in American political culture. The truth of the matter is, though, that both positive and negative liberty have coexisted in the pursuit of individual freedom dating back to the founding. The fact that the Constitution addresses liberty and came to provide protections for specific liberties demonstrates that the founders did see a role for the government in protecting individual rights.[37] In the case of SSM, I contend that both advocates and opponents see a role for the government in actively protecting their freedoms. However, it seems that the idea of negative liberty still can be effective in convincing the other side to temper its views on SSM and related topics.[38] For example, it has been easier in some ways for same-sex advocates to argue against interventionist policies (e.g., sodomy laws) than to argue for the provision and recognition of legal marriage.[39] Calls for privacy and being left alone in the privacy of an intimate relationship resonate across lines that denote sexual orientation.

An obvious divide on the topic of SSM concerns whether or not marriage is considered an individual right and therefore eligible for protection under the Constitution. If marriage is recognized as a fundamental human right, then access should be equal and protected for both homosexual and hetero-sexual couples, as fundamental human rights would be expected to extend to all adult members of the political community. The Ninth Amendment does seem to express constitutional flexibility with regard to the development and recognition of new rights over time. Additionally, we have seen an expansion of rights and reconsideration of rights through both African American civil rights and the advancement and protection of rights for women, as well. If one is inclined to consider marriage as a fundamental right, there is room to do so by way of the Constitution, regardless if one considers marriage an individual right or a collective right by way of assembly.[40] In this case, any failure to allow and protect the right of same-sex couples to marry would be a violation of equal rights and liberty.[41] Further, the significance of marriage as a right grows when one considers the additional rights and benefits that are conferred upon married couples. Through denying the right to marriage and thereby denying same-sex couples of the benefits of marriage, these couples are relegated to second-class citizenship.[42] Such benefits pertain to matters such as immigration, insurance, and healthcare.[43]

Opponents of SSM do not generally recognize these rights claims as being legitimate.[44] They rest their argument on the lack of specific language regarding marriage in the Constitution which would suggest that it is the states' responsibility to determine for themselves what marriage is. That leads to the other important component of any discussion of rights and liberty in the context of federalism and SSM: is this matter about states' rights or individual rights? In the context of federalism, we can deal with either, because federalism provides for a relationship between the states and the national government, the individual citizens and the national government, and the individual citizens and the states. Opponents of SSM argue for the protection of their individual right to religious liberty to the extent that their religious views oppose SSM and also the protection of states' rights against a national determination on SSM as a matter of policy. Advocates of SSM speak in terms of the individual (or collective, if one thinks in terms of couples) right to marry and legitimacy of national authority to that end.

This is a difficult policy issue through which to grapple with individual rights. With competing claims to constitutional protections, the discussion grows contentious quickly, thus explaining the volatility of this matter over the years. The process of identifying and defining new rights and freedoms has never been easy and has been called "more an art than a science."[45] We will return to the matter of persisting issues near the end of this chapter.

Same-Sex Marriage and Federalism

The relationship between federalism and SSM has been complicated due to the high level of activity in this policy area over the last few decades and the frequent mobility with which it has moved back and forth from the state level to the national level. One of the complicating factors when dealing with SSM is that it falls into a category known as morality policy. In this section, we will cover what morality policy is, how it is dealt with in the Constitution, and the general life cycle of morality policy in a federal system. Then we can look more specifically at the compatibility of federalism and morality policy before focusing on the relationship between federalism and SSM.

First, morality policy centers on issues of right and wrong, and positions on such topics are shaped by an individual's values, ethics, and/or faith.[46] Morality policy has three main features that are significant for how the policy is created and implemented. This type of policy is conceptually simple, suggesting that most people have enough information on the topic in order to generate a position of what is right and wrong.[47] Morality policy can be very salient with the general public as these issues are based on values and thus generate a strong emotional response.[48] Lastly, because morality policy matters are simple and salient, they tend to inspire citizen participation at a higher level than we might see with other types of policy.[49] Policymakers are likely to get far more spirited feedback than usual from their constituents regarding both the creation and implementation of morality policy. Given that issues of morality lend themselves to debate, it is important here to seek guidance as to which level might be responsible for such policy in a federal system.

Unfortunately, the guidance found in the Constitution is a bit conflicting, as we have seen in other policy areas. We can find guidance in both the Tenth and Fourteenth Amendments. As we have learned previously, the Tenth Amendment was created as a way to reserve non-specified powers to the state governments. Morality policy has traditionally been reserved to the states in this manner so as to closely reflect the diversity of values that can be found at the state level.[50] It is argued that, due to the high level of variation in opinion on values-based morality questions, the best hope for congruence between policy and public opinion occurs when this policy is created at the state level. The congruence leads to policy stability and the closure of the active policymaking phase.[51] Based on this read of the Tenth Amendment, morality policy would be best created and implemented at the state level. However, civil rights policy development demonstrates that this strategy does not always work well in the interest of protecting individual rights. On the topic of SSM, we once again have a topic that requires us to identify which individuals, in particular, we are interested in protecting. Are we concerned with protecting the individual rights of homosexual people or the individual rights of the people who are opposed to homosexuality on religious grounds? We will return to this issue later in the chapter, but for now we can consider the use of the Fourteenth Amendment to protect those who argue that their rights are being violated, in this case, homosexual people. Beginning in 2015, the Fourteenth Amendment was extended to apply to marriage and interpreted to mean that same-sex couples have a fundamental right to marry and any state restrictions would be in violation of the Fourteenth Amendment's Due Process and Equal Protection Clauses.[52] If one is persuaded that marriage is a fundamental right, then the Fourteenth Amendment protections would render the Tenth Amendment moot with regard to this policy area, but the debate continues on that issue.

Constitutional scholar Lawrence Sager describes the relationship between federalism and morality policy using the concept of life cycle to track how morality policy develops and progresses in a federal system. There are three stages in this life cycle: invention, propagation, and consolidation.[53] In the invention stage, a progressive moral idea will gain support in a few states but may be opposed stridently in others.[54] During this stage, some states will begin engaging in policymaking to advance this new idea. The second stage is propagation. The policymaking efforts gain a higher profile and may be appealing to others in a particular state and beyond to other states.[55] During the propagation phase, what was once a minority viewpoint may no longer be considered such in the more progressive states.[56] The last stage of the life cycle is consolidation, during which the policy in question will become mainstream and the national government may feel inclined to take legislative or judicial action on the matter to create a unified federal policy.[57] This life cycle is easy to follow and understand but there are remaining questions as to how compatible federalism is with morality policy, in general. The life cycle does not include consideration of opponents to the morality policy in question and the tensions that are permitted to linger even after an issue has been "consolidated."[58] Even something as seemingly final as a Supreme Court decision can fail to address the moral tension that persists with these types of issues.[59] The main challenge is that both sides of a morality policy have deeply rooted value-based positions. The way that federalism functions to advance one side of an issue can also serve to help the other side.

Federalism does not just foster one particular type of policy innovation. There could be one type of policy addressing a moral issue going through the life cycle in a certain number of states, perhaps in the same region, and then different policy addressing that same moral issue developing in another region of the country. Due to the nature of morality policy, it is unlikely that proponents of each policy solution will be satisfied with having their policy implemented in a limited geographic region. They will likely want their policy to be implemented far and wide, because their position is "right" while others are "wrong."[60] This sets up persisting tension between the competing perspectives. The invention phase that federalism facilitates can be used to promote both policy innovation and counter-innovations.[61] While this life cycle of morality policy in a federal system can be easily observed, the dynamic is even more complex that the cycle acknowledges. For every policy that successfully navigates this cycle, there are those opposing it during each stage. Those opposing interests are able to shepherd their own policies through that same cycle, and with sympathetic legislators and judges, may be able to move the needle as well.

On the topic of SSM, federalism has played a very important role in the development of policy and it is closely entwined with matters of individual rights. Like civil rights, marriage has both an individual rights component and a social institution component.[62] With civil rights, it was ultimately decided that the institutions rooted in violating the rights of African Americans (e.g., slavery and the racial segregation) were immoral and were thus eliminated. However, with SSM, proponents wish to expand the definition of the institution of marriage to be more inclusive, and in doing so must find a way to make this institution work for the betterment of both individuals and society. SSM is thereby both an individual entitlement and a social entitlement because to exercise this right requires cooperation from others in the recognition and maintenance of the institution of marriage.[63] When we apply the morality policy life cycle to SSM, we can easily see how it has fit the stages. The invention stage began in 1993 with the Hawaii Supreme Court acknowledging that the denial of marriage licenses for same-sex couples was a discriminatory practice, and we can follow the cycle all the way to the consolidation of policy with the 2015 Supreme Court decision of *Obergefell v. Hodges* which applied both the Due Process Clause and Equal Protection Clause of the Fourteenth Amendment to SSM.[64] When we follow the development of SSM policy from the viewpoint of SSM advocates, it is clear that federalism helped move the issue forward toward consolidation.[65]

There are, however, many pieces that are missing from the story if it is told in this limited way. It does seem that in many ways, federalism is compatible with morality policies such as SSM, and we can observe how state sovereignty and issue mobility both served to aid in the development of SSM policy. However, those who are opposed to "moral innovation" and want to maintain the status quo can utilize federalism to advance those ends as well.[66] The life cycle model has been called limited in how it describes the development of morality policy, but it is just limited in how it is applied. Morality policy cuts both ways, and for every position that is "moral" there is a counter-position calling it "immoral." Federalism does allow the development of morality policy the way the life cycle model describes, but it is not limited in who can use it or how it is used. The matter of SSM is an excellent example of how federalism is a method of power distribution and tool for policy development that functions the way people want it to function. Federalism can be used in a progressive way but is not necessarily progressive. When opponents of SSM were unable to amend the Constitution in the 2000s, several states took action to limit the rights of same-sex couples.[67] This was an act facilitated by federalism, and it was done to maintain the status quo.

There is no doubt that federalism has been a significant component of the SSM movement, and its use by both those for and against SSM has fueled the tension and complexity of this policy issue.[68] This is also a very timely issue with key legislative and judicial actions taking place in recent years. It seems that the challenge implicit in the relationship between federalism and morality policy is determining how to bring about stability on the topic. Federalism can be used to support innovation and the spread of new ideas and progressive moral policies that reflect the diversity of the United States, and it is agreed that the policy congruence that comes about as a result can be stabilizing.[69] However, given the nature of morality, both advocates and opponents of the policy are not likely to be satisfied with the geographic limitations of federalism. Advocates for the policy are going to believe that the policy position is morally correct, and they will be inclined to want it consolidated at the national level. Additionally, any lack of portability in the state-level protections will motivate the advocates as well.[70] Opponents will believe that the policy is morally wrong and will not want it to stand anywhere, even if it is only in a limited geographic area. The perceived solution then, for both sides, is policy consolidation at the national level, but even if one side can achieve that, it only serves to antagonize the opposition and keep the policy phase active.[71]

The relationship between federalism and SSM policy is challenging, and like education, has connection to civil rights policy as well. Beyond what we have discussed thus far regarding the history of marriage, same-sex relationships, and the complicated nature of individual rights on this topic, we can now look more specifically at federalism and SSM policy development.

FEDERALISM AND SAME-SEX MARRIAGE POLICY DEVELOPMENT

Unlike education policy, which is debated largely in terms of which level of government is better suited and more constitutionally situated to oversee it, SSM policy is debated more in terms of identifying rights and then deciding whose rights are more important. There is obvious tension between the levels of government in making these determinations, which is characteristic of a federal system. As evidence of this, we can see a great deal of significant action and movement taking place between the two levels of government over the last several decades. While this degree of back and forth has ultimately led to progress for SSM advocates, there remains a lack of certainty over what the future holds. If opponents of SSM continue to argue convincingly for their perspective on individual rights, it is possible that federalism could provide a path forward for that view as well. As we will discuss toward the end of this chapter, same-sex marriage partners and others in same-sex relationships continue to face threats to their individual rights, and the flexibility and mobility of federalism could keep people on both sides of this debate unsteady for the foreseeable future.

Themes of Same-Sex Marriage Policy Development

The process of SSM policy development has largely been reactive and prone to backlash. As a morality policy, there is little room for compromise, and so we do not necessarily see the cumulative policymaking effect that we see in education policy. In our review of policy actions that are of particular interest through the lens of federalism, we do see some recurrent themes, including the tension between liberty and equality. First, many of the actions we will review have dealt with the tension between liberty and equality and to what extent liberty can or should be inhibited in the pursuit of equal outcomes. This debate is complicated by disagreements over when one should expect to enjoy individual liberty, be it positive or negative, and when and where we should expect equal treatment. This debate, along with many others in American politics, is also challenged by the constant undercurrent of individualism that continually prompts us to take responsibility for our circumstances (which may or may not be under our control) and solve our own problems. At both the state and national level, we have identified and protected liberties for both advocates and opponents of SSM, depending on prevailing legislative or judicial perspectives at a given point in time. At both the state and national level, we have seen equality for same-sex couples both protected and neglected, depending on the prevailing views.

Select Legislative Action

One method of understanding the relationship between federalism and SSM is through evaluating legislative trends to see how state and national legislatures have used their power to shape the development of SSM policy. It should be noted that SSM advocates have historically fared better through litigation than legislation.[72] The key legislative acts that we find in this policy area are typically centered on the priorities of those who oppose SSM. In order to evaluate how federalism has impacted SSM policy development, we will review some legislative actions that have either directly or indirectly had an impact on the rights of same-sex partners. To this end, we will engage in a general review of state legislative action and a more specific review of the Religious Freedom Restoration Act of 1993 and the Defense of Marriage Act of 1996.

The record for state legislative action is rather mixed over time. We have examples of state legislatures using their authority to both promote and inhibit access to SSM. Dating back to the 1970s, there were initially more instances of state legislatures banning SSM. In 1977 alone, legislators in six states voted to prohibit SSM, including Colorado and Florida.[73] As attention turned to domestic partnerships and other variations on civil arrangements during the 1980s, the pressure on legalizing or prohibiting marriage eased for both sides.[74] By the early 1990s, however, the states became active again, culminating in thirty-three states banning SSM by 2014 through either constitutional or statutory means.[75] During this same time interval, seventeen states had chosen to legalize SSM.[76] These state legislative actions for and against SSM were significant for federalism because they signified the willingness of the states to actively regulate a morality policy. The trend of state activity on SSM during this time period is also reflective of the position that morality policy is better decided through democratic processes than by the courts. From what is known of both federalism and morality policy, state-level regulation is logical regardless of whose rights the state is trying to protect. However, the national government also got involved with legislation that sought to protect the rights of the religious opponents of SSM.

There are two significant pieces of legislation that Congress passed into law during the 1990s: The Religious Freedom Restoration Act of 1993 (RFRA) and the Defense of Marriage Act of 1996 (DOMA). The RFRA was passed to keep both the national government and the states from placing restrictions on an individual's exercise of religion unless either level of government could demonstrate that such a restriction promoted a "compelling governmental interest."[77] Certainly, the issue of religious liberty is one that predates the SSM debate.[78] This particular piece of legislation came about a few years after the Supreme Court had ruled in *Employment Division v. Smith* against an exercise of religion for fear that people would use religion to justify all manner of illegal activity.[79] That ruling raised concerns that the national government was not doing enough to actively protect religious freedom.

The Supreme Court ultimately ruled that the RFRA could only apply to the national government, and in response, at least twenty-one states passed state-level RFRAs to apply to state governments.[80] The passage of the national

RFRA and then the subsequent passage of state-level religious freedom legislation are both significant for federalism in the matter of SSM. First, this type of legislation was important for SSM policy because it would come to serve as part of the legal argument that would restrict their access to wedding and family-related services if the religious beliefs of the service providers did not support SSM. Second, it was important from the perspective of federalism because it represented the national government formally prioritizing religious liberty over other rights claims and making it more difficult for the government to restrict activities if they could be tied to the exercise of one's religion. Further, when the Supreme Court struck down the extension of this law to the states in 1997, many states then used their own authority to pass similar legislation to protect the exercise of religion in their own states. These actions represented the states' willingness to take a more active role in protecting religious rights when the national government was limited in its ability to do so.

The second piece of legislation for our review in this context is DOMA. This legislation accomplished several anti-SSM objectives out of fear that if one state legalized SSM then all other states would be forced to recognize those marriages.[81] DOMA defined marriage as the union of a man and woman so as to deny federal legal recognition and a vast array of benefits to married same-sex couples.[82] This definition allowed the national government to deny recognition of all same-sex marriages regardless of the legality of the marriage at the state level.[83] DOMA also allowed each state to define marriage for that state and freed the states from any legal obligation to recognize same-sex marriages performed in other states.[84]

The passage of DOMA was significant for federalism and SSM for several reasons. First, Section 2 of the Act, which allowed the states to define marriage and not recognize marriages granted by other states, was a large boost to state sovereignty in the matter of SSM. The specific inclusion of this section demonstrated that Congress wanted to preserve states' rights on this issue.[85] The national government used its authority to reaffirm the states' authority to regulate morality policy, which had previously been the constitutional norm.[86] Second, in its attempt to bolster state power to resist recognition of same-sex marriages performed in other states, DOMA also appeared to limit state power by encroaching on the Full Faith and Credit Clause of the Constitution.[87] This Clause had been a way to make state-level contracts, court proceedings, and the like, portable across state lines.[88] However, there is a "public policy" exception that does not force states to comply with policies that violate their own state's cultural and legal norms.[89] Again, we see here federalism struggling to protect everyone's rights, whether we are talking about individual rights or states' rights. In this case, the very effort of promoting states' rights using national authority, which would turn out to be problematic on its own, served to diminish other states' rights. In any event, the passage of DOMA was significant in the context of both federalism and SSM and would have a jarring effect on SSM policy development for the next several years.

Select Court Decisions

Our review of federalism and SSM policy development also includes a few select court decisions that have been significant for federalism. Given the level of legislative success that opponents of SSM enjoyed at the state and national level, advocates of SSM turned to the courts over time to make progress for same-sex rights. We will begin our review of significant court cases for SSM and federalism with a case that actually had nothing to do with SSM, *Loving v. Virginia* (1967), but would end up impacting the development of SSM policy. We will also review the cases of *Baker v. Nelson* (1972), *Lawrence v. Texas* (2003), *U.S. v. Windsor* (2013), and *Obergefell v. Hodges* (2015). This is by no means an exhaustive list of significant court cases related to same-sex matters, but it is a representative list to help us better understand the courts' impact on the relationship between federalism and SSM policy development. Court decisions have proven to be an efficient way to shape policy for both advocates and opponents of SSM.

The first court case for our consideration did not actually concern SSM at all but rather interracial marriage. The 1967 case of *Loving v. Virginia* struck down all state laws that prohibited interracial marriages, and at the time of the decision, there were still sixteen states that had these bans known as miscegenation laws.[90] The *Loving* decision was viewed as significant for same-sex advocates because it laid the groundwork for challenging the way states were defining marriage and for whom they were providing marriage protections.[91] In the opinion written by Chief Justice Earl Warren, the ability to marry was identified as a civil right that was connected to the pursuit of happiness.[92] Advocates for SSM saw this as an important precedent upon which they could build an argument for expanding the right of marriage to same-sex couples. It should be noted that not everyone has viewed the *Loving* decision as applicable to SSM. The argument against such application is that miscegenation laws were about promoting white supremacy and the purity of the white race, and a decision to strike those laws down was a move to combat white supremacy.[93] As such, the rationale should not be extended to other matters. However, the opinion was written in such a way that it could be interpreted and applied more broadly. Advocates for SSM saw a clear parallel between white supremacy, and heterosexist supremacy and saw the *Loving* decision as a way to enhance marriage access.[94] This case was significant for federalism because it represented the national government defining marriage as a right. From this point forward, no states could enforce laws that regulated marriage on the basis of race. This was a noteworthy shift in power from the states to the national government.

Another case of note was *Baker v. Nelson* (1972). This case represents the first time the matter of SSM was brought before the Supreme Court. In this case, two men, Jack Baker and Michael McConnell, were denied a marriage license in Minnesota due to a state law that limited licenses to opposite-sex couples.[95] The couple filed a lawsuit based on their belief that the license denial represented a violation of both the Equal Protection Clause and Due Process Clause of the Fourteenth Amendment and their privacy rights by way of the Ninth Amendment and First Amendment.[96] Both a lower court and the Minnesota Supreme Court upheld the license denial, and when the Supreme Court was presented with the case, it dismissed it as the case was not thought to contain a question of federal law.[97]

This case was significant for federalism and SSM, because it set an early precedent that there was no fundamental right to marriage protected by the Constitution. When the Supreme Court said that the case did not contain any federal questions, they were stating that the petitioners' claims of Fourteenth, Ninth, and First Amendment violations were not valid.[98] Therefore, this case left the matter of marriage and SSM at the state level and empowered other states to move forward with new or existing state laws that would define marriage as an institution only permitted for a man and a woman.

The 2003 case of *Lawrence v. Texas* is another important case with regard to federalism and SSM. One of the many legal issues facing same-sex couples was the existence of sodomy laws in all fifty states, referred to in some states as "crimes against nature."[99] As it relates to SSM, it would surely be difficult to move forward with a strong case for SSM in a country where sexual acts not directly related to procreation were legally prohibited in most places. The Court had an earlier opportunity to review such laws in the case of *Bowers v. Hardwick* in 1986 and had chosen at that time to leave such matters at the state level.[100] The Court saw no role for the Constitution in defending or protecting any such rights by way of the Equal Protection Clause. By 2003, the tone of the Court had changed, and it was once again asked to consider whether the state-level prohibition of specific sexual activity between same-sex partners represented a violation of the Equal Protection Clause or the Due Process Clause of the Fourteenth Amendment.[101] The Court ruled that the Texas sodomy law at issue in this case was in fact unconstitutional as a matter of due process.[102]

This case is significant for federalism and SSM because it represents another move by the national government to specifically override state decision-making that was believed to violate the individual right to liberty as provided for by the Due Process Clause of the Fourteenth Amendment.[103]

While this case did not directly deal with SSM, it was another important piece of the story of SSM by prohibiting the states from intervening in the private affairs of adult sexual conduct.[104] As long as the states were still empowered to engage in that level of governmental regulation of private affairs, the path to SSM was legally unclear. The removal of that legal barrier is a significant advance toward the legality of SSM and represents another moment wherein the national government asserted itself over state prerogatives in order to protect individual rights.

Since 2003, there has been a flurry of judicial activity on the matter of SSM, but we will focus our attention on the more recent cases of the *U.S. v. Windsor* (2013) and *Obergefell v. Hodges* (2015). Consistent with other recent judicial action relating to homosexuals and same-sex relationships, both of these cases represented the national government directly facilitating the protection of individual rights of homosexuals. First, the case of *U.S. v. Windsor* challenged the constitutionality of the DOMA provision that marriage under federal law could only be recognized between a man and a woman.[105] This case involved a same-sex couple, Edith Windsor and Thea Spyer, who had been married in Canada and whose marriage was legally recognized by the state of New York but not by the federal government. When Spyer died, her estate was taxed in the amount of $363,000, and since their marriage was not recognized, the marital exemption did not apply.[106] The Court ruled in this case that Section 3 of DOMA was unconstitutional in defining marriage in terms that were designed to deny rights and privileges to same-sex couples as it was a violation of the Fifth Amendment's equal protection provision.[107] However, the Court did not go so far as to deal with Section 2 which gave states the ability to not recognize same-sex marriages.[108] It is also declined to comment outright on the legality of same-sex marriage.[109]

From the perspective of federalism, this case is significant because it represents a limitation on the power of the national government to infringe on individual rights by declaring at least part of DOMA unconstitutional. It does not go so far as to impose restrictions on the states, and in fact, the decision was actually made in deference to traditional state authority over the definition of marriage. The issue the case addressed was the differential treatment that DOMA facilitated given that some couples were allowed certain rights and privileges under state law while others were not. By the government choosing to recognize some legal marriages but not all, they had created a material disadvantage for same-sex couples. This case represented a federalism win for both states' rights and individual rights.

Finally, the case of *Obergefell v. Hodges* (2015) represents a significant moment for both federalism and SSM. Though there had been significant state-level action against SSM in the decades leading up to this decision. By 2015, thirty-seven states had already legalized SSM either through legislation, popular vote, or judicial action.[110] This case was actually a consolidation of cases each challenging SSM bans in a variety of states, including Ohio and Michigan.[111] In this case, the Court ruled that both the Due Process Clause and Equal Protection Clause of the Fourteenth Amendment should be construed to protect same-sex marriage as part of a universal and fundamental right to marry, and that all states would be required to recognize all legally performed marriages.[112]

This case has many implications for federalism and SSM. First, it took the unprecedented step of overriding state-level definitions of marriage with one unified federal definition.[113] Marriage had traditionally been under the purview of state governments, and there had been a reluctance on many levels to apply the ruling in *Loving* to the matter of SSM. Ultimately, however, the fact that marriage had already been acknowledged as a fundamental right would serve to defend an extension of marriage and the rights and privileges therein to couple regardless of their sexual orientation. The states would no longer have the authority to impose more restrictive definitions of marriage.

Second, it represents another attempt to balance the principles of liberty and equality, though with different results than in earlier legislative and judicial actions.[114] In this case, the liberty of the states was constrained in order to enhance individual liberty and equality of homosexual people. The relationship between liberty and equality is a balancing act, for when we allow for an expansion of one group's liberty, it can serve to infringe on the liberty of another group. When the beliefs of one group of people result in the unequal treatment of another group of people, the government may be called upon to determine if that unfair treatment is an acceptable of unacceptable price to pay for the liberty that created it. In this case, the Supreme Court chose the preservation of equality and liberty for same-sex couples over the liberty of the states to deprive them of equality and liberty.

Third, the decision brought at least temporary stability to a matter of morality policy that had grown quite unstable over time due to the policymaking mobility that federalism allows.[115] The swiftness with which judicial action can solve a problem is no guarantee of lasting peace on an issue. In this case, however, it did overcome one challenge of federalism and that is a lack of predictability and inconsistency in policy creation and implementation.

Like education policy development, the path of SSM policy development has been reactive, though it has shown a more even trend line toward national dominance on this issue, whether for SSM or against it. From the perspective of federalism on SSM, we are more interested in where the relevant power is exerted and which level of government is able to maintain control over the issue, not necessarily what the results of those decisions were. This is particularly true in the matter of SSM, where people have made arguments for constitutionally protected individual rights on both sides of the issue. The judicial and legislative evidence does support a general shift in support for SSM, or at least a shift in favor of less governmental intervention in limiting personal decisions. However, there is also plenty of evidence that support for SSM, like we see with other morality policies, has done as much to generate a more vibrant opposition as it has done to encourage more support. This type of whipsawing back and forth is facilitated by a federal system. Additionally, even in light of a Supreme Court decision, the decentralization of policymaking in a federal system can continue to create challenges for the treatment and experience of same-sex couples.

FEDERALISM AND SAME-SEX MARRIAGE TODAY

Like both civil rights and education policy development, SSM poses continual challenges in a federal system with regard to balancing liberty and equality and settling on acceptable definitions of each. Whereas education policy debates are still centered more specifically on which level of government is better equipped to manage it, SSM issues are more complicated, in that they require policymakers to decide whose individual rights we are most interested in protecting and which liberties, if any, should be given up to facilitate equality. These underlying debates are more a feature of morality policies, and we will surely see them arise in the next chapter as well.

At the present time, the national government asserted its authority through the establishment of one definition for marriage and the decision to protect the rights of same-sex couples to marry and enjoy the privileges thereby provided. The states, however, especially those with majorities opposed to SSM, are still exploring ways to balance the liberty of homosexual couples with the religious liberties of the opponents. Even in light of the *Obergefell* decision, the anti-SSM culture is still quite active and impacts both same-sex related policies and the overall experience of same-sex couples in this country. There are a number of persistent issues in SSM and related policy development that are significant for federalism, including the ongoing debate between religious liberty and equal treatment. A review of this issue will serve to facilitate a consideration of how well individual rights are protected in the realm of SSM policy. Once we conclude this review, we can move forward to evaluate how well federalism has functioned to protect individual rights in this policy area.

Unfortunately, the *Obergefell* decision was not able to settle the debate regarding religious liberty and equal treatment. In fact, the decision included language to address concerns on both sides. The Court concluded that marriage was a fundamental right that must be extended to people regardless of sexual orientation based on the Fourteenth Amendment, but also held that the First Amendment would continue to protect religious organizations in their opposition to homosexuality.[116] We have a seemingly unresolvable clash of constitutional principles, as proponents of SSM see the interpretation of the Fourteenth Amendment as evidence that the Constitution can and does change to accommodate cultural transformations. Opponents argue that the First Amendment protections are explicit and intended, while SSM is a "judicially created right" that should be subordinated to those which are clearly spelled out.[117] To better understand this debate, we can briefly review each side's position beginning with the argument for religious liberty.

Religious liberty—both the freedom to exercise religion and the freedom from the establishment of state-sanctioned religion—is protected by the First Amendment. There are those who argue that the *Obergefell* decision significantly diminished the existence of religious liberty by deciding that marriage was a fundamental right protected by the Constitution.[118] Therefore, any effort to enforce public accommodation of SSM represents a violation of both the Free Exercise and Establishment Clauses of the Constitution.[119] Where majorities exist that support this position, the state can take action. There is a path for claims of religious freedom violations by way of the federal RFRA and state-level religious freedom acts, where available.[120] However, these efforts have not always been successful in protecting religious liberty. There is the persisting belief that the states were robbed of their constitutional right to define marriage for their own jurisdictions and this has fueled the desire to assert state authority where and when possible.[121] Federalism affords to the states opportunities to shape religious liberty as it pertains to SSM, but that also creates a challenge, in that advocates have to work to make these changes in each state. Over half of the states have their own version of the RFRA, but efforts have failed in other states.[122]

In addition, when a same-sex couple believes that have been treated unfairly, the possibility of a legal challenge will arise, thus contributing to the instability of this policy area. The challenge, however, is that it becomes a court decision that may or may not align with the desired outcome of the petitioner, and there is fear that the current judicial trend is not consistently supportive of the religious position.[123] Ultimately, the courts must decide between two different acknowledged rights and choose which one takes precedence.[124] Since the Supreme Court has already taken the liberty of establishing a binding federal definition of marriage, the belief is that federalism has already been compromised and cannot yield a truly fair outcome regarding SSM and religious liberty.[125]

On the other side of this debate are the advocates for SSM who continue to defend the establishment and extension of marriage rights on the grounds of due process and equal protection. Their position is that marriage as a social construction is "fluid and mobile," and having a document and policies in place to reflect that makes sense in the spirit of affording equal rights regardless of sexual orientation.[126] Now that marriage has been recognized as a fundamental right, any attempts to limit the rights and privileges connected to that status are viewed as blatant discrimination. The language of "marriage conscience protection" to advance religious liberty and anti-gay policy positions is a veiled attempt at engaging in deliberate sexual orientation discrimination.[127] Any laws that provide religious exemptions to providing same-sex couples with publicly available accommodations or services are a direct threat to the progress that has been made to diminish or prohibit sexual orientation discrimination.[128]

Further, those who argue for the protection of equal rights in the context of sexual orientation and SSM contend that their position is most reflective of the liberal ideology at the foundation of American governance which includes principles of both individual freedom and equal treatment under the law.[129] Specifically, if an action does not result in demonstrable harm to another, there is no need for the government to engage in regulation.[130] Such a position is also consistent with the promotion and protection of minority rights, moral pluralism, and human rights, in general.[131] The fact that a specific right is not explicitly identified in the Constitution does not preclude it from being defined by the courts at a later date, and marriage is a right that has already been extended in ways that the Constitution is silent on regarding race and even imprisonment.[132]

Lastly, proponents of equal rights in the context of sexual orientation argue that civil marriage through the states has long since parted ways with its religious origins.[133] Other laws and regulations that had religious foundations have gone away as well, including laws prohibiting adultery and blasphemy.[134] It only makes sense for restrictions on equal treatment for individuals regardless of sexual orientation be prioritized even if it comes into conflict with other individuals' privately held religious beliefs.

This debate poses a challenge for federalism because the decentralization of policymaking power allows for these types of debates to continue endlessly, especially in a circumstance such as this wherein both sides of the debate have constitutional footing. Both sides can make arguments for the protection of individual rights and both sides can utilize provisions in the Constitution that either explicitly or implicitly protect their own position. After the *Obergefell* decision, much of the backlash and discussion has centered on how to protect individuals with strong anti-gay religious views from facing discrimination and having their liberty violated through compulsion to cooperate with same-sex marriage accommodations.[135] Every state has the ability to fine-tune legislation to address this debate and to take additional measures to promote either side of this issue, religious liberty or equal treatment. Such laws will surely result in legal challenges, and so it will go. Federalism provides a multitude of opportunities to create and implement policy, and so a multitude of opportunities will be taken. In the matter of morality policy, the possibility of shifting out of the active phase of policy-making is low, and so a true finish line here is elusive.

Since there is an argument for the protection of individual rights both for and against SSM, it is hard to identify a scenario in this context where I could argue that individual rights are not being protected. At both the national and state level, efforts have been made and continue to be made in the spirit of protecting individual rights. The conflict we keep coming back to concerns whose individual rights we are more interested in protecting. Due to the special nature of this topic, I cannot carry out the same type of rights analysis as I did with civil rights and even with education, though that was modified slightly as well. At various points in time and in various ways, both the national government and state governments have protected and violated individual rights. Therein lies the true complication with regard to federalism and SSM. It is with this challenge in mind that we move forward to our main question: Has federalism advanced or diminished the protection of individual rights with regard to SSM?

Three-Part Test

The first question of my three-part test is: Are individual rights in the context of SSM protected somewhere in our political system? The answer is yes: individual access to SSM and the benefits and privileges thereof is currently protected in the American political system by the national government as a result of the *Obergefell* decision. The long-term stability of this protection is in question, however, as judicial decisions are not typically effective in resolving tensions on morality policy.[136] Judicial decisions provide a policy solution but not necessarily resolution of a moral conflict. The imposition of a national solution is viewed by some as "non-federal" in the sense that it does not truly accommodate diversity but rather picks one position and then imposes it on everyone.[137]

Individual rights are also protected at the state level with regard to religious liberty and religious conscience objections to SSM where there is a religious liberty law in place. It should be noted that not all states have such laws, and so it could be argued that some individuals in some states do not have equal access to these types of protections. This, of course, is a feature of a federal system. These laws do have the potential to create more policy stability at the local level through a higher of congruence between policy and local preferences, while not technically infringing on the right of same-sex couples to get married. However, the opportunity that states have to develop religious liberty protections has the additional effect of reducing the liberty of same-sex couples to the extent that they may be denied access to publicly available accommodations and services related to weddings, adoptions, and other family-related matters.

Second, is there reason to believe that this protection was enhanced through federalism, as demonstrated by issue mobility between levels of government to seek protections for individual rights? The answer is yes. With regard to access to SSM, the mobility allowed by federalism permitted the states to move forward with legalization ahead of a federal law. As a result, individual rights for same-sex couples were enhanced. In each phase of the life cycle of SSM policy development, individual rights were expanded in general. Though there were a few backlash intervals (e.g., the passage of DOMA), the development of SSM policy was able to navigate federalism to a new realization of individual rights protection.

With regard to the religious liberty angle, I am inclined to say that federalism has worked there as well. For example, when individuals sought protections under the RFRA, and those protections were not extended to the states, they were able to put state-level legislation in place to protect religious liberty. Even in the *Obergefell* decision, the Court was unwilling to infringe on First Amendment protections for religious liberty and stated as much. For each group of individuals, the policy mobility allowed by federalism permitted each group to find protections at some point, indicating that federalism has been successful in protecting individual rights with regard to SSM.

Lastly, is there reason to believe that this protection will be lasting in a federal system, demonstrated by issue symmetry between the state and national level? The answer to this question is mixed. There are varying degrees of issue symmetry between the states and the national government. Overall, I would say there is currently a lack of symmetry, which is expected when trying to address issues of morality at the national level. One of the long-term challenges of any morality policy is finding some degree of lasting stability.

One of the most significant ways that state power can be utilized in a federal system is with regard to morality policy.[138] The types of "intense conflict" that accompany moral debates are best resolved with the smallest audience in mind so as to increase the chance that the resolution will actually be acceptable to a majority of the people impacted.[139] In a situation where the national government has inserted itself in a meaningful way, it could be that we will be caught in a perpetual conflict, particularly "in a country as heterogeneous and religious as the United States."[140]

Given that SSM is currently defined by the national government and against the wishes of some states, the decision has served to protect the individual rights of same-sex couples, but it may have also cast SSM into a constantly active policymaking phase due to the incongruence between policy and public opinion in some places.[141] Additionally, moral progress of any type is thought to be vulnerable in a federal system because of the numerous ways it can be challenged.[142]

Another possibility, though, is that the concrete change brought about through the nationwide legalization of SSM could bring about a shift in public opinion over time.[143] As opponents adjust to a new legal definition of marriage, they may find that the existence of SSM does not infringe on their religious liberty to the extent they feared it might. In the event that public opinion shifts in the states where there is more opposition, it is possible that those state legislators and courts might shift as well. In such a case, congruence would increase, and the long-term protection of individual rights could be more sustainable. For SSM advocates, it would be sustainable because the right to marriage would be protected, and for religious liberty advocates, it would be sustainable because their consideration of liberty and its threats would shift.

CONCLUSION

In the matter of SSM policy, I conclude that American federalism has allowed for the protection of individual rights. Time will tell if the protections are lasting, and if they are, for whom. Given that individuals on both sides of the debate are able to make constitutionally grounded arguments (though how persuasive they are will depend largely on one's own opinion about SSM), I am not willing or able to dismiss the rights claims of one group over another based on my own assessment of the policy itself.[144] The primary need is to balance the demand for liberty with the calls for equality. Federalism allowed for the invention and propagation of SSM policy, but it also allows for counter-policy to develop as well.[145] There are at least two sides to every morality issue, and federalism as a method of power distribution does not discriminate between the sides. Anyone willing to navigate the system creates a possibility of arriving at a desired policy outcome. Even in the development of SSM policy, advocates had to work to find venues that were more conducive to advancing their cause, and federalism provides that opportunity.

If we are to learn from history, though, there a few lessons to recall with regard to morality policy, in general, and SSM policy, in particular. First, the conflicting civil and religious views of marriage have deep roots that persist beyond the determination of the *Obergefell* Court. With all of the support that same-sex couples have received, there are many people who still subscribe to a religious view of marriage that precludes homosexuality and SSM.[146] Second, other legally marginalized groups, whose movements extend further back into American history than the gay rights movement, continue to face challenges. Progress with regard to both race and gender have been subject to backlash and setbacks, and SSM advocates should anticipate continued backlash from opponents until such a time as those opinions shift or subside.[147] Federalism also leaves the door open to shifting views about the balance between liberty and equality and whose liberty we should be collectively protecting. The relationship between federalism and SSM policy is complicated and dynamic and provides an enlightening policy study into both the functioning of American federalism and the role of moral debate in the United States.

NOTES

1. Kindregan, "Same-Sex Marriage: The Cultural Wars and the Lessons of Legal History," 427.
2. Cleves, "What, Another Female Husband?" 1055.
3. Ibid., 1056; See also *The Homosexual in America* by Donald Webster Cory for an impactful treatment of the topic by a homosexual man in the 1950s.
4. Kindregan, "Same-Sex Marriage: The Cultural Wars and the Lessons of Legal History," 433.
5. Moats, *Civil Wars*, xii.
6. O'Connor and Yanus, "'Til Death—or the Supreme Court—Do Us Part," 294.
7. Pierceson, *Same-Sex Marriage in the United States*, 39.
8. Kindregan, "Same-Sex Marriage," 430.
9. Ibid.
10. Ibid.
11. Ibid.
12. Ibid.
13. Ibid., 431, 434.
14. Pierceson, *Same-Sex Marriage in the United States*, 37–38.
15. Ibid., 41.
16. Ibid., 24.
17. Ibid., 26.
18. Ibid.
19. Ibid., 24.
20. Ibid.
21. Ibid., 25.
22. Ibid., 24.
23. Ibid.
24. Ibid., 26.
25. Ibid.
26. Gibson, *Same-Sex Marriage and Social Media*, 77.
27. Ibid.
28. Ibid.
29. Pierceson, *Same-Sex Marriage in the United States*, 37.
30. Gibson, *Same-Sex Marriage and Social Media*, 78.

31. Pierceson, *Same-Sex Marriage in the United States*, 7.

32. Ibid.

33. Ibid.

34. Ibid.

35. Ibid.

36. Ibid.

37. For more thoughts on this, please see Ch. 4 of Walls, *Individualism in the United States*.

38. Pierceson, *Same-Sex Marriage in the United States*, 19.

39. Ibid., 18.

40. Williams, "Same-Sex Marriage and Equality," 589.

41. Ibid., 594.

42. Chamie and Mirkin, "Same-Sex Marriage: A New Social Phenomenon," 539.

43. Ibid.

44. Josephson, "Citizenship, Same-Sex Marriage, and Feminist Critiques of Marriage," 278.

45. Yoshino, "A New Birth of Freedom?" 179.

46. Hollander and Patapan, "Morality Policy and Federalism," 1.

47. Mooney, "The Decline of Federalism and the Rise of Morality-Policy Conflict in the United States," 174.

48. Ibid.

49. Ibid.

50. Ibid., 172.

51. Ibid., 178.

52. Hollander and Patapan, "Morality Policy and Federalism," 7.

53. Sager, "Symposium: Dual Enforcement of Constitutional Norms," 1387–1388.

54. Ibid., 1387.

55. Ibid.

56. Ibid., 1388.

57. Ibid.

58. Hollander and Patapan, "Morality Policy and Federalism," 6–7.

59. Ibid., 2.

60. Ibid., 16–17.

61. Ibid., 16.

62. Ibid., 2.

63. Ibid.

64. Ibid., 5.

65. Ibid.

66. Ibid., 6–7.

67. Ibid., 7.

68. Pierceson, *Same-Sex Marriage in the United States*, 6.

69. Mooney, "The Decline of Federalism and the Rise of Morality-Policy Conflict in the United States," 178.

70. Knauer, "Federalism, Marriage Equality, and LGBT Rights," 112.

71. Mooney, "The Decline of Federalism and the Rise of Morality-Policy Conflict in the United States," 178.

72. Pierceson, *Same-Sex Marriage in the United States*, 17.

73. Ibid., 41–42.

74. Ibid., 46.

75. Pickerill and Bowling, "Polarized Parties, Politics, and Policies," 376.

76. Ibid.

77. "Religious Freedom Restoration Act," *Encyclopaedia Britannica.*

78. Gibson, *Same-Sex Marriage and Social Media*, 33.

79. *Employment Div. v. Smith*, 494 U.S. 872 (1990).

80. Gibson, *Same-Sex Marriage and Social Media*, 33.

81. "Defense of Marriage Act," *Encyclopaedia Britannica.*

82. Knauer, "Federalism, Marriage Equality, and LGBT Rights," 99.

83. Pickerill and Bowling, "Polarized Parties, Politics, and Policies," 376.

84. Dry, *Same Sex Marriage and American Constitutionalism*, 34.

85. Ibid.

86. Pickerill and Bowling, "Polarized Parties, Politics, and Policies," 376.

87. O'Connor and Yanus, "'Til Death—or the Supreme Court—Do Us Part," 304.

88. Ibid.

89. Ibid.

90. *Loving v. Virginia*, 388 U.S. 1 (1967); Pierceson, Same-Sex Marriage in the United States, 28.

91. Kindregan, "Same-Sex Marriage: The Cultural Wars and the Lessons of Legal History," 435.

92. Ibid.

93. Novkov, "The Miscegenation/Same-Sex Marriage Analogy," 345.

94. Pierceson, Same-Sex Marriage in the United States, 28.

95. Pierceson, *Same-Sex Marriage in the United States*, 28; *Baker v. Nelson*, 291 Minn. 310, 191 N.W.2d 185 (1971).

96. *Baker v. Nelson*, 291 Minn. 310, 191 N.W.2d 185 (1971).

97. Ibid.

98. Pierceson, *Same-Sex Marriage in the United States*, 29.

99. Cory, *The Homosexual in America*, 281.

100. *Bowers v. Hardwick*, 478 U.S. 186 (1986)

101. *Lawrence v. Texas*, 539 U.S. 558 (2003).

102. Kindregan, "Same-Sex Marriage: The Cultural Wars and the Lessons of Legal History," 442.

103. Ibid.

104. Josephson, "Citizenship, Same-Sex Marriage, and Feminist Critiques of Marriage," 278.

105. *United States v. Windsor*, 570 U.S. 744 (2013).

106. Ibid.

107. United States v. Windsor, 570 U.S. 744 (2013).

108. Knauer, "Federalism, Marriage Equality, and LGBT Rights," 108.

109. Pickerill and Bowling, "Polarized Parties, Politics, and Policies," 392.
110. Gibson, *Same-Sex Marriage and Social Media*, 32.
111. Ibid.
112. *Obergefell v. Hodges*, 576 U.S. __ (2015).
113. Knauer, "Federalism, Marriage Equality, and LGBT Rights," 95.
114. Ibid.
115. Gibson, *Same-Sex Marriage and Social Media*, 33.
116. *Obergefell v. Hodges*, 576 U.S. __ (2015).
117. Weeden, "Marriage Equality Laws are a Threat to Religious Liberty," 226.
118. Ibid., 211.
119. Ibid., 212.
120. Ibid., 217.
121. Ibid., 226.
122. Ibid., 231.
123. Ibid., 218.
124. Ibid.
125. Ibid., 226.
126. Eskridge, "*A History of Same-Sex Marriage*," 1485.
127. NeJaime, "Marriage Inequality," 1177.
128. Ibid., 1179.
129. Pierceson, *Same-Sex Marriage in the United States*, 9.
130. Ibid.
131. Ibid., 10.
132. Ibid.
133. Kindregan, "Same-Sex Marriage: The Cultural Wars and the Lessons of Legal History," 437.
134. Ibid.
135. Gibson, *Same-Sex Marriage and Social Media*, 121.
136. Hollander and Patapan, "Morality Policy and Federalism," 18.
137. Ibid., 20.
138. Mooney, "The Decline of Federalism and the Rise of Morality-Policy Conflict in the United States," 187.
139. Ibid.
140. Ibid.
141. Ibid.
142. Hollander and Patapan, "Morality Policy and Federalism," 8.
143. Pierceson, *Same-Sex Marriage in the United States*, 5.
144. Unlike with civil rights, in which case I am more than happy to say that no one has the right to enslave someone or discriminate against them on the basis of race.
145. Hollander and Patapan, "Morality Policy and Federalism," 9–10.
146. Kindregan, "Same-Sex Marriage: The Cultural Wars and the Lessons of Legal History," 435.
147. Valdes, "From Law Reform to Lived Justice," 7.

SUGGESTED READINGS

Gibson, Rhonda. *Same-Sex Marriage and Social Media.* London and New York: Routledge, 2018.

Hollander, Robyn and Haig Patapan. "Morality Policy and Federalism: Innovation, Diffusion and Limits." *Publius* 47, no. 1 (2016): 1–26.

Mooney, Christopher Z. "The Decline of Federalism and the Rise of Morality-Policy Conflict in the United States." *Publius* 30, no. 1 (2000): 171–188.

Pierceson, Jason. *Same-Sex Marriage in the United States.* Lanham, MD: Rowman and Littlefield, 2013.

Weeden, L. Darnell. "Marriage Equality Laws are a Threat to Religious Liberty." *Southern Illinois University Law Journal* 41, no. 2 (2017): 211–236.

Chapter 7

Federalism and
Physician-Assisted Death

My goal in choosing topics to include in this study was to cover both established policy topics and then also newer topics that were not as developed. Physician-assisted death (PAD) came to my mind as a newer topic that does not have the established history of civil rights or education but is increasingly relevant to the American population as life expectancies grow and attitudes toward pain management and medical treatment evolve. At the same time, the opposition to PAD is driven by a powerful religious and moral component, which will not likely subside in the foreseeable future. Federalism appears to be the perfect answer to such a situation, but as we learned in the last chapter, morality policy poses a unique set of challenges to a federal system, and PAD would certainly be classified as such.

In this final policy chapter, we will take the opportunity to learn more about the history of PAD and how this topic has been relevant for the individual and for American federalism. Following a similar framework as we used with civil rights, education, and same-sex marriage, we will engage in a select review of legislative and judicial actions that have been impactful from the perspective of federalism, review the condition of PAD today, and then conduct an assessment of the impact of federalism on individual rights in the area of PAD. This is a sensitive topic, and while the goal here is not to develop an argument for or against PAD, I will define what liberty means in this context and ultimately what it means to protect individual rights in this area.

PHYSICIAN-ASSISTED DEATH

Given the topics I have selected for this study, it seems that all roads lead back to civil rights. It is remarkable how much the African American civil rights movement has influenced thinking about the individual and the role of the government in protecting individual rights. Both the civil rights movement and the women's liberation movement have been credited for shifting thinking about individual autonomy and providing the foundation for how to consider the concept of "patient rights" when making medical decisions, particularly end-of-life medical decisions.[1] As with these other movements, public opinion has played a role in shaping the governmental policy response. While legislative actions are intended to be more directly reflective of public opinion in any one state or congressional district, judicial decisions are also impacted by the major overtones of political culture at any given point in time. With regard to PAD, public opinion has shifted more favorably toward allowing people with terminal illnesses the ability to decide the circumstances of their own death with the help of their doctor.[2] The opinion of the medical community has also shifted in a way significant for the PAD movement. As we will discuss, the practice of PAD is not quite as new as the policies regulating it. There is evidence that the practice of administering life-altering medication to the terminally ill has long been established, though not documented or formalized. In recent decades, however, the opinion of the medical community has shown greater outward acceptance of the use of aggressive pain management strategies to alleviate the pain of the terminally ill, even if such treatment hastens their passing.[3] We can see evidence of the growing acceptance for such treatment in the proliferation of palliative care facilities in the United States.[4] Fifty years ago, there was only one such facility that provided palliative care to terminal cancer patients, and by 2010, there were approximately 5,000 such facilities or programs with over one million patients.[5] Though the offer of and legality of palliative care does not specifically extend to provisions for PAD, the rationale that provides for it can be used to justify other types of medical interventions for those who are dying and have no quality of life remaining.

Clearly, these are difficult questions, thus the lack of a unified governmental policy is not necessarily surprising. Even with public opinion growing increasingly supportive for PAD, only a handful of states have legalized the practice, whether through their state legislatures, citizen initiatives, or judicial mandates. The laws that support PAD are known generally as "death with dignity" statutes, and there are currently nine states and Washington, DC, with such laws in effect: California, Colorado, Hawaii, Maine, New Jersey, Oregon, Vermont, and Washington.[6] Montana has also legalized death with dignity but through a court decision. There is also one county in New Mexico that has legalized PAD. As of March 2020, there were seventeen additional states that had some type of death with dignity bill on their agenda.[7] While consideration of the practice has grown, a vast majority of states still prohibit PAD, with twenty-four states not planning any consideration of the topic in the current year.[8] One of the ongoing challenges of PAD is understanding the terminology and exactly what the issue is and what the various proposals are. Though our purpose cannot be to flesh out a comprehensive review of this topic and all of the debate surrounding it, we can make progress toward understanding the terminology and gaining a sense of what this matter is generally about.

In reviewing the literature on this topic, it becomes apparent that there is no broad consensus regarding the terminology that is used. I have settled on PAD for the purposes of this chapter, but I have also already introduced the death with dignity language as well. Other terms that are used include physician-assisted suicide and euthanasia, and we will review those as well. As we will see, the way this whole matter is framed makes a difference to how it is understood and accepted (or not). We will also establish how these actions differ from other ways individuals are empowered to make end-of-life choices. For the purposes of general discussion, however, I will be defaulting to the term PAD as opposed to physician-assisted suicide or death with dignity, as I find it to be the more morally neutral term.

The PAD debate is about whether or not terminally ill adults have a right to obtain the assistance of their doctor to end their lives.[9] The patient coordinates with a doctor to obtain a drug that, when taken, will cause death.[10] The doctor provides the drug or a prescription to obtain the drug, and then the patient is actually the one who ingests the drug, thus causing their own death.[11] If the doctor were to actually administer a lethal dose of medication with the patient's consent, that would be considered voluntary euthanasia.[12] Euthanasia has been a more contentious idea than PAD, in that fear persists that voluntary euthanasia could easily shift toward involuntary euthanasia. Though PAD involves both the patient and physician, the focus of PAD policymaking has served to emphasize the role of the individual patient. This emphasis is consistent with American political culture and has proven easier to promote than a scenario wherein the doctor plays a larger role. The terms physician-assisted suicide or PAD and voluntary euthanasia are separate matters from the ability of a patient to refuse life-support or to ask that life-support be discontinued, as these practices have long since been legally supported.[13] These practices are also distinct from indirect euthanasia, which refers to the use of pain medication to alleviate pain in the terminally ill to the extent that such use may hasten death.[14] For example, this category would include the use of morphine in a palliative care setting.

While the history of PAD policy does not go back that far, the debate over suicide dates back to ancient Greece and can also be found in early Christian thought.[15] Both of these sources yielded solid opposition to the practice, labeling suicide as "unnatural" and "sinful," respectively.[16] Over time, though, and after the Enlightenment, in particular, the role of religion in shaping preferences and thoughts on moral issues began to diminish in favor of reason.[17] The willingness to consider suicide in a more rational way led many people away from the previous practice of rejecting it in any circumstance. People became willing to accept that there were some situations in which a rational person could decide that death was preferable to life. However, the act of suicide was still considered a crime in many places where the law was based on a religious foundation. As with all other policy areas and subjects, the early American colonists brought with them British law and norms to create colonial policy, and suicide was no exception to this practice.[18] Suicide was considered a crime under British common law, and as such, all attempts to commit suicide were crimes as was helping another person to commit suicide.[19] In both eighteenth-century England and America, attitudes began to change toward the criminalization of suicide.[20]

The first PAD-related legislation was a bill introduced in the state of Ohio in 1906 entitled "An Act Concerning Administration of Drugs etc. to Mortally Injured and Diseased Persons," which was soundly defeated.[21] It would be decades before the first formal pro-euthanasia group was founded in 1938 by a Unitarian minister named Charles Potter.[22] It was originally called the Euthanasia Society of America and then changed to the Society for the Right to Die.[23] They came together to build on the support that public opinion was showing for both mercy deaths and increased individual discretion over end-of-life decisions.[24] The movement toward increased individual autonomy over such matters would only grow during the coming decades spurred by both an increasing desire for individual rights protections and a desire for the government to be less invasive in personal decision making.[25]

PAD and the Individual

With regard to individual liberty, what does it mean for the individual to be protected with regard to PAD policy? On the topic of individual liberty and PAD, it is important to acknowledge an important point: any person can end their life at any time, regardless of the willingness of any outside party to assist or any laws regulating such an act. Additionally, there are other options one can utilize to end their life in a medical setting, including simply discontinuing medical treatment or refusing food and water. Unfortunately, all of these options—suicide, outright death from an illness, and starvation or dehydration—are highly unpleasant and objectionable ways to die.[26] The main purpose of PAD policy has been to use the government to protect the rights of individuals, not only to die, but to die in a manner of their choice when confronted with a terminal prognosis and the rights of medical professionals who wish to help them pursue that end. The issue is discussed by advocates in terms of rights, specifically the right to individual liberty over a personal life decision.[27] Due to the collaborate nature of PAD, individual liberty in this context only makes sense in the positive: the freedom to work with a medical professional to make end-of-life decisions due to a terminal condition. The alternate approach to liberty in such a scenario would involve the government leaving medical decisions to doctors and patients without intervention. That would be a version of negative liberty: freedom from intervention. However, given the fact that aiding in someone's death in any capacity would likely be breaking an existing law, the only practical way to understand liberty here is in a positive sense through which the government forges a path to enable free activity. There is a degree to which current policy is aligned with this thinking, and it specifically concerns the execution and recognition of advance healthcare directives. Individuals have the ability to execute a legal document that states what type of treatment they wish to have should they not be conscious or competent to make end-of-life decisions.[28] Additionally, individuals can exercise their freedom to refuse life-sustaining care. However, if people wish to create a path for PAD, that requires them to come together to agree that the individual freedom to seek assistance in ending their life supersedes any other moral, ethical, or religious concerns the community has regarding the preservation of life. Each state then must decide how far individuals can go in making such decisions. How much individual liberty will the law afford in this context?[29] Again, this is not just the freedom to die, but the freedom to die in a controlled environment with maximum comfort.

For proponents of PAD, it is clear that the individual of relevance to any discussion of rights is the individual who has the terminal prognosis. The desired role for the government is to protect and promote the individual's right to die under the umbrella of the right to privacy.[30] This argument is usually made in terms of autonomy, and contends that being an autonomous individual requires, at the very least, the ability to make decisions about whether to live or die.[31] The preservation of individual autonomy is what protects the individual from others who might wish to impose their own values and sense of what is best onto them.[32] However, opponents of PAD argue that the patients are not the only individuals of relevance and that consideration must be given to others who are impacted by these policies. They believe that policies that advance patient autonomy in this respect do so at the cost of societal and community wellness.[33] They criticize individualism as the ideological component of American political culture that drives this notion of autonomy. Critics prefer the government to function as a tool for protecting people from engaging in life-threatening activities, not as a tool to enable such activities.[34] They consider what is best from the perspective of loved ones and medical professionals and determine that those interests are not served by PAD and must come before the preferences of a terminally ill patient who no longer wishes to live. They do not see this as a privacy issue since its impact is so far-reaching.[35]

In the matter of PAD, the group of individuals that have the most relevance are the patients themselves. These policies are designed to maximize their individual choice to persist with a terminal condition or die in a humane way in a controlled medical environment. Clearly, there is much debate over whether or not this should be a protected right and a form of positive liberty that is afforded to the terminally ill. There are those who believe that the community impact should come first, and further believe that stopping PAD yields a net benefit for the community. While I do not suggest this argument is wholly without merit, I do not think it is consistent with either American political culture or the classical liberal ideology that serves as its foundation. Individualism as the founders understood it had both positive and negative components, and in this case, I am inclined to define individual liberty in the context of PAD policy in positive terms. Due to the nature of death and the legal implications of being involved in another person's death, the government has a role to play to ensure that individuals have maximum latitude to make their own healthcare decisions and this should extend to the medical decision to end one's life in the context of terminal illness.

PAD and Federalism

In the context of federalism, we should first look to the Constitution for any possible guidance on how the national and state governments are intended to proceed with this type of policy. Like other topics, we have discussed herein, the Constitution does not directly deal with the topic of PAD. Though many people refer to PAD under the umbrella of the "right to die," there is no such identified right enumerated anywhere in the Constitution.[36] PAD advocates have used the Due Process Clauses in the Fifth Amendment and Fourteenth Amendment to protect the liberty needed to justify ending one's life with medical assistance.[37] There has also been an attempt to create a right to die under the right to privacy that was created when the Supreme Court decided the case of *Griswold v. Connecticut* (1963).[38] The argument is that where there is a right to privacy, there can also be a right to make your own personal decisions regarding your life.[39] As we have discussed with the other policy topics, the Fourteenth Amendment has been subject to interpretation numerous times as its applicability has been tested from one policy area to another. While the amendment prohibits the limitation of liberties, the way it is interpreted can be done broadly or narrowly depending on the perspective of those involved.[40] A narrow interpretation of the Fourteenth Amendment would limit its application to specific liberties that have long since been recognized by the states.[41] In the case of PAD, we can find no such tradition. A broad interpretation would allow for those recognized liberties and any other liberties that might rest upon the same set of values as previously recognized liberties.[42] In the case of PAD, we could argue for individual autonomy and the ideological tradition of American individualism. The general acknowledgment of individual rights and their fundamental importance to American governance and political culture could be used then to support the extension of such freedom to a right to die.[43] The Supreme Court has acknowledged that the Fourteenth Amendment does protect liberty that extends to personal autonomy and has used that interpretation to allow individuals to refuse life-support when cognitively able to do so.[44] Since the Constitution does not provide us with particularly clear guidance on PAD, we can learn more about federalism and PAD through observing how the national government and state governments have generally addressed these matters before we review more specific actions in the next section.

First, the national government has played a role in this policy area, but it has been limited. The matter of PAD has simply never been established as part of the national agenda.[45] PAD advocates have criticized the lack of national action as critical in shaping the future of PAD, because the national government does not wish to engage in setting nationwide policy on this matter. This means that individuals who reside in states where PAD is illegal will continue to face infringements on their personal liberty. When the national government has acted, either through its courts or Congress, the end result has been to defer to the states and encourage further policymaking at the state level. Proponents of this action would cite the existence of federalism as justification for allowing the states to move forward with whatever policies they deem appropriate. However, PAD advocates contend that this refusal on the part of the national government to actively engage in PAD policy is more the result of partisan politics and the distinct differences between Democratic and Republican judges on right-to-die matters.[46] With the large number of Republican federal judges, PAD advocates contend that the national government is not likely to make any progressive moves on this policy anytime soon.[47] Absent an egregious violation of federal law, the federal courts have not and will not be eager to intervene in these matters.[48] This notwithstanding, the state courts have taken guidance from other federal court decisions to determine how to proceed with their own cases. This has led to an interesting dynamic wherein the state courts have been relied upon to settle these conflicts within each state, but yet the U.S. Constitution is relied upon to make the main arguments for and against PAD.[49] Based on the recognition of a "liberty interest" in the Fourteenth Amendment and the establishment of privacy rights by way of *Griswold* and *Roe v. Wade* (1973), the state courts have agreed to provide a right to die for conscious and competent patients, including the refusal of nourishment, and the right of others to make decisions for people who are either of unconscious or incompetent.[50] This practice of relying on the U.S. Constitution in the absence of relevant state-level legislative action or case law is known as the "federalization" of constitutional law at the state level, and it is observable in the matter of right-to-die policy.[51]

With the lack of national action and the need for some type of policy response regarding PAD and other related policy matters, the state courts and legislatures have been active. While the state courts have been prone to rely on the U.S. Constitution, the state legislatures have allowed for more variety and diversity in their lawmaking to address the wishes of their constituents.[52] The states have also looked to one another to formulate policy and move forward either to advance or stymie PAD policy.[53] In general, the state courts have been more progressive than the state legislatures.[54] However, legislatures in all fifty states have been proactive in passing legislation regarding advance healthcare directives for end-of-life care that are designed to maximize individual control over these decisions.[55] There is also the option of the initiative process for citizens to directly engage in policy development when either the legislature or courts have not acted at all or have not acted in a satisfactory manner.[56] Citizen initiatives have been a very impactful method of policymaking on PAD issues, especially earlier in the policy's development.

In keeping with traditional thinking about morality policy, the national government has refrained from acting too frequently or decisively on matters of PAD, preferring to maintain state sovereignty on such matters. In the absence of national action, the state courts and legislatures have engaged in policymaking, and where the state-level governments have been unwilling or unable to act, the citizens have directly involved themselves in the policymaking process. Thus, the existence of a federal system has been an integral part of the PAD policymaking process. Beyond our basic understanding of how federalism and PAD have functioned together thus far, we can now talk more specifically about federalism and the development of PAD policies.

FEDERALISM AND PAD POLICY DEVELOPMENT

An individual's views on life or death matters are traditionally influenced by notions of morality, ethics, and religion. As a morality policy, PAD is not prone to compromise, and there are typically two options that are polar opposite: either we use the government to allow terminally ill patients the option of PAD and protect those medical professionals who assist them from criminal prosecution or we restrict this choice by using the government to make PAD illegal and threaten medical professionals with criminal prosecution. PAD advocates have taken opportunities to promote favorable policy at the state level, and that is where they have had success so far. However, PAD is only available in a limited number of states. The lack of availability creates hardships and a restriction of individual liberty for terminally ill people who live in states where PAD is not available. From the perspective of maximizing individual freedom, a policy made at the national level would create uniformity and increased access. However, SSM policy development demonstrates that imposing uniform policy on morality issues can lead to chronic instability and activity on that policy matter. Opponents of PAD would certainly prefer to limit availability to only those states who have the critical mass of support to make the policy reasonable in that particular place. If proponents of PAD are able to continue in the propagation phase of the morality policy life cycle and spread support for PAD from state to state, then it is reasonable to think there can ultimately be a national policy that is enforceable at the state level and thus more stable.

Themes of PAD Policy Development

The process of PAD policy development has been somewhat slow over the last several decades, mostly due to the reasonable reluctance of the national government to move the policy forward in a progressive way and the strength of religious organizations who have worked diligently to advance a more protective and paternalistic view of the government as it relates to the individual. I do not think these PAD opponents would say that they want to limit individual rights, but they believe that restricting individual action is the path to protecting the individual in this case. There have been significant decisions made regarding PAD at the national and state level in the way of citizen initiatives, legislative action, and judicial action. In conducting a select review of significant actions from the perspective of federalism, there are a few themes to note. These include notions of morality and the tension over which branch of government is best suited to decide morality policy. First, morality is a running theme through actions intended to provide some regulation or guidance on matters of PAD policy. Both advocates for and opponents of PAD can draw on moral arguments to support their side. There is the ongoing debate as to how significant individual autonomy is, and what efforts should be made to balance it with other moral concerns. The argument for autonomy is based on the idea that individuals should be protected in their ability to make their own decisions and that extends to how they die.[57] The opposing view is that individual autonomy is overemphasized at the cost of societal stability, and that people need to give up some of those freedoms for the betterment of the whole. Again, this assumes that allowing the terminally ill to choose to die in a medical setting creates such a threat. Next, there is the moral consideration of "best interest" and who is able to determine such an interest and for whom. Advocates of PAD have continually argued that individual patients are the ones best positioned to determine what is in their best interest and should be trusted to carry out whatever plans line up with that assessment. Individuals have a "special expertise" in matters concerning their own health and should be able to proceed based on that knowledge.[58] On the contrary, opponents argue that any assessment that leads one to believe they should die is an incorrect assessment. Dying by choice is a bad decision, and any decision that results in death cannot possibly be in one's best interest.[59] A final moral issue concerns the sanctity of life. There is an ongoing debate as to whether or not human life is inherently sacred. This element draws heavily from religious beliefs that only God can take life and that actions taken by people to end a life are sinful, even if the action is to take one's own life. The main question here is—even if we can concede that individual autonomy is politically significant and should be protected and that dying is in the patient's best interest because they are terminally ill with no hope of recovery—does a voluntary death still violate the sanctity of life?[60]

A second recurring theme in PAD policy development is the debate over whether or not legislatures or the courts are more appropriate for deciding morality policy. There is skepticism about the role of litigation in moving the issue forward out of concern that those decisions are not necessarily in line with what the majority of people want. Nonetheless, advocates of PAD have expressed frustration with the unwillingness of the federal courts to push the issue forward for the benefit of terminally ill individuals nationwide.[61] They argue that the reluctance of the courts does not have anything to do with a great respect for federalism and state sovereignty but is reflective of the ideological predispositions of conservative judges who believe in the sanctity of life.[62] As a result, these judges have chosen to either not hear cases or, when they have heard cases, defer to the states. In light of these issues, legislative acts can be effective in moving policy forward at the state level, but there are state legislatures who are not particularly keen to get in on this debate either. As a result, citizen initiatives have been a powerful tool for PAD advocates, and these are facilitated by a federal system as well. Our review of key actions will give a sense of how each level of government has influenced this policy issue and affected the protection of individual rights.

Select Citizen Initiatives

One way we can better understand the relationship between federalism and PAD is through learning more about citizen initiatives and the role they can play in the policymaking process. Though the specific processes will vary from state to state, the basic idea of a citizen initiative is providing the people within a state with an opportunity to make policy for themselves. There will be a process in place through which anyone can potentially place a policy issue directly on the ballot. Though American politics, national and state, relies primarily on principles of representation, citizens initiatives are one way the people can engage in direct policymaking. In the case of PAD, there is an extensive history of groups like the Hemlock Society attempting to bypass state legislatures and formulate policy through organizing these types of initiatives.[63] Though this method has been successfully utilized in multiple states, we will review the first successful citizen initiative, the Oregon Death With Dignity Act of 1997 (ODWDA).

The ODWDA was passed in November 1994 but was not implemented until October 1997 due to legal challenges.[64] The law created a process through which terminally ill patients could get prescriptions for lethal doses of medication that they would then ingest on their own. The law does specifically prohibit euthanasia, defined as any process through which a doctor would directly administer the lethal dose.[65] Oregon was the first state to legalize PAD, and as such, took care to make sure the law was conservatively written so as to draw fewer challenges: it is only intended to be available to very small population of individuals, it is not referred to as "suicide," and it contains many procedural safeguards to limit its use.[66] The safeguards include an age restriction limiting the option to patients eighteen and older, a residency requirement, a competency requirement, and the additional requirement that death is likely within six months.[67] In practice, the law has achieved its goal of being a limited option. From 1997 to 2019, only 2,518 people received prescriptions, and then only 1,657 of those individuals went on to ingest the medication and die.[68] A majority of the doctors that participate in PAD have chosen to remain anonymous because of the continued stigma surrounding PAD and the fear of negative repercussions from policy opponents.[69]

The ODWDA is significant from the perspective of federalism for a few reasons. First, it represents the first citizen initiative passed to legalize PAD. Such a development is only possible in a federal system wherein the states have the sovereignty to develop their own policies. This state-level facilitation of direct democracy is significant for bringing individual citizens into the political process in a meaningful way. Through the creation of this state law, the people of Oregon were able to make PAD policy that was consistent with what a majority of voters wanted, even if it is not something that would be appropriate for the entire country. The congruence between policy and state-level support is significant for policy stability, federalism allows for that, and the people of Oregon were able to capitalize on these factors. Second, though the law was passed, the implementation was impacted by national law. This is also a byproduct of federalism that is worth noting. There were some conflicts between state and federal law, as federal law prohibited federal healthcare systems and physicians from participating in PAD.[70] For example, veterans who were patients of Veterans Administration hospitals would not have access to PAD.[71] In this case, even though the state of Oregon had the ability to create PAD policy for that state, not all Oregonians had access due to the involvement of the national government in some aspects of healthcare delivery in that state.

Select Legislative Action

Another method of understanding the relationship between federalism and PAD is to evaluate a selection of impactful national and state-level legislative acts.[72] The legislatures are responsible for the creation of policy, and this ideally is the first governmental step to address public issues. If the national or state legislatures are able to address such matters adequately, then the courts will not necessarily need to get involved. There are examples of legislation at both the national and state level that have been impactful for the relationship between federalism and PAD. They do not all directly involve PAD but are still important for the issue and the principles of federalism. We will review examples of national legislation, including the Patient Self-Determination Act of 1990 and the Act for the Relief of the Parents of Theresa Marie Schiavo. At the state level, we will review the California End of Life Option Act of 2015.

The first piece of legislation for our review is the Patient Self-Determination Act of 1990 (PSDA). The PSDA was created to institutionalize the concept of patients' rights and provide a legal path through which individuals could have some control over their end-of-life care. Though this law does not provide for PAD, it did provide for the creation of, and adherence to, advance healthcare directives regarding end-of-life care.[73] This law was very important for the PAD movement, however, because it was the first formal recognition of an individual right to die, though it was limited to allowing people to die of natural causes without life-sustaining care.[74]

The passage of the PSDA was significant for the relationship between federalism and PAD for a few reasons. First, the law represents the assertion of national authority over a morality issue. In this case, the issue of individual autonomy and its relationship to self-determination created an opportunity for Congress to act in a way that protected all individuals, regardless of their state of residence. Given the primacy of individual rights in American political culture, this extension to a limited exercise of self-determination in healthcare matters was reasonable. In many established policy areas, protection of such rights has fallen under the purview of the national government, despite the ability of the states to provide same. Second, it created a baseline for end-of-life self-determination that, at minimum, all states would have to comply with. For some states, where support for PAD was particularly low, this legislation raised the floor toward greater individual autonomy in healthcare decisions.

A second piece of legislation for our consideration that was particularly noteworthy for federalism and PAD was the Act for the Relief of the Parents of Theresa Marie Schiavo ("Schiavo Relief Act") of 2005. This law came about as the result of an extended legal battle in the state of Florida. Terri Schiavo had suffered a stroke which left her in a persistent vegetative state (PVS).[75] Her husband wished to disconnect life-support, which would have left her to die of starvation or dehydration. Her parents did not believe she was in a PVS and wished to keep her alive with the feeding tube that was inserted. A legal drama played out at the state level with involvement of the state courts, the state legislature, and the state's governor, Jeb Bush. Ultimately, the decision was made and upheld at the state level to remove the feeding tube.[76] There were two attempts (one by Governor Bush and one by Ms. Schiavo's parents) to appeal the matter to the U.S. Supreme Court, which were denied both times. When it appeared that options to save her life at the state level had been exhausted, Congress passed the Schiavo Relief Act, so that the federal courts would have jurisdiction over the matter.[77] The Act granted federal jurisdiction over the case and removed some procedural obstacles that would have encouraged federal deference to the previous decisions made by the state courts.[78] The Act vacated the state court proceedings, without having to show that anything was mishandled, and gave the parents the opportunity to ask a federal court judge to order the feeding tube reinserted.[79] The parents did so, and their request was denied. Terri Schiavo died in the following days.

While this matter was quite unique, it is significant for federalism and the right-to-die movement, broadly understood. First, it demonstrated the willingness of the national government to intervene on a matter directly related to the potential death of a chronically incapacitated patient. Despite the fact that the state government had effectively processed the case and arrived at a decision, the national government provided Terri Schiavo's parents with the opportunity to engage the national government to help save their daughter's life. Though the legislative branch and the federal judiciary were not necessarily in agreement here, this action ran contrary to the idea that the states should and would be left alone to address matters of death and the right to die. Second, it is significant for federalism because it represents the national government using its power to undercut state-level governance out of a belief that the state was not doing its job to protect the life of one its residents. Although national intervention in state matters was not new, it was a significant move relative to PAD policy. Advocates had been urged time and again to use state processes as those were better suited to deal with such issues. The intervention of the national government in this case was a jolt to the balance of power that a healthy federal system requires. In this case, it is worth noting that Ms. Schiavo, who was only twenty-six at the time of her incapacitation, had not completed an advance healthcare directive. The lack of this document began the years of fighting between her husband and parents over what she would have wanted in this scenario.

A third piece of significant legislation for the relationship between federalism and PAD is the California End of Life Option Act (EOLA), passed in 2015. This law was the first state law providing for PAD that was introduced and passed in the state legislature, though many other states had attempted to do this.[80] The EOLA allows a doctor to prescribe a lethal dose of a drug to a terminally ill patient who meets other specified criteria but may not help in any way with the actual administration of the dose.[81] The criteria include patient competency to communicate with and make an "informed decision" regarding their death.[82] Additionally, the patient must be able to prove that they are a California resident.[83]

This legislation was significant for federalism because it represented the first time a state legislature used its authority to create a law allowing PAD rather than relying on the citizens to proceed with ballot initiatives. Legislators do not always wish to enter into these types of moral debates. This inaction can then place pressure on other actors to move policy forward. If state legislators are unwilling to act, the pressure to create policy can shift upward to the national government or downward to the citizens. In this case, where the national government had expressed an unwillingness to actively engage, state legislatures became viable venues for the creation of PAD policy. At the time the California EOLA passed, it was hypothesized that this type of action in a state as large and diverse as California could have a propagating effect and might encourage other states to follow suit.[84] In fact, that hypothesis was correct, and in the few years between the passage of the EOLA and this writing, four other states have passed similar laws.

Select Judicial Decisions

Our review of federalism and PAD policy development also includes a few select court cases that have impacted how federalism has functioned in these matters to protect individual rights. Advocates for PAD have sought to make progress through both the federal and state courts. These decisions have had an impact on how, and more importantly for federalism, where these matters should and will be decided. This is not an exhaustive list of court cases, but they serve to set the tone for how such matters have been handled by courts. Our review will include the cases of *Cruzan v. Director, Missouri Department of Health* (1990), *Washington v. Glucksberg* (1997), and *Gonzales v. Oregon* (2006). These court decisions have been impactful for the development of PAD policy and on working through the questions of what should be decided where and for whom.

One significant court case for our consideration is *Cruzan v. Director, Missouri Department of Health* (1990).[85] This case, while not directly a PAD case, was the first time the Supreme Court addressed right-to-die issues. This case was about the conditions under which one could refuse medical treatment but is known as a right-to-die case.[86] In this case, Nancy Cruzan had been in a car accident and suffered injuries that left her in a PVS. After several weeks with a feeding tube, her parents requested that the life-support be discontinued. However, the hospital was unwilling to do so without the approval of the state courts to discontinue life-support. In the absence of any "clear and convincing" documentation that Ms. Cruzan would have wanted the feeding tube withdrawn, the decision was made to leave it in and continue life-support.[87] After the Missouri Supreme Court had ruled in favor of the state and against the Cruzan family, they appealed to the U.S. Supreme Court.[88] The Court did ultimately uphold an individual's right to die, however, they also acknowledged that the states had an obligation to protect the lives and safety of their residents.[89] In the opinion, Chief Justice John Rehnquist stated that the right to die came from the Due Process Clause of the Fourteenth Amendment, but in order to be exercised, it must be clear that it is the individual's will to die and then it must be balanced against the state's interests.[90] As such, the Court upheld the state's position that protected Ms. Cruzan's life and rejected her parents' request.[91]

The *Cruzan* case is significant from the perspective of federalism. It represents the first decision made by the U.S. Supreme Court on this policy. Any time the national government intervenes on morality policy, it represents a jolt to the principles of federalism. Historically, such matters are within the jurisdiction of the states, and so when the national government sees fit to intervene, it is noteworthy. Though the Supreme Court did ultimately rule in favor of the state's ability to make its own rules dealing with the rights of surrogates to make decisions for incapacitated individuals, it also made the bold move of asserting a constitutionally supported position in favor of a right to die.[92] It was this decision that led to the introduction and passage of the Patient Self-Determination Act which would enable individuals nationwide to document their end-of-life wishes in a way that would be acknowledged by healthcare professionals should they become incapacitated. In this way, the decision was both a move to protect states' rights while also carving out a role for the national government for the protection of individual rights.

While right-to-die advocates thought the *Cruzan* decision was a significant step toward to the protection of PAD, the case really only addressed the right to refuse treatment.[93] The Court had not yet stated anything explicitly about PAD, though it would take the opportunity to in 1997 when it chose to hear appeals related to two PAD cases: *Washington v. Glucksberg* and *Vacco v. Quill*. The *Glucksberg* case was from the state of Washington and *Vacco v.*

Quill was out of New York state, but both involved state laws that prohibited PAD and physicians who had sued the state for violating a constitutional right based on the Due Process Clause of the Fourteenth Amendment to choose death in extraordinary medical circumstances. The *Quill* case brought the additional claim that allowing the refusal of treatment but not allowing PAD was a violation of the Equal Protection Clause because it afforded a right only to those terminally ill patients who required life-support and not those terminally ill patients who did not require life-support. The Court decided in favor of the states' ability to ban PAD, and additionally ruled that there was no violation of the Equal Protection Clause.[94] The Court went on to identify six interests that state governments were obligated to protect, including the preservation of life, the prevention of suicide, and the avoidance of a "slippery slope" scenario wherein PAD could turn into doctor-led euthanasia.[95] Even though the Court was reluctant to intervene in the states' ability to protect these interests, the decision also made clear that any such laws would not inhibit a patient's access to palliative care.[96]

For right-to-die activists, the opportunity to have this matter ruled upon by the Supreme Court was long overdue, and many of them felt comforted by what they thought the *Cruzan* case signaled: the belief that people had broad latitude to choose death in a medical setting. In reality, the *Cruzan* decision had only granted quite narrow latitude to choose death, as became apparent in the *Glucksberg* and *Quill* cases. The decision of the Court in these matters was significant in shaping the future of the relationship between federalism and PAD policy development. First, we find significance in the willingness of the national government to get involved in this matter. The acceptance of these cases encouraged those who wished to promote the protection of individual rights in these matters and threatened those who wished to preserve states' rights. This leads to the second reason why this decision was significant: the Court made it clear that it wished the states to work these issues out on their own. The Court did go so far as to reject the existence of a constitutional right to PAD; however, it was equally clear that the states needed to make this decision for themselves on a state-by-state basis and those decisions needed to be supported at the state level.[97] The Court was ultimately unwilling to settle this matter beyond effectively handing it back to the states.[98] There is yet another reason why this decision was significant for federalism and PAD, and this reason extends more specifically to the concept of individual rights and their relationship to states' rights. The decision seems to signal a rather limited interpretation of individual rights as compared to states' rights.[99] Through the articulation of several specific state interests that exist on right-to-die matters, the Court set up a tension between individual rights and the rights of each state to protect those interests.[100] While this decision allowed states to pursue policy best suited for each state, it also raised questions regarding individual autonomy and created the potential for a stronger role for the states in limiting that autonomy.

The final case in our focused review is *Gonzales v. Oregon* (2006). This case provides an opportunity to see the interplay between the states and the national government on the topic of PAD by way of executive action. In 2001, then-Attorney General John Ashcroft issued a memorandum (the "Ashcroft Directive") creating a rule that prohibited physicians from prescribing any federally controlled substances for the purposes of PAD, as assisting suicide was not deemed to be a "legitimate medical purpose" under the Controlled Substances Act (CSA).[101] At the time, Oregon was the only state that allowed PAD, and so it was written that doctors in Oregon who prescribed such controlled substances could have their medical licenses suspended.[102] This case resulted when the State of Oregon, a doctor, pharmacist, joined by a number of terminally ill individuals sued in federal district court to stop implementation of the rule.[103] That court ruled that the Ashcroft Directive was an illegal use of national authority in a matter that was to be regulated by the states.[104] Upon appeal to the U.S. Ninth Circuit Court and then the U.S. Supreme Court, that decision was affirmed out of a strong concern for federalism and the balance of power between the states and the national government.[105]

This decision was almost exclusively about federalism and the view the federal courts held regarding the preferred relationship between federalism and PAD policymaking. It reinforced the thinking of the *Glucksberg* Court, in that it rejected the assertion of national authority over PAD. The decision did not deal directly with any normative questions regarding PAD but focused rather on what role the national government should play regarding medical regulation.[106] The opinion recognized the fact that PAD was a current topic actively debated at the state level and that the national government should not intervene in any way that could shape or resolve the issue for the states.[107] This decision both strengthened the position of the states while also creating some uncertainty for the individual. As with all matters of federalism, the increase in state sovereignty can allow for both the creation of moral policy appropriate for a limited population while also creating a possible threat to individuals who might not be protected in their access to PAD.[108]

Overall, judicial activity on matters of PAD has functioned almost exclusively to promote states' rights and minimize the role of the federal government. The resistance of the national government to rule on matters of morality has been very evident in this policy area, and the interpretation of individual rights has been quite limited to the actual choices and actions of the individual as expressed and carried out by that individual person. The courts have been unwilling to extend those rights to others on behalf of the individual in any meaningful way.

FEDERALISM AND PAD TODAY

Since the matter of PAD has been left to the states, there are many policy-centered issues that remain and challenges that have resulted from using state-led policy development. One example of a challenge is the development of "death tourism." Also known as suicide tourism, this is a direct result of how PAD has been managed in the context of American federalism. Death tourism is part of a larger international phenomenon known as medical tourism that can cover all manner of medical treatment that is either unavailable or unaffordable in one's own place of residence.[109] Medical tourism is a feature of the globalization of healthcare, and from the position of choice, it is not inherently problematic.[110] The concept of death tourism is based on traveling to a jurisdiction where some form of PAD or voluntary euthanasia is legal. In the American context, people can travel from one state to another seeking these services. This practice began with the passage of the Oregon law, and thus the term "Oregon transplant" was coined to refer to such patients.[111] The idea of merging death with tourism is still a relatively new idea, and there has not been a great deal of research done on this topic.[112] From the perspective of federalism and individual rights, there are a few issues that we can explore.

First, the need to travel could be prohibitive for the terminally ill people who may wish to benefit from PAD services. One of the benefits of federalism is purportedly that the policies of the states can more effectively meet the needs of the people. The corollary to this is that people can go to the states where the policies best meet their own needs. In the case of PAD, the need to travel may not be feasible. If there is an individual who wishes to explore PAD options, but that individual cannot afford to travel or is too sick to travel, then they cannot access that service.

Second, the idea that an individual would not be eligible for the rights conferred in one state until they become a legal resident creates an additional burden for that individual in seeking PAD. These residency requirements are not insurmountable, but they then serve to limit access to PAD to residents and those who have the resources relocate to that state. Within the confines of federalism, these laws were created for the benefit of the residents of those respective states, and so the inclusion of residency requirements might seem logical at first. However, in most other contexts, people are immediately under the jurisdiction of the state they are physically in. In this case, the terminally ill individual must jump through a number of hoops to benefit from the state PAD policy upon arrival in a state where it is legal.

The combination of federalism, the desire to address PAD policy at the state level, and the nationwide demand for PAD policy has created a scenario in which terminally ill people must, if they can, become an "Oregon transplant" to obtain the medical care they desire.[113] This situation also creates a mixed bag of results with regard to individual rights. Again, with the national government yielding control over this matter to the states, its power is generally moot in this discussion. The states that have legalized PAD are actively protecting the individual rights of the residents of those respective states, however the inclusion of residency requirements, even with a shortened time duration to establish residency, serves to limit the general rights of terminally ill Americans who wish to obtain access to PAD services. Those states with no provisions for PAD, again, are not protecting the individual rights of the patients.

The only solution that federalism offers to address this challenge is for the national government to take control over this policy area. Given the history of litigation on this topic, that is highly unlikely. Not only is there is an extensive and well-documented history of the national government deferring this policy matter to the states, the national government is well aware of the challenges that develop when it chooses to weigh in on morality policy. A decision is made, but the matter is not settled, as federalism provides a path for advocates and opponents alike. I can think of no better example of this than the topic of abortion that was decided in 1973 and persists today as a highly divisive and volatile topic in American politics and for federalism, in particular. Another possible solution would be the spread of pro-PAD policy state-by-state until a greater national consensus was achieved and most, if not all, Americans would have access to PAD programs.

Our focused review of judicial and legislative actions on PAD has shed light on how federalism has been used to address PAD. However, shifting responsibility to the states only leads to more questions and more possibilities—both good and bad—for the individual. As we saw in our review of education policy, it seems that PAD has been addressed largely in terms of states' rights and not always in terms of individual rights. The Supreme Court has now asserted repeatedly both a recognition of limited individual rights and a need to balance those with the duties and obligations of the states. That position sets up tension between both the individual and the national government and the individual and the state in the event that the individual seeks access to PAD services and cannot easily obtain them.

FEDERALISM, PAD, AND INDIVIDUAL RIGHTS

It is difficult to imagine a topic more personal or more connected to the concept of self-determination than life and death. In American political culture, we have always recognized life as a natural right, but what about the choice to die? If the individual has a right to live, does that individual have a right to die? If so, then under what conditions will this be permitted? It is also a topic that is largely driven by emotion and religious views. Policymaking decisions have been made in the narrowest manner possible from the way individual rights are understood in this context to which level of government is expected to take the lead on making the policy. Individuals and states have sought direction from the national government by way of legislation and court decisions but have not received much guidance in return. Over the last several years, the states have created policies that suit the majority of people in each state, whether that is to create PAD policy or keep the issue off the agenda. For our purposes, we must assess if federalism has served to advance or diminish the protection of individual rights with regard to PAD policy.

Three-Part Test

The first question of my three-part test is: Are individual rights in the context of PAD protected somewhere in our political system? The answer is yes: individual access to PAD services is currently protected in the American political system in several states, the District of Columbia, and one county in New Mexico. Due to the freedom that Americans have to travel as they wish, these services are available to all with the restriction of various residency requirements in each state. While the national government is not expected to expand individual access to PAD, there is the possibility in a federal system that more states will institute PAD policy thus increasing individual access and increasing individual autonomy regarding right-to-die matters. Of course, it is also possible that no other states may choose to allow PAD, which would impact accessibility for citizens living in states where PAD is not available. It is also possible that states where it is currently legal could change their policy. However, this possibility is not supported by the current trend data toward greater legalization.

Second, is there reason to believe that this protection was enhanced through federalism, as demonstrated by issue mobility between levels of government to seek protections for individual rights? The answer is yes. PAD has been considered at both the national and state level, and it has settled where it can develop most stably. In the short term, there is the loss of individual rights for those living in states where PAD is illegal, and particularly for those who do not have the resources or wherewithal to travel for PAD services. Over the last several years, more states have created their own PAD policies, and as long as that is the trend more Americans wish to see, a further expansion of those rights would be expected.

One possible threat that federal mobility poses to individual rights is the possibility of the national government taking some nullifying action that would restrict the implementation of PAD at the state level. This threat is not supported by past behavior of the Supreme Court. The Court has had the opportunity to act one way or the other on PAD and has deferred to the states on the basis of federalism. Overall, the sovereignty that federalism allows for the states has facilitated the development of PAD as it exists today. Even with limitations in place, I would say that the policy mobility that federalism allows has enhanced individual rights in this policy area.

Lastly, is there reason to believe that this protection will be lasting in a federal system, demonstrated by issue symmetry between the state and national level? The answer to this question is a bit more difficult that in the other policy areas, mostly because the national government has reserved regulation of PAD to the states. The Supreme Court has established that there is a constitutionally protected right to refuse medical treatment by way of the Fourteenth Amendment, but there is not a constitutional right to PAD. Beyond that, the Court has left it to the states to decide for themselves based on their own state constitutions, court cases, and statutory laws. I suppose to that extent then, we can say there is issue symmetry: it has been decided that the states will take the lead on PAD policy with limited guidance from the national government, and what guidance it has issued is legally binding.

As long as there is state-level support for PAD in any of the fifty states, then the protections will be lasting. They can become more or less accessible to terminally ill individuals, but the protections will exist somewhere. If the current public opinion data trends continue, we should expect support to grow. We also know from our study of morality policy that if there is any clear path to long-term policy stability, it will more likely be by way of policy development on a state-to-state basis. Based on this assessment, I do expect to see federalism facilitate the lasting protection of individual rights in PAD policy.

CONCLUSION

In the matter of PAD policy, I conclude that American federalism has allowed for the limited protection of individual rights. Given the likely expansion of these protections and the ability that some individuals have to travel to obtain these services, I feel this is a reasonable conclusion. The work that has been done through citizens initiatives, the legislatures, and the courts has brought this policy a long way from its highly moral, ethical, and religious beginnings. According to a May 2018 Gallup Poll, 72 percent of Americans supported some form of PAD.[114] It only stands to reason that support for PAD and the protections it creates for individual rights will continue to grow and spread to other states through state-level legislation and citizen initiatives. Additionally, though the current position of the national government is to leave this policy matter to the states, that does not preclude the Supreme

Court, in particular, from taking up future cases that relate to individual claims of right-to-die violations at the state level.

While there is much that can still be done at the state level to facilitate the protection of individual rights regarding PAD policy, I believe that federalism has been used thus far to that end. Matters of life and death are important to all Americans, and the role that the government should play in regulating those matters has been controversial since the topic of PAD first became politically salient in this country. The policy mobility and inconsistency that federalism allows can be viewed as a limitation on individual rights in this policy area, however, I am inclined to think that federalism has allowed this policy to develop in a way that is sustainable and agreeable to state populations one at a time. One of my main concerns in this area is the extent to which the individual has been lost at times in the larger debate between the national government and the state governments over who gets to decide the individual's fate. Knowing that federalism provides for a direct link between the national government and the individual citizens and that the national government has a role to play in protecting the individual's natural rights, it can be a bit disconcerting that the national government has been content to leave such a primary protection to the states' discretion. However, the national government has provided at least some guidance to allow for a baseline understanding of a right to die and what individuals can do to make sure their wishes are followed even if they can no longer speak for themselves. The limited access of PAD to people who are able to administer lethal doses of medication to themselves and the fear of the slippery slope toward involuntary euthanasia continue to pose challenges in this policy area, and debates over voluntary euthanasia will continue. It will take another culture shift to allow for the policy to move in that direction, and there is a great deal of fear and resistance to slow that shift. However, all signs currently point to federalism allowing for increasing protections for individual rights in the area of PAD policy development.

NOTES

1. Urofsky, *Lethal Judgments*, 25.
2. Ball, *At Liberty to Die*, 3.
3. Ibid.
4. Palliative care refers to end-of-life care that is focused on providing comfort and alleviating pain when a patient has a terminal diagnosis.
5. Ball, *At Liberty to Die*, 3.
6. "Take Action in Your State," *Death With Dignity*.
7. Ibid.
8. Ibid.

9. Svenson, "Physician-Assisted Dying and the Law in the United States," 3.

10. Emanuel, "Whose Right to Die?"

11. Ibid.

12. Ibid.

13. Ibid.

14. Ibid.

15. Urofsky, *Lethal Judgments*, 7–8.

16. Ibid.

17. Ibid., 11.

18. Gorsuch, *The Future of Assisted Suicide and Euthanasia*, 29; Urofsky, *Lethal Judgments*, 9.

19. Urofsky, *Lethal Judgments*, 10.

20. Gorsuch, *The Future of Assisted Suicide and Euthanasia*, 31.

21. Emanuel, "Whose Right to Die?"

22. Cox, *Hemlock's Cup*, 60; Urofsky, *Lethal Judgments*, 25.

23. Cox, *Hemlock's Cup*, 60.

24. Urofsky, *Lethal Judgments*, 25.

25. Gorsuch, *The Future of Assisted Suicide and Euthanasia*, 43.

26. Svenson, "Physician-Assisted Dying and the Law in the United States," 4.

27. Urofsky, *Lethal Judgments*, 98.

28. Dworkin, *Life's Domain*, 180.

29. Ibid.

30. Clark, *The Politics of Physician Assisted Suicide*, 39.

31. Dworkin, *Life's Domain*, 190.

32. Ibid., 223.

33. Urofsky, *Lethal Judgments*, 17.

34. Ibid.

35. Clark, *The Politics of Physician Assisted Suicide*, 39.

36. Ibid., 38.

37. Ball, *At Liberty to Die*, 1.

38. This case involved a state law that prohibited the use of birth control, and the Court decided that there was an expectation of privacy in marital affairs and intimate relations. Thus, it was not reasonable to enforce a law of this nature based on the right to privacy. Though there is no explicit protection for privacy listed in the Constitution, it can be derived from the First, Fourth, and Ninth Amendments.

39. Clark, *The Politics of Physician Assisted Suicide*, 38.

40. Humphry and Clement, *Freedom to Die*, 295.

41. Ibid., 295–296.

42. Ibid., 296.

43. Urofsky, *Lethal Judgments*, 14.

44. Ibid.

45. Clark, *The Politics of Physician Assisted Suicide*, 68.

46. Ball, *At Liberty to Die*, 164.

47. Ibid., 167.

48. Urofsky, *Lethal Judgments*, 57.

49. Hoefler, "Diffusion and Diversity," 153.
50. Ibid., 157.
51. Ibid., 158.
52. Ibid., 153.
53. Ibid., 158.
54. Ibid., 161.
55. Urofsky, *Lethal Judgments*, 40.
56. Clark, *The Politics of Physician Assisted Suicide*, 78.
57. Bullock, "Assisted Dying and the Proper Role of Patient Autonomy," 12.
58. Ibid., 14.
59. Dworkin, *Life's Domain*, 192.
60. Ibid., 194.
61. Ball, *At Liberty to Die*, 167.
62. Ibid.
63. Urofsky, *Lethal Judgments*, 98.
64. "Oregon's Death with Dignity Act: The First Year's Experience," 1.
65. Ibid.
66. Svenson, "Physician-Assisted Dying and the Law in the United States," 6.
67. "Oregon Death with Dignity Act: 2019 Data Summary," 4.
68. Ibid.
69. Ibid., 10.
70. Ibid., 9.
71. Ibid.
72. Urofsky, *Lethal Judgments*, 40.
73. Clark, *The Politics of Physician Assisted Suicide*, 26.
74. Ibid.
75. There was some disagreement among the doctors who evaluated her whether or not she was truly in a VPS.
76. Caminker, "Schaivo and Klein," 530.
77. Ibid.
78. Ibid., 535.
79. Ibid., 546.
80. Petrillo et al., "California's End of Life Option Act," 828.
81. Goralka and Dhillon, "Department: Practice Tips: Guidance on California's End of Life Option Act," 11.
82. Ibid.
83. Ibid.
84. Petrillo et al., "California's End of Life Option Act," 829.
85. *Cruzan v. Director*, Missouri Department of Health, 497 U.S. 261 (1990).
86. Pappas, *The Euthanasia/Assisted-Suicide Debate*, 87.
87. *Cruzan v. Director, Missouri Department of Health*, 497 U.S. 261 (1990).
88. Urofsky, *Lethal Judgments*, 60.
89. Ibid.
90. Ibid., 60–61.
91. Ibid.

92. Ibid., 62.

93. Humphry and Clement, *Freedom to Die*, 297.

94. Ibid., 295; Svenson, "Physician-Assisted Dying and the Law in the United States," 5.

95. Humphry and Clement, *Freedom to Die*, 298.

96. Ibid., 308.

97. Ibid., 297.

98. Ibid., 307.

99. Ibid., 295.

100. Ibid.

101. Sclar, "U.S. Supreme Court Ruling in Gonzales v. Oregon Upholds the Oregon Death With Dignity Act," 639; Gorsuch, *The Future of Assisted Suicide and Euthanasia*, 219.

102. Sclar, "U.S. Supreme Court Ruling in Gonzales v. Oregon Upholds the Oregon Death With Dignity Act," 639.

103. Ibid.

104. *Gonzales v. Oregon*, 546 US 243 (2006).

105. Sclar, "U.S. Supreme Court Ruling in Gonzales v. Oregon Upholds the Oregon Death With Dignity Act," 640.

106. Gorsuch, *The Future of Assisted Suicide and Euthanasia*, 219.

107. Ibid.

108. Sclar, "U.S. Supreme Court Ruling in Gonzales v. Oregon Upholds the Oregon Death With Dignity Act," 640.

109. Cohen, "Traveling for Assisted Suicide," 373.

110. Ibid., 374.

111. Ball, *At Liberty to Die*, 2.

112. Yu et al., "Defining Physician-assisted suicide tourism and travel," 2.

113. Ball, *At Liberty to Die*, 172.

114. Lane, "Lifting the U.S. ban on euthanasia is like opening a Pandora's box."

SUGGESTED READINGS

Ball, Howard. *At Liberty to Die: The Battle for Death with Dignity in America*. New York, NY: New York University Press, 2012.

Clark, Nina. *The Politics of Physician Assisted Suicide*. New York, NY: Garland Publishing, Inc., 1997.

Emanuel, Ezekiel J. "What Is the Great Benefit of Legalizing Euthanasia or Physician-Assisted Suicide?" *Ethics* 109, no. 3 (1999): 629–642.

Humphry, Derek and Mary Clement. *Freedom to Die: People, Politics, and the Right-to-Die Movement*. New York, NY: St. Martin's Press, 1998.

Urofsky, Melvin. *Lethal Judgments: Assisted Suicide & American Law*. Lawrence, KS: University Press of Kansas, 2000.

Part III

CONCLUSIONS

What does federalism mean for the protection of individual rights in the United States? Does it serve to protect individual rights or does a federal system make the protection of individual rights more difficult? In the final section of the book, I provide both a summary and final assessment of this question. In chapter 8, I will revisit the arguments contained in chapter 3 for and against this compatibility of federalism and individual rights and see what evidence we can find in our policy studies to support or refute those positions. Additionally, I will summarize the individual findings from the policy studies and make a final determination based on an aggregation of those findings. Finally, in chapter 9, we can explore current challenges to federalism and the protection of individual rights in light of my conclusions. We will also consider ways in which federalism could be better utilized moving forward with a consistent and deliberate objective of protecting the individual.

Chapter 8

American Federalism and Individual Rights

The introductory study of American politics always contains some treatment of the principles of American democracy. There is a generally agreed upon list and many people have some familiarity with terms such as majority rule and minority rights, separation of powers, individual rights, and federalism, even if they cannot readily explain in detail what they are. Beyond that, those who study and teach these concepts are accustomed to seeing them grouped together which makes it is easy to assume they always work together in a complementary way. The American identity has always held a component of civic nationalism in which one subscribes to these principles of governance and believes that they represent a more desirable form. While the underlying political ideology of American politics welcomes and promotes open discussion of political ideals, it can be uncomfortable at times to challenge some of these principles and that discomfort can extend to challenging assumptions about their compatibility. It was my own work on individualism that first led me to question those assumptions. After extensively studying the concept of American individualism and discovering all of the internal contradictions and challenges therein, I began to wonder how well these founding principles of American democracy have actually worked together. The founders put together a list of political ideas based on ideological ideals, some of which—like federalism—had not been thoroughly tested. Clearly, the hope was that these principles could and would work together to provide a solid organizational and procedural foundation for a new democratic republic, but what if some of those principles worked at cross purposes? What would that mean for policymaking over time? What could those conflicts explain about struggles this country has faced in trying to address and solve public issues?

When I first began to narrow down the policy areas that I would cover in this book, I considered questions of both relevance and my own interest in the topics.[1] There are even more topics that have become relevant to federalism since I began writing, and I will address a couple of those in the final chapter. In this chapter, I wish to bring together all of the individual policy studies into one unified analysis of federalism and individual rights. Through our study of each of these policy areas—civil rights, education, same-sex marriage, and physician-assisted death—we can find many common themes. These themes are not exclusively topics of federalism, but they represent issues that American federalism must contend with across many policy areas. Through developing a better understanding of these persistent themes, we may be able to better anticipate the issues that will arise in the course of new policy development as it relates to federalism and the protection of individual rights. Our study of the individual policy areas also provides us with the opportunity to test some of the claims presented in chapter 3 regarding the relationship between federalism and individual rights and how well-suited federalism actually is to protecting individual rights. We can then engage in a summary discussion of the findings regarding each of our policy areas, a concluding discussion on the persisting tension between individual rights and states' rights in a federal system, and an ultimate conclusion about the relationship between federalism and individual rights.

First, one of the most interesting aspects of writing about all of these various topics from the perspective of federalism and individual rights is the extent to which common themes kept presenting themselves. Such recurring themes include the discernment of private from public issues, the debate between equality versus liberty, the question of rights prioritization and identification, and of course, the determination of which level of government is most suitable for addressing each policy matter.

The first recurring theme is one that is integral to any discussion of governmental policy: which issues are truly public and which are private? The government is only charged with addressing public issues, those issues that concern all or most of us, while we as individuals are charged with finding solutions to our own private problems. One of the underlying issues that we see in every policy area we have studied is the debate over whether or not the matter is truly public and in need of a governmental solution or if it is best left in the private realm. In civil rights policy, the prevailing view had been that the subjugation of African Americans into enslavement was a private economic matter that the government had no role in regulating. Beyond the overt racism and inhumanity that allowed slavery to persist for so long was this view that it was not a public issue. The first step toward establishing a role for the government was to place it in the hands of the states to regulate, as that would at least leave the issue closer to the people. The states that wished to maintain slavery could, and those that did not wish to could abolish it. It was not until the Civil War that the national government asserted its powers in this domain, and the matter of civil rights was formally established as a public issue that justified governmental action. We see this same tension in education policy, whereby the matter was initially private and then slowly transitioned into a public issue subject to control by the localities, states, and national government.

The newer policy areas of SSM and PAD have been particularly challenging with regard to the public versus private debate. The topics of both marriage and death are intensely personal, and yet they both require external cooperation in order to maximize individual freedom. If one could truly be left alone to marry the person of one's choice, regardless of gender and sexual orientation, and if one could be left alone to die in the manner of one's choosing, then the government would not have a role to play in these private matters. However, due to the need for external cooperation, the government's role was established in both issues thereby making them public issues. While we have identified our "individual of concern" in each of these matters, there are other interested parties. The government has had to mediate these competing concerns in order to arrive at policy solutions that are acceptable given public support and constitutional and statutory provisions.

A second recurring theme concerns matters of equality versus liberty, and again we see this across the policy areas. The reality of American culture is that many people feel empowered to stridently hold and express their own views. The freedom of expression is protected by the Constitution, and it is foundational to the American conception of the individual rooted in classical liberal theory. However, this leads to the challenge of determining where one person's freedom ends and the next person's freedom begins. When the first person does not hold others in equal regard and their actions reflect that unequal consideration, to what extent should they be able to express and act on that belief before it is viewed or felt as an infringement on the next person's freedom? If the government assumes a role in promoting and enforcing equality in any policy area, there will be a corresponding decrease in the liberty of those who were treating others unfairly. We see this in education with regard to school funding. If a state decides that it is fair to allow schools to be funded based on local property taxes, the wealthy areas have more money to spend on education than the poor areas do. If the state courts rule that this funding structure violates a state's constitutional obligation to provide education, and the funding structure changes, the people living in the wealthier districts may feel that their rights are being violated in the name of creating more equal educational opportunities for children across the state.

In the case of SSM, there is very clear tension between same-sex couples wishing to have equal access to marriage and the rights and privileges thereof, while others assert that the equality same-sex couples want comes into direct conflict with their religious liberty. While the Supreme Court has legalized same-sex marriage, questions of religious liberty have persisted as people have tried to sort out at the state level where the lines are between equality and liberty. Does requiring a baker to bake a wedding cake for a same-sex couple represent a violation of that baker's religious liberty? What if the individual is a pastor who is asked to officiate over a same-sex wedding or a caseworker at an adoption agency? Are requests for these services violations of religious liberty? And if they are, is it worth infringing on individual religious liberty to the extent that it promotes equality for same-sex couples or not?

The next theme deals with rights issues: the prioritization of existing rights and the determination of new rights. Of the policy areas we have studied, SSM is the best example of the struggle of prioritizing rights, because both advocates for and opponents of SSM have asserted constitutional arguments for their positions. The question then becomes: Which right is more important? That is a very difficult question to answer, and that is one of the reasons why tensions persist in matters of SSM even in the years after it has been "settled" by the Supreme Court. The next rights issue concerns the process of rights identification. The language of rights is deeply engrained in American political culture, and there far more claims to rights than there are legally recognized and protected rights.[2] There are times when new rights are identified and then granted legal protection, and this happened with civil rights and SSM. However, there are other times when rights are claimed but the courts are unwilling to grant those rights legal protection, such as the denial of a constitutionally recognized right to PAD. The Supreme Court has been willing to concede a right for the individual patient to refuse care, but there is no such right to have a physician assist in any way. This has led to the equal protection arguments that rest on the idea that only those patients on life-support have the right to choose death while others do not, though both groups may have terminal diagnoses.

Finally, there is the perennial question of which level of government is best situated to address different policy issues. In some cases, we have arrived at a fairly stable answer to the question. Of the policy issues we have examined herein, civil rights policy is the best example of a policy area that has been addressed most stably and consistently at the national level. Civil rights have been addressed specifically through constitutional amendment and through other constitutionally protected powers. PAD policy has settled at the state level due to the reluctance of the national government to weigh in on a morality policy it believes should be resolved by the states. In other policy matters, there can be an answer to the question, but also persisting instability because of issue asymmetry. SSM policy is an example of this combination answer whereby the right to marry has been recognized and yet those at the state level still have the ability to impact the access to or enjoyment of that right. A final possibility is the lack of a consistent answer or settling of the policy at one level of government or another. Education is an example of this type of scenario wherein we continue to bounce the issue back and forth due to conflicting views regarding where it should be managed and continually shift control over those policy decisions.

The identification of these common themes can help provide a framework through which we can anticipate issues in policy development in others as they pertain to individual rights and federalism. While these themes are not specific to federalism, they are issues that develop when trying to protect individual rights in a federal system.

FEDERALISM AND INDIVIDUAL RIGHTS

In addition to identifying these common themes, our policy studies also allow us to conduct a review of the compatibility claims regarding federalism and individual rights. Of course, I can only extend these arguments to the four policy areas covered herein, and so the conclusions I make should only be generalized with great caution and to very similar policy types. Recalling chapter 3, we reviewed some of these arguments made for and against the compatibility of federalism with the protection of individual rights. One argument for this compatibility is the connection and interdependence of these concepts. Federalism allows for individuals to seek protection whether they are in the majority or the minority, and it expands the opportunities for rights protection based on location. Specifically, if the national government will not provide a protection for a certain right, then some state or states can provide that protection if they choose. Our policy studies support this first argument for compatibility. In the instance of SSM, this policy has enjoyed both minority and majority support, and during both times was able to find legal protection at some level of government. With PAD policy, even though the national government does not recognize a constitutional protection, there are a number of states that have moved forward with laws establishing access to PAD.

A second argument for the compatibility of federalism and individual rights is the balancing effect that the national government and state governments can have on each other in order to protect individual rights. The national government can intervene when states violate individual rights, and the states can assert their authority when the national government does not wish to act. Another possibility is the cooperation between the states and national government to protect rights. We can find some evidence to support some but not all of these claims. The balancing scenario was demonstrated through the development of civil rights policy. Too many states were choosing to violate the individual rights of African Americans, and so the national government chose at various points in time to act to protect those rights. In the matter of PAD, we can see the states asserting their authority to protect PAD when the national government has made it clear that it does not wish to set a federal policy on the matter. The only policy that we have discussed that would fall in the third scenario of individual rights protected through a cooperative effort is education. Based on my review, I am reluctant to say that federalism and individual rights were compatible in this policy area. The attempts at cooperation have led to a lack of accountability, predictability, and stability that have not served to protect the individual rights of the students to a quality education.

A final argument for the compatibility of federalism and individual rights is the ability of the state to provide rights "sanctuaries" for individuals who prefer another state's policies over those in their home state. The two policy areas from our study that would fit here are education and PAD, but I am unconvinced that the ability to move to another state is adequate evidence that these concepts are compatible. With education policy, one could theoretically move to another school district or another state if they felt that schools in another jurisdiction had access to more generous funding. The assumption here is that one would be moving from a poorer area to a more affluent area to have access to better resources. I am not sure that this is as easily done as it is said. If a person is living in an area with more poverty, they too might live in poverty and not have the resources to move or change schools. We have already seen this scenario play out in areas with open enrollment where all of the families who can move their kids to resource-rich schools do and the only kids who are left are the ones who do not have the resources to leave for alternate educational opportunities. PAD is another policy area that has created sanctuaries for individuals, in this case dealing specifically with end-of-life care and the decision to die. However, as I pointed out in chapter 7, the burden of traveling and establishing residency could be prohibitively high for a terminally ill individual and not truly a viable option for protecting that individual's rights.

Our policy studies provide mixed support for the pro-compatibility arguments. A review of the arguments against the compatibility between federalism and individual rights will help us develop a broader view on this matter. Some of these arguments we can evaluate by way of the policy studies, while other arguments speak to more foundational issues. One argument against compatibility is the lack of a conceptual link between federalism and individual rights. This position rejects any idea that the founders chose a federal system with the intent of protecting individual rights. With all due respect to this position, I do not find it convincing. As I explained in chapter 1, there is evidence of this intent by way of both the ideological influence that classical liberalism had on the founders and passages within the *Federalist Papers* that support the connection between these principles and the intent that a federal system would serve to protect individual rights.

Another argument against the compatibility of these concepts concerns how the development and recognition of rights can occur in a federal system. Classical liberalism recognizes the natural rights of life, liberty, and property as fixed rights. Any government based on liberal principles is bound to protect natural rights and then expand those concepts to other rights that are desired by the people living under that government's jurisdiction. In a federal system, there is the possibility of both rights and "rights:" those rights that the national government recognizes and protects and those "rights" that exist under the limited jurisdiction of individual states. In the case of PAD, terminally ill people who live in PAD-legal states enjoy a right to die, while terminally ill people in other states do not. In this case, PAD clearly does not rise to the level of a constitutionally protected right, and that could be construed as a deprivation of rights to people living in non-PAD states. Given that rights should be fixed and not relative in a liberal society, perhaps it would be more appropriate for a policy to be promoted to the federal level if it involves individual rights protections and has been approved be a certain number of states. I do agree that there are some conceptual problems with having a relative rights structure in a liberal political system.

Another argument against the compatibility of federalism and individual rights is the failure that federalism has suffered in the course of protecting individual rights. Unfortunately, it is difficult to refute this argument. While I can find examples in all of the policy areas we have covered, there is no more glaring a failure than with civil rights policy. It was in a federal system that slavery was able to exist and persist. Federalism allowed for the both the national government and many states to ignore or severely limit the application of the Constitution to civil rights. Federalism empowered the states to actively persist in discriminatory and racist policies for one hundred years after slavery had ended. There was nothing inherent in federalism that stopped these individual rights violations from occurring.

A final argument against compatibility is the erosion of the meaning of federalism which has led to an almost exclusive focus on states' rights to the exclusion of the individual rights. Clint Bolick, an associate justice on the Arizona Supreme Court, made this argument in his 1993 book, *Grassroots Tyranny*, in which he contends that the founders intended the concepts to be linked, but modern politicians have failed to keep these concepts linked based on their own issue agendas and preferences. Federalism has not led to the preservation of individual rights due to "the abandonment of the traditional principles of federalism."[3] The focus has moved from federalism as a tool to protect individual rights to federalism as a way for liberals to support national action to achieve specific economic or social objectives and for conservatives to support state's rights even if both actions serve to diminish individual rights.[4] He contends that neither group uses a preference of individual liberty to guide their choice of policymaking venue.[5]

The connection between federalism and individual rights was broken when the states could not be trusted to protect individuals in civil rights matters and the national government was forced to permanently intercede in such matters by way of the Fourteenth Amendment.[6] This perpetuated a strong "states' rights" movement that does not necessarily make sense from the perspective of federalism which supports the existence of state powers and individual rights but not "states' rights."[7] In current times, conservatives are not using states' rights arguments to protect individual freedom but rather to find an easier path to majoritarianism at the state level to achieve specific policy goals.[8] Liberals then may seem more willing to use the power of the national government to bring about regulation to protect individual rights without considering how those actions could also impede individual freedom.[9] Federalism and individual rights are ultimately incompatible because there is not anything intrinsically protective about federalism for individual rights. The meaning of federalism has changed over time into something quite different from what the founders intended. Had the concepts been more compatible, perhaps it would not have been so easy for this to occur.

I can also find mixed support for the arguments against the compatibility of federalism and individual rights. These general points help place our thinking about federalism and individual rights in a critical context, entertaining the ideas of both compatibility and incompatibility. Now that we have had the opportunity to study specific policy areas, we can address the question of rights protection on a policy-by-policy basis.

Civil Rights

In the area of civil rights policy, I do believe that federalism has led to the protection of individual rights. Though opponents of civil rights progress have prioritized their own individual rights in matters of slavery, racial segregation, and racial discrimination, the individuals of concern for this study are clearly African Americans. When the three-part test is applied, I find that civil rights are currently protected in the American political system at the national level; there is reason to believe that the issue of civil rights was enhanced through federalism due to the issue mobility we can observe from one level of government to another; and, there is reason to believe that protections for the individual by way of civil rights policy are likely to be lasting at the national level, though the lack of symmetry in this policy area will keep tension between the levels of government. In essence, there will be pushback on national authority when and where possible to diminish certain protections.

We are already seeing this with regard to voting rights. The protection of individual rights in the context of African American civil rights requires continued action as long as racist and discriminatory attitudes continue. I believe that the federal structure of the U.S. government is what ultimately allowed the individual to be protected in the context of civil rights policy. Further, of the policy areas addressed herein, I believe that civil rights protections are likely the strongest due to how the U.S. Constitution has been used to both establish and protect those rights. The Constitution is difficult to amend, and due to principles of *stare decisis* and the adherence to precedent, the current supportive judicial interpretation regarding civil rights is not likely to drastically change.

Education

In the area of education policy, I do not believe that individual rights have been protected. Though there are many groups of individuals who have a vested interest in education policy—parents, educators, administrators, and politicians—the individuals of interest in this study are the students. When I applied the three-part test to this policy area, I found mixed results. The answer to the first question—Are individual rights in education policy protected somewhere in our political system?—is yes: individual access to education is currently protected in the American political system at the national level regarding the prohibition of racial segregation and overtly discriminatory practices, and individual access to education is also protected at the state level through state constitutions. However, it is not clear that issue mobility has served to protect individual rights. With regard to race, the ability of the national government to insert itself into state matters and to prohibit racial segregation in the schools indisputably enhanced the protection of individual rights regarding education. The same can be said with regard to poverty. However, the mobility of this issue between levels of government has inhibited the facilitation of equitable access to quality education for all students. Even when the national government has taken a more aggressive stance to standardize education policy, it has largely been at the mercy of the states to effectively implement the policy. Finally, while I do believe that protections for the individual are likely to be lasting at the national level with regard to racial discrimination and poverty, I also believe that there is enough asymmetry in this policy area to keep tensions high between the levels of government which leads to a degree of instability. In the current political environment, wherein the national government is asking the states to take the lead on education policy, the degree of variability and standardization is bound to increase to the detriment of individual rights. The states are capable of creating and implementing policies that set high standards and maintain equitable access to quality education for our students, but there is no consistent way to hold them accountable. Of the policy areas we have reviewed, education policy appears to be the least protective of individual rights. There seems to be too much volatility in its regulation, and the frequent passing of this policy back and forth has led to a decrease in overall accountability and momentum toward any lasting reform or improvements. Unfortunately, the students pay the price for this indecision and it results in a decrease in their individual rights in this policy area.

Same-Sex Marriage

In the area of same-sex marriage policy, I do believe that federalism has allowed for the protection of individual rights. Like the other policy areas, there are multiple groups of individuals with an interest in these policy actions and outcomes. Unlike the other areas, however, it is not so easy to prioritize the rights claims of one group over the other due to the nature of this issue. One's personal opinions regarding homosexuality and same-sex marriage will largely determine with which group of individuals one is concerned. If one is of the opinion that religious liberty should supersede marriage liberty and equal protection, then they are primarily concerned with the religious rights of individuals who oppose SSM. If one is more inclined to think that liberty in marriage and equal protection is either more impor-tant than religious liberty or is of the opinion that the protection of SSM is not in conflict with religious liberty, then they would prioritize the rights of individuals who are in favor of SSM. The three-part test yields some mixed results: yes, individual access to SSM and the benefits and privileges thereby provided are currently protected in the American political system by the national government; yes, federal issue mobility enhanced the protection of individual rights because the states could move forward with legalization ahead of a federal law. Federalism also allowed for the rights of religious opponents to be protected as well when the national government was able, for a time, to institute a federal definition of marriage. Further, when SSM opponents sought protections under the RFRA, and then those protections were not extended to the states, they were able to put state-level legislation in place to protect religious liberty. Even when SSM was legalized, the Court was unwilling to infringe on the First Amendment's protections for religious liberty. Federalism served to protect the individual rights of both advocates and opponents of SSM over time, which makes matters a bit more challeng-ing to assess than in the other policy areas.

The question of lasting protection is mixed as well. There are varying degrees of issue symmetry between the states and the national government. Some states had already legalized SSM before *Obergefell*, while others were enforcing

RFRA-type laws. Overall, there is currently a lack of symmetry, and this can be expected to lead to some policy instability as opponents of SSM look for other legal avenues to protect their religious liberty. It is possible that public opinion could shift, and symmetry could increase thus enhancing the long-term protection of individual rights. For SSM advocates, it would be sustainable because the right to marriage would be protected, and for religious liberty advocates, it would be sustainable because they would no longer believe that their religious liberty was being threatened. By way of this analysis, I conclude that American federalism has allowed for the protection of individual rights. As this is a newer policy area, we will have to wait to see if the protections are lasting and for whom. Given that individuals on both sides of the debate have made constitutionally grounded arguments, I am not able to dismiss the rights claims of one group out of hand. Federalism has been used as a tool to advance policy on both sides of this issue for the protection of individual rights.

Physician-Assisted Death

In the area of PAD, I believe that federalism has led to the protection of individual rights. There are several groups of impacted individuals, including the patients, their families and loved ones, and the medical personnel who could be involved with ending the patient's life. While all of these groups have distinct interests, the purpose of PAD policy has always centered on maximizing the individual choices of the terminally ill patients. This takes the shape of protecting the rights of individuals to die in a manner of their choice and the rights of medical professionals who wish to help them pursue that end. The individual of primary concern is the patient, and the individual of secondary concern is the physician. Application of the three-part test yields consistently positive results. First, individual rights in the context of PAD are currently protected in the American political system in several states, the District of Columbia, and one county in New Mexico. Access to others who do not live in those particular places may also gain access, though I do not view this opportunity as optimistically as others might due to the potential obstacles and burdens in place. Second, I believe that access to PAD-related individual rights have been enhanced through federalism by way of issue mobility. PAD has been considered at both the national and state level, and it is currently regulated at the state level where it can develop most stably. Over time, an increasing number of states have created their own PAD policies, and as long as that is the trend more Americans wish to see, a further expansion of those rights would be expected. Lastly, there is reason to believe that this protection will be lasting. The national government has consistently demonstrated that it does not wish to intervene in this policy area. As long as there is state-level support for PAD in any of the fifty states, then the protections will be lasting.

Access to those services can vary, but the protections will exist somewhere. Additionally, if the spread of PAD policy continues from state to state, this is arguably the most stable way for morality policy to develop. Based on current trends, I do expect to see federalism facilitate the lasting protection of individual rights in PAD policy. There is the potential for these protections to grow, however the policy mobility and inconsistency that federalism allows can be viewed as a limitation on individual rights in this policy area. Of the policy areas consider in this study, PAD is an example of a policy area through which federalism provides limited protections. Unlike the other areas, we cannot yet consider access to PAD a constitutionally protected right nor should we expect that to occur anytime in the near future. As such, the protections are limited to any one state's desire to recognize a right to die by way of PAD.

ARE FEDERALISM AND THE PROTECTION OF INDIVIDUAL RIGHTS COMPATIBLE?

Through our review and analysis of civil rights, education, same-sex marriage, and physician-assisted death policies, it is clear that there are instances where federalism has enhanced the protection of individual rights and instances where it has not. This leads to the conclusion that federalism and the protection of individual rights can be compatible, if federalism is used to that end. The use of federalism to protect individual rights is not automatic or self-executing. There must also be a commitment among political actors to the preservation of individual rights. Federalism is a neutral tool, perhaps more neutral than the founders themselves realized. It can be used for good or for ill, depending on your perspective. If those responsible for national and state-level governance wish to use federalism to protect individual rights, then it can be used in that way, and we have evidence that it has been used in that way. However, if the desire is there to restrict individual rights, federalism can be used in that way as well.

The founders were interested in the protection of individual rights and envisioned a role for the government in developing and maintaining these protections. While there were debates as to which level of government should be more dominant, the purpose of American federalism was to build a consistent path toward the protection of the individual.[10] The Constitution was written to balance three main objectives that the founders had in mind: establishing a national government that was powerful enough to create and implement meaningful policy, allowing the reservation of significant powers to the states, while also protecting and preserving individual rights against infringement by the government and others.[11] We can see in that document efforts to carry out all of these objectives, but the ultimate success of these provisions would depend largely upon the intent of the individuals charged with their execution. As we have seen through the course of U.S. history, the mere presence of these constitutional features has not been enough to protect individual rights. Yes, there must be a division of powers established in the Constitution, and we see that division by way of the powers delegated to the national government and those powers reserved to the states. Beyond that division, however, we must also see the division of power result in a balance that limits the power of both levels of government.[12] That has not consistently happened. Additionally, in those policy areas where the states have been left to oversee and regulate the day-to-day affairs of their residents, the state governments must proceed with the preservation of individual rights in mind.[13] That has not consistently happened, either. Further, at the insistence of the Anti-Federalists, the Constitution provides a listing of individual rights out of a belief that such a list could be utilized to adequately protect the individual.[14] That has also not consistently happened. There is nothing inherent in a federal structure that leads to the protection of individual rights. It is a tool that functions in whatever manner the user intends.

NOTES

1. It is much easier to write about things you are interested in!
2. For a discussion of the role of rights in American political culture, see Mary Ann Glendon, *Rights Talk: The Impoverishment of Political Discourse*. New York: The Free Press, 1991.
3. Bolick, *Grassroots Tyranny*, 7.
4. Ibid.
5. Ibid., 16.
6. Ibid., 15.
7. Ibid., 17.
8. Ibid., 22.
9. Ibid., 36.
10. Ibid., 42.
11. Ibid.
12. Ibid., 53.
13. Ibid.
14. Ibid.

SUGGESTED READINGS

Bolick, Clint. *Grassroots Tyranny: The Limits of Federalism*. Washington, DC: Cato Institute, 1993.
Nathan, Richard P. "There Will Always Be a New Federalism." *Journal of Public Administration Research and Theory: J-PART* 16, no. 4 (2006): 499–510.

Chapter 9

The Future of Federalism and Rights

There is a challenge in ending a book of this nature, because the relationship between federalism and individual rights is ongoing. I cannot tell you how this story ends nor can I even give a solid yes or no answer to the research question I have endeavored to answer. It is possible for federalism to protect individual rights if the key political players involved in decision making wish for it to do so. Of course, in order for them to wish that, they must agree that federalism was originally intended to protect rights and can and should continue to do so. There have been past efforts to evaluate and implement federalism more thoughtfully and intentionally, but those efforts have not lasted. In this chapter, I will review an example of such an effort, discuss some of the persisting threats to individual rights in a federal system, and conclude with thoughts about how this work can move forward.

THE ADVISORY COMMISSION ON
INTERGOVERNMENTAL RELATIONS

There was a time when the condition of American federalism was on the minds of the top politicians in the United States. By condition, I do not simply mean the existence of federalism or the practice of federalism, but its health, functionality, and ability to do what it was intended to do. One such person was President Dwight Eisenhower. In the early 1950s, he was primarily concerned with the ways in which national authority had begun encroaching on state and local authority. He wished to investigate if it would be possible to give some of these responsibilities back to the states, together with some funding to offset their costs.[1] Beyond finding more immediate solutions to the imbalance of power President Eisenhower identified, there developed the larger goal of better monitoring and maintaining the federal system. By 1959, legislation was introduced in both the House and Senate to create an Advisory Commission on Intergovernmental Affairs (ACIR) and this was passed into law by the end of that year with tremendous congressional support.[2] As an advisory commission, ACIR was expected to review a multitude of issues related to federalism and then make recommendations based on their research. The commission was comprised of twenty-six members, including members of the federal legislative and executive branches, state governors, mayors, and individuals outside of the government with content expertise.[3] ACIR was asked to make recommendations on a variety of topics, including problems that were common to all levels of government, new and developing public problems that would require cooperation among levels of government, and the most effective and efficient distribution of tasks between the levels of government.[4] Over the thirty-seven years that ACIR was active, they had a prolific publishing record, including 130 policy reports with recommendations, twenty-three public opinion polls, and the quarterly magazine, *Intergovernmental Perspective*.[5] These publications would prove to be useful to those beyond the originally intended audience. At the time ACIR began its work, there were few college courses offered in intergovernmental relations and even fewer scholarly materials to support such coursework. The publications that ACIR generated filled this void and promoted the development of college-level intergovernmental relations curriculum.[6] ACIR would thus come to have two important roles. First, the commission served an educational role for both those in and outside of government; and second, the commission provided a venue in which people could come together to have meaningful discussions about those issues impacting intergovernmental relations.[7] This commission met several times per year for the duration of its existence to provide active and meaningful support to the national government on all matters of federalism.[8] The many reports and recommendations generated by ACIR are still valuable and informative today.[9]

The creation of ACIR was not only a wise and timely idea but the work it did was tremendously valuable to the maintenance of a healthy federal system. However, over the years, not everyone would remain focused on the importance of federalism and the active maintenance that such a system requires in order to remain balanced and focused on the protection of individual liberty. By 1996, ACIR would find itself mired in partisan politics and unable to do its job in any remotely independent way. Rather than maintaining its own budget to carry out research and make recommendations as it saw fit, the commission had been reduced to doing work for hire for a variety of other bureaucratic agencies.[10] After suffering numerous struggles in getting members appointed and procuring an independent budget, the ACIR ceased to be on September 30, 1996.[11] From that point forward, there would no longer be a central "hub" to bring together people from all levels of government to address general issues of federalism.[12] However, the lack of venue should not be interpreted as a lack of need. By the mid-1990s, federalism was as relevant a topic as it had ever been as members of both parties were supportive of devolution and shifting power pack to the states in some way. Many Americans were impacted by changing ideas about federalism whether they knew it or not, especially those Americans who benefited from social welfare programs. If the condition of American federalism was in flux, then why would this be the time the national government would decide to shutter the one commission that was created to actively monitor federalism and make recommendations for its functionality? Several reasons have been proposed, though none of them are particularly satisfactory in justifying the termination of such an important advisory group. Reasons put forth include the need for budgetary reductions, the increase of partisanship in matters of intergovernmental affairs, and the development of other issue-specific venues in which matters of federalism could be addressed.[13] The more pointed issue that is cited for the commission's termination concerned the politics surrounding a report it drafted on federal mandates.[14] While the commission had previously released critical reports, it seems they underestimated both the degree to which this report would be criticized and the extent to which special interests interpreted it as a personalized commentary about how their issues should be managed.[15] Once the report became politicized in this way, ACIR became a liability for the Clinton Administration and a sitting duck for congressional Republicans who wished to defund it.[16] This was a sad and unceremonious end for a commission that was, and is still, very much needed.

Given the dynamic nature of a federal system and the challenges that persist in managing policy to best protect individual rights, a new ACIR-type organization would be busy from the start providing much needed guidance and recommendations to politicians on all levels.[17] Looking exclusively at the policy areas discussed in this book, there are countless contributions such an organization could make. For example, education policy is experiencing an awkward transition now as we have moved from an era of elevated national regulation to a time in which the Education Secretary would not be opposed to the elimination of the Department of Education. A new organization could make recommendations on how best to move forward based on the extensive amount of experience the United States now has with regard to regulating education policy. Additionally, it would be beneficial to work toward a more consistent method of creating and executing morality policy. We have examples of regulating issues of morality at both the national level and state level, but there does not seem to be much rhyme or reason as to how these decisions are made. Perhaps a more coherent federalism strategy could inform all decision-makers when choosing where to best regulate an activity, if at all. Further, a centralized organization could help re-center the focus of federalism on protecting individual rights so that Americans could reliably expect those principles of American democracy to work together in a compatible way. Federalism requires maintenance and continual deliberation regarding its functionality and ability to protect individual rights. Given how inconsistently some policy areas have been handled in recent years, there is cause for concern that perhaps the connection between federalism and individual rights is not nurtured to the extent that it should. There are always new policy issues on the horizon, and it is not clear to what extent the government is proactively planning for how to deal with those issues.

PERSISTING THREATS TO INDIVIDUAL RIGHTS IN A FEDERAL SYSTEM

We could engage in a review of other specific policy areas that either currently pose or will soon pose new challenges for the protection of individual rights in a federal system. However, it would be more inclusive and a broader use of the space remaining to speak in terms of themes. Persisting threats to the protection of individual rights can be grouped according to four main themes: policy ownership, issue asymmetry, social individualism, and crisis response.

The first area of trouble has to do with policy ownership: whose job is it to protect individual rights? In the course of American policy development, we have not come up with a consistent response and it shows. In a federal system, many laws, benefits, and rights are contingent upon where one lives due to the ability of the states and cities to create policy for those living in those jurisdictions.[18] The issue of relative rights has been the persistent issue here, however, as many individuals have to come to believe that rights should be universal and never limited to the confines of a state's particular jurisdiction. This tension connects back to the founders' intent for the protection of individual rights. The founders and other state-level politicians of that era believed that states could and should play a large role in the protection of rights, and we have evidence of this belief by virtue of the state-level protections included in state constitutions.[19] What is known now that could not have been known at the founding is how difficult that task would prove to be with regard to civil rights. There were concerns after the Civil War that the southern states could not be trusted to implement consistent protections for the individual rights of African Americans.[20] This doubt led to the ratification of the Reconstruction Amendments, and even those constitutional amendments struggled to provide the protections they were intended to provide. In the years to follow, the national government would insert itself on matters of individual rights protections in numerous policy areas, including labor rights and racial segregation and discrimination.[21] Once the national government became associated with the protection of individual rights and was able to accomplish it to a degree that the states either could not or did not want to, it became challenging to return to the expectation that the states could be trusted with such a significant task. That leads to an ongoing issue for federalism and individual rights today.

We do not consistently protect rights at either level of government. Rather, some individual rights are protected by the national government and some are protected by the states, and this leads to confusion and dissatisfaction with federalism in general. This negativity is felt primarily by those who see rights protected in a different way than they wished or expected. For example, someone who believes that the right to PAD should be constitutionally protected and yet is only offered protections in certain states may feel frustrated by federalism. Another type of dissatisfaction may be felt by someone who believes marriage should be regulated at the state level, and yet finds that the Supreme Court has protected marriage nationwide under the U.S. Constitution. While this flexibility does have the potential of maximizing individual rights by allowing the policies to move where they can be optimized, we are continually faced with the challenges and debate that follow that policy mobility. The movement is not smooth or easy. It is fraught with conflict and litigation and legislation and citizen action. All of this energy spent on deciding where policy should be decided could possibly take away from the energy needed to construct actual policy solutions. Identifying this challenge does not move us forward much toward solving it, unfortunately. Would an intentional return to state-held protections be more a more stable approach to rights protections or would it be more restrictive? Even if there was a concerted effort made to give states more responsibility in protecting individual rights again, would the states be willing to do it? Historically, there is not much evidence of state-level enthusiasm for rights protection. For those who believe that state-level protections are more desirable, there will always be opponents to various rights protections no matter who creates and implements them. There are people who live in PAD states who are passionately opposed to PAD. It is doubtful they feel better about it or more accepting of it because it came from the state government instead of the national government. No matter what the policy or where it came from, there will always be people who will bristle at regulations designed to protect individual rights. In education policy, it is difficult to think of a single component that generated more debate and disdain than Common Core curriculum standards, and the creation of those standards was a collaborate state-level initiative. Understanding that there will never be one policy that satisfies everyone's interests, it may represent progress if we could agree which level was better positioned and equipped to protect individual rights.

Issue asymmetry is another persisting challenge to American federalism. In 1965, Charles Tarlton speculated as to a relationship between symmetry and the success of federalism, and his thoughts on this relationship are still important today. He described symmetry as the "extent to which component states share in the conditions and thereby the concerns more or less common to the federal system as a whole.[22] Tarlton then suggested that a symmetrical system that would best utilize federalism as a method of power sharing. In the case where the component states did not share these common concerns and conditions, the functionality of federalism would vary dramatically across the system.[23] In a country such as the United States wherein you have a multitude of component states and their populations are not organized in any particular way, the potential is higher for conflict between the states and the national government.[24] Some states will fall in line and share those common conditions and concerns while others will not. Tarlton contended that in such a situation, federalism would not be an effective tool to unify those states under a common political authority.[25] This runs contrary to the conventional wisdom that would consider federalism as the ideal system to bring together such a diverse group of states.[26]

Though I am writing in a different time than Professor Tarlton was, I am inclined to agree that the United States is an asymmetrical system and it is not even the "ideal" type of asymmetry he describes whereby there is some pattern or way to understand the differing interests of the component states. These states are somewhat haphazard in their origins and their composition, their populations, and their policy preferences. Over time, mobility has increased to allow people to settle wherever they want, and that creates even more diversity of opinion and preference. That asymmetry will continue to create conflict, particularly in instances when the national government engages in morality policy

Another ongoing challenge for American federalism is the transformation of individualism into a social ideal. Social individualism has grown in the United States over the last several decades, and it assumes that no one individual is able to understand or address societal problems.[27] Due to natural limitations, we are only able to speak as to what is best for each of us individually and not for others.[28] This application of individualism does not readily see a role for the government in solving problems, and runs counter to the concept of political individualism of the founders that supported the use of both the national government and the state governments to protect individual rights.[29] Further, social individualism is based on the idea of negative liberty which defines freedom in terms of being left alone.[30] Laws should only be used to create a "sphere of unencumbered action" in which people can do what they think is best.[31]

Social individualism poses a few challenges for federalism. First, if Americans are more inclined now than in the past to reduce the role of governmental intervention into their private affairs, then which level of the government can act in a way that will be perceived as less threatening to rights? As we saw in the SSM and PAD policy studies, there can exist multiple groups of people with vested interests in a policy area. To allow one group access to the rights they desire can lead another group to feel that their rights are being infringed upon. How does federalism accommodate the concerns of the social individualist? Is it less intrusive to carry out rights protections at the state level? Perhaps in the big picture, but probably not to people living in a state that has implemented policy they find invasive. Second, to the person who is less likely to trust the government to identify and protect individual rights, federalism may by definition appear more threatening to freedom. Instead of being regulated by one level of government, any individual person at one time must adhere to local, state, and national laws on all manner of activities. Though federalism was initially thought the ideal way to protect the individual by providing opportunities for the states to act, the reality that the national government has assumed a significant role in rights protection may make the whole proposition seem more threatening to individual freedom.

A final challenge to American federalism is the management of national crises. When a national crisis occurs, federalism is oddly positioned to address it. A national crisis brings awareness to our interconnectedness and the ability of one set of circumstances to affect the entire country. The COVID-19 pandemic is an example of such a crisis that has generated this awareness.[32] When there is a national crisis, whether it is related to health or national security or perhaps a natural disaster, we as individuals suffer threats to our rights including life, liberty, and property. When we consider that a national crisis impacts the entire country, it may seem logical to think that the national government is the level best positioned to protect individual rights. However, American federalism is not structured in that way. Though the media attention may be on what the president or members of Congress have to say, most of the plans in place to deal with the crisis will likely come from the state government, as is the case with COVID-19.[33]

The constitutional reservation of police powers to the state and local governments explains the limited role the national government plays. These powers allow the states to lead the way in protecting the health and wellness of the people in their state, and that applies to the spread of disease and the use of quarantines to limit that spread.[34] In Ohio, Governor Mike DeWine and the Director of Health Dr. Amy Acton have used their authority to delay the 2020 primary election, to close non-essential businesses, and to order people to stay at home unless they must leave out of necessity.[35] There are many examples of state government using those powers to move quickly in support of their residents and in some cases taking actions the national government would ultimately mimic.[36] For example, states took the lead on declaring states of emergency and on suspending foreclosures.[37] The effectiveness that states can demonstrate when seeking to protect the health and safety of their residents is not surprising given the key advantages that states have over the national government. These advantages include knowledge of local resources, hazards, and priorities, and the ability to quickly correct mistakes that are made in the course of mitigating the crisis.[38] However, not all states are as effective as they could be, and this leads to some of the challenges.

First, under federalism, states must not and do not act consistently. During the COVID-19 crisis, some governors performed quickly and appropriately to save lives and provide enhanced access to healthcare, unemployment benefits, and rent and bill relief, while others were very slow to act, if they have acted at all.[39] After states were moving to enact stay-at-home orders and calling for social distancing practices to keep people in public at least six feet apart, the governor of Oklahoma posted a picture of himself and his family on social media dining at a crowded restaurant.[40] The Florida governor declined to close beaches during the height of the spring break tourist season, deferring to the counties and cities to make the decisions, which they were slow and reluctant to make. These examples of negligent behavior notwithstanding, there is an argument to make for the benefits of experimentation during a crisis, and there is utility in trying different solutions during an extended crisis to develop some best practices moving forward.[41] Surely, as this crisis continues, there will be more good and bad examples set by the states that we will all learn from.

Second, even in a situation where the national government would like to act or the states would like for it to act, the national government has little to no authority to tell the states what to do.[42] In the case of a healthcare crisis, many people falsely view the Centers for Disease Control (CDC) as a component of the federal bureaucracy capable of setting and implementing policy, but it not structured or staffed to do anything of that magnitude.[43] The national government cannot compel the states to take less action if they are thought to be doing too much, and the states cannot be compelled to do more if they are not doing enough. President Trump had announced in a press conference that he wanted businesses to reopen by a certain date, but he had no authority to enforce such a mandate.[44] Likewise, the national government is very limited to compel states that are not doing anything to take more actions to protect the health of the people living in that state.[45] At the time of this writing, President Trump has announced on Twitter that the president has overriding authority to reopen the economy, even at the objection of state governors.[46] Only time will tell how this federalism dispute will be resolved.

A national crisis presents challenges in many forms, and the continued protection of individual rights can be particularly hard in a federal system. A national crisis would seem to demand a national response, but American federalism is not structured to provide that response in all circumstances. In the event of a national security threat, the national government would be most empowered to act. However, even in the case of the 9/11 terrorist attacks, federalism created challenges for providing national support for state and local needs. In the event of a natural disaster, states can request federal help to provide for victims of that disaster, and the Federal Emergency Management Agency (FEMA) is set up to provide support for those efforts.

In the event of a health crisis, the national government has limited formal authority to address the issues, but perhaps greater capacity. FEMA has a COVID-19 response page on its website, and the agency has begun disbursing funds to the states. The states have more formal authority, but perhaps less capacity. Tensions have grown between President Trump and state governors over what the states can and should be doing and what the national government should provide. Public health is under the purview of the states, but the states will face many challenges in delivering the services and protections that the people are going to need.[47] Those people are the ones that are going to pay for that variability by way of their individual rights.

Whereas national security issues and natural disasters have more established protocol for facilitating federal cooperation between the national government and the states, it appears that there was not an adequate plan in place for a health crisis to ensure that all Americans regardless of their state of residence would have equal access to life and liberty protections. It could be that, in the case of a health crisis, an expanded role for the national government could be beneficial.[48] However, such a statement could only be true under the condition that the national government would take more significant steps toward protecting individual rights than the states, and this is not guaranteed. In the COVID-19 crisis, there are many examples of individual states taking more precautions to protect individuals than the national government has wished to take. Restricting the power of the state governments in this particular scenario could serve to further restrict protections for the individual. As with so many other policies, we are left to debate which level of government is best positioned to protect individual rights. In the event of a crisis, that challenge is magnified.

CONCLUSION

This categorization of the persisting threats to individual rights in a federal system is by no means exhaustive, and the opportunities for continued research in this area are endless.[49] There are many ways that the work contained in this book can be extended. The same organizational structure and evaluative process by way of my three-part test could be applied to other policy areas to build on the conclusions I have drawn about American federalism regarding civil rights, education, SSM, and PAD policy. Additionally, work could be done to expand the policy discussions contained herein. There are far more legislative, judicial, executive, and citizen actions that were significant for federalism and individual rights in each of these policy areas than I was able to include here. Anyone with a particular interest in any of those policy areas individually could use the work herein as a springboard to develop more expansive works on those topics as they relate to federalism and individual rights.

Another possibility for future research would be to connect this work to the existing literature on public opinion and its effects on the practice of federalism. Specifically, a study of survey data to look for a connection between attitudes about individual rights and preferences for centralized or decentralized policymaking could be helpful in explaining those preferences. When it comes to morality policy, in particular, there does not seem to be a consistent pattern in place. Previous research has shown strong connections between party identification, ideology, and federalism preference.[50] However, these preferences do not seem to align quite as cleanly regarding the protection of individual rights. There are morality policies that have risen to the level of protection under the U.S. Constitution and others that have not. There are policies that did not rise to that level of protection in the past but would go on to enjoy heightened protections in the future. Civil rights and SSM are two policy areas that were handled much differently over the course of time and a changing political culture. Investigating the extent to which federalism preferences have an ideological foundation by way of individual rights views could shed more light on how those preferences have developed both at the party level and the individual level.

The purpose of this book from the very beginning was to investigate the relationship between federalism and individual rights. There is a debate over whether or not federalism was intended to protect individual rights and whether it should protect individual rights. My goal was to discover whether it actually does serve to protect individual rights in practice. I have always thought that if American founding principles served at cross purposes, then the stability of the political system could be vulnerable. The work I have done shows when and how federalism and the protection of individual rights have chafed against each other. I have also found examples where these principles have worked in harmony to maximize protections for individual rights. American federalism protects individual rights to the extent that we want it to and no further than that. There is nothing about federalism that automatically makes it protect individual rights, and it is used in countries that do not have the individualistic culture that the United States has. However, if the political culture in place values the protection of individual rights, then federalism provides ample opportunities to provide those protections. The maintenance of a federal system intended to protect individual rights requires the continued diligence of all members of government, both at the national and state level, and the citizens whom they serve.

NOTES

1. McDowell, "Advisory Commission on Intergovernmental Relations in 1996: The End of an Era," 111–112.
2. Ibid., 112.
3. Chi, "The Contributions of the U.S. Advisory Commission on Intergovernmental Relations," 231.
4. McDowell, "Advisory Commission on Intergovernmental Relations in 1996: The End of an Era," 112.
5. Ibid.
6. Ibid., 114.
7. Nathan, "ACIR: A Gap That Needs to Be Filled," 233.
8. Chi, "The Contributions of the U.S. Advisory Commission on Intergovernmental Relations," 231.
9. Ibid., 233.
10. McDowell, "Advisory Commission on Intergovernmental Relations in 1996: The End of an Era," 111.
11. Ibid.
12. Chi, "The Contributions of the U.S. Advisory Commission on Intergovernmental Relations," 231.
13. McDowell, "Advisory Commission on Intergovernmental Relations in 1996: The End of an Era," 121–122, 125.
14. Kincaid, "The U.S. Advisory Commission on Intergovernmental Relations," 183.
15. Ibid., 187–188.
16. Ibid.
17. Nathan, "ACIR: A Gap That Needs to Be Filled," 234.
18. Tarr and Katz, "Introduction," x.
19. Ibid., xii.
20. Ibid., xiii.
21. Ibid.
22. Tarlton, "Symmetry and Asymmetry as Elements of Federalism," 861.
23. Ibid., 867.
24. Ibid., 869–870.
25. Ibid., 872.
26. Ibid., 874.

27. Walls, *Individualism in the United States*, 116.

28. Ibid.

29. Ibid.

30. Ibid., 117.

31. Ibid.

32. Hollo, "With the Climate Crisis and Coronavirus Bearing Down on Us, the Age of Disconnection is Over."

33. "Florida's Governor Dissents on Lockdowns," *Wall Street Journal*.

34. Chemerinsky, "Op-Ed: Trump Doesn't Have the Authority to Order the Country Back to Work by Easter."

35. Ibid.

36. Povich, "Governors Leapfrog Feds on Coronavirus Response."

37. Ibid.

38. Olson, "Federalism and the Coronavirus Lockdown."

39. Rozell, "Gov. Larry Hogan's Coronavirus Leadership Trumps Trump's."

40. Ibid.

41. "Florida's Governor Dissents on Lockdowns," *Wall Street Journal*.

42. Olson, "Federalism and the Coronavirus Lockdown."

43. Gerson, "Coronavirus Demands Strong Federal Response."

44. Chemerinsky, "Op-Ed: Trump Doesn't Have the Authority to Order the Country Back to Work by Easter."

45. Rozell, "Gov. Larry Hogan's Coronavirus Leadership Trumps Trump's."

46. Trump, *Twitter*, April 13, 2020.

47. Gerson, "Coronavirus Demands Strong Federal Response."

48. Ibid.

49. For those interested in such research, the journal *Publius* is an international journal exclusively dedicated to the topic of federalism, and it publishes scholarship from a variety of disciplines. I cited articles from this journal extensively in writing this book and am so thankful for this community of scholars who have worked to keep interest and progress in this area of study alive.

50. Dinan and Heckelman, "Stability and Contingency in Federalism Preference," 234.

Bibliography

Abraham, Henry J. *Freedom and the Court: Civil Rights and Liberties in the United States.* New York and Oxford: Oxford University Press, 1988.

Alexander, William Paul. "The Measurement of American Federalism." In *The Development of American Federalism,* edited by William Riker, 99–112. Norwell, MA: Klewer Academic Publishers, 1987.

Bailyn, Bernard. *The Ideological Origins of the American Revolution.* Cambridge, MA and London: The Belknap Press of Harvard University Press, 1967, 1992.

———. *To Begin the World Anew.* New York, NY: Alfred A. Knopf, 2003.

Baker v. Nelson, 291 Minn. 310, 191 N.W.2d 185 (1971).

Ball, Howard. *At Liberty to Die: The Battle for Death with Dignity in America.* New York, NY: New York University Press, 2012.

Ball, Terrance, Richard Dagger and Daniel O'Neill. *Political Ideologies and the Democratic Ideal.* New York: Longman, 2014.

Beasley, Dorothy Toth. "Federalism and the Protection of Individual Rights: The American State Constitutional Perspective." In *Federalism and Rights,* edited by Ellis Katz and G. Alan Tarr, 101–121. Lanham, MD: Rowman & Littlefield Publishers, Inc., 1996.

Beer, Samuel. "The Rediscovery of American Federalism." In *Principles and Practice of American Politics: Classic and Contemporary Readings,* edited by Samuel Kernell and Steven S. Smith, 85–109. Washington, DC: CQ Press, 2000.

Berger, Raoul. *Federalism: The Founders' Design.* Norman: University of Oklahoma Press, 1987.

Bolick, Clint. *Grassroots Tyranny: The Limits of Federalism.* Washington, DC: Cato Institute, 1993.

Bond v. United States, 564 U.S. 211 (2011).

Bond v. United States, 572 U.S. 844 (2014).

Bowers v. Hardwick, 478 U.S. 186 (1986).

Bowling, Cynthia J. and J. Mitchell Pickerill. "Fragmented Federalism: The State of American Federalism 2012–13." *Publius* 43, no. 3 (2013): 315–346.

Bowman Kristi. "The Failure of Education Federalism." *University of Michigan Journal of Law Reform* 51, no. 1 (2017): 1–53.

Breton, Albert. "Federalism and Decentralization: Ownership Rights and the Superiority of Federalism." *Publius* 30, no. 2 (2000): 1–16.

Brown v. Board of Education, 347 U.S. 483 (1954).

Brown v. Board of Education, 349 U.S. 294 (1955).

Bullock, Emma C. "Assisted Dying and the Proper Role of Patient Autonomy." In *New Directions in the Ethics of Assisted Suicide and Euthanasia*, edited by M. Cholbi and J. Varelius, 11–25. International Library of Ethics, Law, and the New Medicine 64, DOI 10.1007/978-3-319-22050-5_2.

Camera, L. "DeVos: I'd be Fine Ditching the Education Department." *US News*, February 17, 2017. Accessed February 25, 2020. https://www.usnews.com/ne ws/articles/2017-02-17/betsy-devos-id-be-fine-if-we-could-ditch-the-education-de partment.

Caminker, Evan. "Schaivo and Klein." *Constitutional Commentary* 332 (2005): 529–551. https://scholarship.law.umn.edu/concomm/332.

Chamie, Joseph and Barry Mirkin. "Same-Sex Marriage: A New Social Phenomenon." *Population and Development Review* 37, no. 3 (2011): 529–551.

Chi, Keon S. "The Contributions of the U.S. Advisory Commission on Intergovernmental Relations." *State & Local Government Review* 36, no. 3 (2004): 231–233.

Civil Rights Cases, 109 U.S. 3 (1883).

Clark, Nina. *The Politics of Physician Assisted Suicide*. New York, NY: Garland Publishing, Inc., 1997.

Cleves, Rachel Hope. "What, Another Female Husband?": The Prehistory of Same-Sex Marriage in America." *The Journal of American History* 101, no. 4 (2015): 1055–1081.

Cohen, I. Glenn. "Traveling for Assisted Suicide." In *Euthanasia and Assisted Suicide: Global Views on Choosing to End Life*, edited by Michael J. Cholbi, 373–391. Santa Barbara, CA: Praeger, 2017.

Cole, Richard L., Rodney V. Hissong and Enid Arvidson. "Devolution: Where's the Revolution?" *Publius* 29, no. 4 (1999): 99–112.

Conlan, Tim. "From Cooperative to Opportunistic Federalism: Reflections on the Half-Century Anniversary of the Commission on Intergovernmental Relations." *Public Administration Review* 66, no. 5 (2006): 663–676.

Corwin, Edward S. "The Passing of Dual Federalism." *Virginia Law Review* 36, no. 1 (1950): 1–24.

Cory, Donald Webster. *The Homosexual in America: A Subjective Approach*. New York: Greenberg, 1951.

Cox, Donald. *Hemlock's Cup: The Struggle for Death with Dignity*. Buffalo, NY: Prometheus Books, 1993.

Cruzan v. Director, Missouri Department of Health, 497 U.S. 261 (1990).

Cumming v. Richmond County Board of Education, 175 U.S. 528 (1899).

D'Alemberte, Talbot. "Rights and Federalism: An Agenda to Advance the Vision of Justice Brennan." In *Federalism and Rights*, edited by Ellis Katz and G. Alan Tarr, 123–138. Lanham, MD: Rowman & Littlefield Publishers, Inc., 1996.

Dallman, Scott and Anusha Nath. "Education Clauses in State Constitutions Across the United States." Federal Reserve Bank of Minneapolis, January 8, 2020. Accessed February 27, 2020. https://www.minneapolisfed.org/~/media/assets/arti cles/2020/education-clauses-in-state-constitutions-across-the-united-states/educ ation-clauses-in-state-constitutions-across-the-united-states.pdf?la=en.

Death With Dignity. "Take Action in Your State." Accessed March 21, 2020. https:// www.deathwithdignity.org/take-action.

Diamond, Martin. "The Federalist's View of Federalism." In *Essays in Federalism*, edited by The Institute for Studies in Federalism, 21–64. Claremont, CA: Claremont Men's College, 1961.

Dinan, John and Jac C. Heckelman. "Stability and Contingency in Federalism Preferences." *Public Administration Review* 80, no. 2 (2020): 234–243.

Dry, Murray. *Same Sex Marriage and American Constitutionalism: A Study in Federalism, Separation of Powers, and Individual Rights.* Philadelphia: Paul Dry Books, 2017.

Dworkin, Ronald. *Life's Domain: An Argument about Abortion, Euthanasia, and Individual Freedom.* New York, NY: Vintage Books, 1993.

Dye, Thomas R. and Ronald Keith Gaddie. *Politics in America.* Boston: Pearson, 2016.

Edwards, George C. and Martin P. Wattenberg. *Government in America: People, Politics, and Policy.* Boston: Pearson, 2016.

Eisinger, Peter. "Imperfect Federalism: The Intergovernmental Partnership for Homeland Security." *Public Administration Review* 66, no. 4 (2006): 537–545.

Elazar, Daniel J. *Exploring Federalism.* Tuscaloosa, AL: The University of Alabama Press, 1987.

———. "Federal-State Collaboration in the Nineteenth-Century United States." In *American Federalism in Perspective*, edited by Aaron Wildavsky, 190–222. Boston: Little, Brown and Company, 1967.

———. "Federalism, Diversity, and Rights." In *Federalism and Rights*, edited by Ellis Katz and G. Alan Tarr, 1–10. Lanham, MD: Rowman & Littlefield Publishers, Inc., 1996.

Emanuel, Ezekiel J. "Whose Right to Die?" *The Atlantic*, March 1997. Accessed January 31, 2020. https://www.theatlantic.com/magazine/archive/1997/03/whose -right-to-die/304641/.

Employment Div. v. Smith, 494 U.S. 872 (1990).

Encyclopaedia Britannica. "Defense of Marriage Act." Accessed March 1, 2018. https://www.britannica.com/topic/Defense-of-Marriage-Act.

———. "Religious Freedom Restoration Act." Accessed January 1, 2020. https://ww w.britannica.com/topic/Religious-Freedom-Restoration-Act.

Eskridge, William N., Jr. "A History of Same-Sex Marriage." *Virginia Law Review* 79, no. 7 (1993): 1419–1513.

Francis, Megan Ming. *Civil Rights and the Making of the Modern American State.* New York, NY: Cambridge University Press, 2014.

Finn, Chester E., Jr. and Michael J. Petrilli. "The Failures of US Education Governance Today." In *Education Governance for the Twenty-First Century: Overcoming the*

Structural Barriers to School Reform, edited by Paul Manna and Patrick McGuinn, 21–35. Washington, DC: Brookings Institution Press, 2013.

"Florida's Governor Dissents on Lockdowns; Republican Ron DeSantis Draws Liberal Ire for Resisting 'Shelter in Place'." *Wall Street Journal (Online)*, March 26, 2020. https://search-proquest-com.ezproxy.bgsu.edu/docview/2383269644?a ccountid=26417.

Gerson, Michael. "Coronavirus Isn't the Next Katrina. It's Worse." *The Washington Post*, March 10, 2020. https://search-proquest-com.ezproxy.bgsu.edu/docview/23 74967823?accountid=26417.

Gerstle, Gary. *Liberty and Coercion: The Paradox of American Government from the Founding to the Present*. Princeton and Oxford: Princeton University Press, 2015.

Gerston, Larry. *American Federalism: A Concise Introduction*. Armonk, NY and London, England: M. E. Sharpe, 2007.

Gibbons v. Ogden, 22 U.S. 1 (1824).

Gibson, Rhonda. *Same-Sex Marriage and Social Media*. London and New York: Routledge, 2018.

Glazer, Nathan. "Federalism and Ethnicity: The Experience of the United States." *Publius* 7, no. 4 (1977): 71–87.

Gleason, Bob. "The Transformation in American Politics: Implications for Federalism." United States Advisory Commission Intergovernmental Relations Report. Washington, DC, 1986.

Glendening, Parris N. and Mavis Mann Reeves. *Pragmatic Federalism: An Intergovernmental View of American Government*. Pacific Palisades, CA: Palisades Publishers, 1984.

Gonzales v. Oregon, 546 U.S. 243 (2006).

Goralka, John M. and Kiran K. Dhillon. "Department: Practice Tips: Guidance on California's End of Life Option Act." *Los Angeles Lawyer* 39, no. 11 (2017): 11–15.

Gorsuch, Neil. M. *The Future of Assisted Suicide and Euthanasia*. Princeton, NJ: Princeton University Press, 2006.

Greene, Jack P. *Peripheries and Center: Constitutional Development in the Extended Polities of the British Empire and the United States, 1607–1788*. Athens, Georgia and London: The University of Georgia Press, 1986.

Grodzins, Martin. *The American System: A New View of Government in the United States*. Chicago, IL: Rand McNally, 1966.

Hail, Michael and Stephen Lange. "Federalism and Representation in the Theory of the Founding Fathers: A Comparative Study of U.S. and Canadian Constitutional Thought." *Publius* 40, no. 3 (2010): 366–388.

Hamilton, Alexander, James Madison and John Jay. *The Federalist Papers*. ed. Clinton Rossiter. New York: New American Library, 1961.

Heart of Atlanta Motel, Inc. v. United States, 379 U.S. 241 (1964).

Heise, Michael. "From No Child Left Behind to Every Student Succeeds: Back to a Future for Education Federalism." *Columbia Law Review* 117, no. 7 (2017): 1859–896.

———. "The Political Economy of Education Federalism." *Emory Law Journal* 56, no. 1 (2006): 125–157.

History. "Black Codes." Accessed October 10, 2019. https://www.history.com/topics /black-history/black-codes.

———. "How the History of Blackface is Rooted in Racism." Accessed February 15, 2019. https://www.history.com/news/blackface-history-racism-origins.

———. "Jim Crow Laws." Accessed February 21, 2020. https://www.history.com/t opics/early-20th-century-us/jim-crow-laws.

Hobbes, Thomas. *The Leviathan.* New York: Touchstone, 1962 (1651).

Hoefler, James M. "Diffusion and Diversity: Federalism and the Right to Die in the Fifty States." *Publius* 24, no. 3 (1994): 153–170.

Hollander, Robyn and Haig Patapan. "Morality Policy and Federalism: Innovation, Diffusion and Limits." *Publius* 47, no. 1 (2016): 1–26.

Hollo, Tim. "With the Climate Crisis and Coronavirus Bearing Down on Us, the Age of Disconnection is Over." *Guardian News & Media Limited,* March 27, 2020. Accessed April 1, 2020. https://search-proquest-com.ezproxy.bgsu.edu/docview /2383707652?OpenUrlRefId=info:xri/sid:summon&accountid=26417.

Hornbeck, Dustin. "Seeking Civic Virtue: Two Views of the Philosophy and History of Federalism in U.S. Education." *Journal of Thought* 51, no. 3–4 (2017): 52–68.

Howard, A. E. Dick. "Does Federalism Secure or Undermine Rights?" In *Federalism and Rights,* edited by Ellis Katz and G. Alan Tarr, 11–28. Lanham, MD: Rowman & Littlefield Publishers, Inc., 1996.

Humphry, Derek and Mary Clement. *Freedom to Die: People, Politics, and the Right-to-Die Movement.* New York, NY: St. Martin's Press, 1998.

Jacobs, Nicholas. "An Experimental Test of How Americans Think About Federalism." *Publius* 47, no. 4 (2017): 572–598.

Josephson, Jyl. "Citizenship, Same-Sex Marriage, and Feminist Critiques of Marriage." *Perspectives on Politics* 3, no. 2 (2005): 269–284.

Katz, Ellis. "United States of America." In *Distribution of Powers and Responsibilities in Federal Countries,* edited by Akhtar Majeed, Ronald L. Watts and Douglas M. Brown, 296–321. Montreal, QC: McGill-Queen's University Press, 2006.

Kesler, Charles. "*Introduction to The Federalist Papers.*" In *The Federalist Papers,* edited by Clinton Rossiter, vii–xxxi. New York: New American Library, 1961.

Kincaid, John. "From Cooperative to Coercive Federalism." *The Annals of the American Academy of Political and Social Science* 509 (1990): 139–152.

———. "The U.S. Advisory Commission on Intergovernmental Relations: Unique Artifact of a Bygone Era." *Public Administration Review* 71, no. 2 (2011): 181–189.

Kincaid, John and Richard L. Cole. "Is Federalism Still the 'Dark Continent' of Political Science Teaching? Yes and No." *PS: Political Science and Politics* 47, no. 4 (2014): 877–883.

Kindregan, Charles P. "Same-Sex Marriage: The Cultural Wars and the Lessons of Legal History." *Family Law Quarterly* 38, no. 2 (2004): 427–447.

Knauer, Nancy J. "Federalism, Marriage Equality, and LGBT Rights." In *Controversies in American Federalism and Public Policy,* edited by Christopher P. Banks, 93–113. New York: Routledge, 2018.

Kramer, Liz. "Achieving Equitable Education through the Courts: A Comparative Analysis of Three States." *Journal of Law & Education* 31, no. 1 (2002): 1–51.

Kreimer, Seth F. "Federalism and Freedom." *The Annals of the American Academy of Political and Social Science* 574 (2001): 66–80.

Krislov, Samuel. "American Federalism as American Exceptionalism." *Publius* 31, no. 1 (2001): 9–26.

LaCroix, Alison L. *The Ideological Origins of American Federalism.* Cambridge, MA: Harvard University Press, 2010.

Lane, Charles. "Lifting the U.S. Ban on Euthanasia is Like Opening a Pandora's Box." *The Washington Post (Online)*, September 23, 2019. Accessed January 31, 2020. https://www.washingtonpost.com/opinions/lifting-the-us-ban-on-euthanasia -may-be-more-complicated-than-you-think/2019/09/23/f0151198-de3b-11e9-8dc8 -498eabc129a0_story.html.

Latzer, Barry. *State Constitutions and Criminal Justice.* New York: Greenwood Press, 1991.

Lawrence v. Texas, 539 U.S. 558 (2003).

Locke, John. *Two Treatises of Government.* London: Cambridge University Press, 1988 (1698).

Loving v. Virginia, 388 U.S. 1 (1967).

Mahon, J. Patrick. "Cumming v. Board of Education of Richmond County." *Britannica*. Accessed December 11, 2019. https://www.britannica.com/topic/Cu mming-v-Board-of-Education-of-Richmond-County.

Manna, Paul. *School's In: Federalism and the National Education Agenda.* Washington: Georgetown University Press, 2006.

Marbury v. Madison, 5 U.S. 137 (1803).

McConkie, Pace Jefferson. "Civil Rights and Federalism Fights: Is there a 'More Perfect Union' for Heirs to the Promise of Brown?" *Brigham Young University Law Review* 1996, no. 2 (1996): 389–405.

McCulloch v. Maryland, 17 U.S. 316 (1819).

McDonald, Forrest. *Novus Ordo Seclorum: The Intellectual Origins of the Constitution.* Lawrence, KS: University Press of Kansas, 1985.

McDowell, Bruce D. "Advisory Commission on Intergovernmental Relations in 1996: The End of an Era." *Publius* 27, no. 2 (1997): 111–127.

McGovern, Shannon K. "A New Model for States as Laboratories for Reform: How Federalism Informs Education Policy." *New York University Law Review* 86, no. 5 (2011): 1518–1537.

McGuinn, Patrick. "From No Child Left Behind to the Every Student Succeeds Act: Federalism and the Education Legacy of the Obama Administration." *Publius* 46, no. 3 (2016): 392–415.

McLaughlin, Andrew C. "The Background of American Federalism." *The American Political Science Review* 12, no. 2 (1918): 215–240.

Miller, Lisa L. "Criminal Justice." In *Federalism in America*, edited by Joseph R. Marbach, Ellis Katz and Troy E. Smith, 139–140. Westport, CT: Greenwood Press, 2006.

Miller, Loren. *The Petitioners: The Story of the United States Supreme Court and the Negro.* Cleveland and New York: Meridian Books/The World Publishing Company, 1966.

Moats, David. *Civil Wars: The Battle for Gay Marriage*. Orlando, FL: Harcourt, 2004.

Mooney, Christopher Z. "The Decline of Federalism and the Rise of Morality-Policy Conflict in the United States." *Publius* 30, no. 1 (2000): 171–188.

Murrin, John. "1787: The Invention of American Federalism." In *Essays on Liberty and Federalism*, edited by John M. Murrin, David E. Narrett, Ronald L. Hatzenbuehler and Michael Kammen, 20–47. College Station, TX: Texas A&M University Press, 1988.

Nagel, Robert F. "On the Decline of Federalism." *Daedalus* 135, no. 1 (2006): 127–130.

Nathan, Richard P. "ACIR: A Gap that Needs to be Filled." *State & Local Government Review* 36, no. 3 (2004): 233–234.

NeJaime, Douglas. "Marriage Inequality: Same-Sex Relationships, Religious Exemptions, and the Production of Sexual Orientation Discrimination." *California Law Review* 100, no. 5 (2012): 1169–1238.

Nugent, John D. *Safeguarding Federalism: How States Protect Their Interests in National Policymaking*. Norman, OK: University of Oklahoma Press, 2009.

Obergefell v. Hodges, 576 U.S. __ (2015).

O'Connor, Karen and Alexandra Yanus. "'Til Death—or the Supreme Court—Do Us Part." In *The Politics of Same-Sex Marriage*, edited by Craig A. Rimmerman and Clyde Wilcox, 291–311. London: The University of Chicago Press, 2007.

Olson, Walter. "Federalism and the Coronavirus Lockdown; Trump Can't Order the Country Back to Normalcy by April 30 or any Day. That's for States to Decide." *Wall Street Journal (Online)*, March 30, 2020. https://search-proquest-com.ezproxy.bgsu.edu/docview/2384319047?accountid=26417.

"Oregon's Death with Dignity Act: The First Year's Experience." Department of Human Resources, Oregon Health Division, Center for Disease Prevention and Epidemiology. 1999. https://www.oregon.gov/oha/ph/providerpartnerresources/evaluationresearch/deathwithdignityact/documents/year1.pdf.

"Oregon Death with Dignity Act: 2019 Data Summary." Public Health Division, Oregon Health Authority. 2019. https://www.oregon.gov/oha/ph/providerpartnerresources/evaluationresearch/deathwithdignityact/documents/year22.pdf.

Ostrom, Vincent. *The Meaning of American Federalism*. San Francisco, CA: ICS Press, 1991.

Oyez. "Bond v. United States." Accessed March 31, 2020. https://www.oyez.org/cases/2010/09-1227.

Pappas, Demetra M. *The Euthanasia/Assisted-Suicide Debate*. Santa Barbara, CA: Greenwood, 2012.

Patrick, Barbara. "Fiscal Federalism, Performance Policies, and Education Reforms: Are States Using Performance Policies to Improve Workforce Quality?" *Politics & Policy* 40, no. 4 (2012): 593–628.

Petrillo, Laura A., Elizabeth Dzeng and Alexander K. Smith. "California's End of Life Option Act: Opportunities and Challenges Ahead." *Journal of General Internal Medicine* 31, no. 8 (2016): 828–829.

Pickerill, J. Mitchell and Cynthia J. Bowling. "Polarized Parties, Politics, and Policies: Fragmented Federalism in 2013–2014." *Publius* 44, no. 3 (2014): 369–398.

Pickerill, J. Mitchell and Paul Chen. "Medical Marijuana Policy and the Virtues of Federalism." *Publius* 38, no. 1 (2008): 22–55.

Pierceson, Jason. *Same-Sex Marriage in the United States*. Lanham, MD: Rowman and Littlefield, 2013.

Pinder, Kamina Aliya. "Federal Demand and Local Choice: Safeguarding the Notion of Federalism in Education Law and Policy." *The Journal of Law and Education* 39, no. 1 (2010): 1–35.

Plessy v. Ferguson, 163 U.S. 537 (1896).

Posner, Paul L. "Unfunded Mandates Reform Act: 1996 and Beyond." *Publius* 27, no. 2 (1997): 53–71.

Povich, Elaine S. "Governors Leapfrog Feds on Coronavirus Response." *TCA News Service*, March 23, 2020. https://search-proquest-com.ezproxy.bgsu.edu/docview /2381740162?accountid=26417.

Reagan, Michael D. and John G. Sanzone. *The New Federalism*. New York and Oxford: Oxford University Press, 1981.

Riker, William. *Federalism: Origin, Operation, and Significance*. Boston and Toronto: Little, Brown and Company, 1964.

———. *The Development of American Federalism*. Norwell, MA: Klewer Academic Publishers, 1987.

Rivlin, Alice M. "Rethinking Federalism for More Effective Governance." *Publius* 42, no. 3 (2012): 387–400.

Roberts, Patrick S. "Dispersed Federalism as a New Regional Governance for Homeland Security." *Publius* 38, no. 3 (2008): 416–443.

Robertson, David Brian. *Federalism and the Making of America*. New York and London: Routledge, 2012.

Robinson, Kimberly Jenkins. "The High Cost of Education Federalism." *Wake Forest Law Review* 48, no. 2 (2013): 287–331.

Rose, Shanna and Greg Goelzhauser. "The State of American Federalism 2017–2018: Unilateral Executive Action, Regulatory Rollback, and State Resistance." *Publius* 48, no. 3 (2018): 319–344.

Rozell, Mark J. "Gov. Larry Hogan's Coronavirus Leadership Trumps Trump's -and Many Others|COMMENTARY." Tribune Publishing Company, LLC, March 19, 2020. Accessed April 1, 2020. https://search-proquest-com.ezproxy.bgsu.edu/ docview/2379288445?OpenUrlRefId=info:xri/sid:summon&accountid=26417.

Rubin, Edward L. and Malcolm M. Feeley. "Federalism and Interpretation." *Publius* 38, no. 2 (2008): 167–191.

Rutherglen, George. "The Thirteenth Amendment, the Power of Congress, and the Shifting Sources of Civil Rights Law." *Columbia Law Review* 112, no. 7 (2012): 1551–1584.

Sager, Lawrence G. "Symposium: Dual Enforcement of Constitutional Norms: Cool Federalism and the Life-Cycle of Moral Progress." *William & Mary Law Review* 46 (February 2005): 1385–1397.

San Antonio Independent School District v. Rodriguez, 411 U.S. 1 (1973).

Scavo, Carmine, Richard C. Kearney and Richard J. Kilroy, Jr. "Challenges to Federalism: Homeland Security and Disaster Response." *Publius* 38, no. 1 (2008): 81–110.

Schapiro, Robert A. *Polyphonic Federalism: Toward the Protection of Fundamental Rights*. Chicago and London: The University of Chicago Press, 2009.

Sclar, David. "U.S. Supreme Court Ruling in Gonzales v. Oregon Upholds the Oregon Death With Dignity Act." *Journal of Law, Medicine & Ethics* 34, no. 3 (2006): 639–645.

Severino, Carrie. "Justice Kennedy: Federalism Exists to Secure Individual Liberty." *National Review*, June 17, 2011. Accessed May 14, 2018. https://www.national review.com/bench-memos/justice-kennedy-federalism-exists-secure-individual-li berty-carrie-severino/.

Sidlow, Edward and Beth Henschen. *GOVT 10*. 10th edn; Instructor edn. Boston, MA: Wadsworth/Cengage Learning, 2019.

Slaughterhouse Cases, 83 U.S. 36 (1873).

Somin, Ilya. "The Supreme Court of the United States: Promoting Centralization More Than State Autonomy." In *Courts in Federal Countries: Federalists or Unitarists?* edited by Nicholas Aroney and John Kincaid, 440–481. Toronto, Buffalo, and London: University of Toronto Press, 2017.

Spackman, S. G. F. "American Federalism and the Civil Rights Act of 1875." *Journal of American Studies* 10, no. 3 (1976): 313–328.

Storing, Herbert J. *What the Anti-Federalists Were For*. Chicago and London: The University of Chicago Press, 1981.

Sundquist, Christian B. "Positive Education Federalism: The Promise of Equality after the Every Student Succeeds Act." *Mercer Law Review* 68, no. 2 (2017): 351–387.

Svenson, Arthur G. "Physician-Assisted Dying and the Law in the United States: A Perspective on Three Prospective Futures." In *Euthanasia and Assisted Suicide: Global Views on Choosing to End Life*, edited by Michael J. Cholbi, 3–28. Santa Barbara, CA: Praeger, 2017.

Tarlton, Charles D. "Symmetry and Asymmetry as Elements of Federalism: A Theoretical Speculation." *The Journal of Politics* 27, no. 4 (1965): 861–874.

Tarr, G. Alan. "The Past and Future of the New Judicial Federalism." *Publius* 24, no. 2 (1994): 63–79.

Tarr, G. Alan and Ellis Katz. "Introduction." In *Federalism and Rights*, edited by Ellis Katz and G. Alan Tarr, ix–xxiii. Lanham, MD: Rowman & Littlefield Publishers, Inc., 1996.

Troy, Daniel E. "The Unfunded Mandates Reform Act of 1995." *Administrative Law Review* 49, no. 1 (1997): 139–147.

Trump, Donald (@realDonaldTrump). "For the Purposes of Creating Conflict and Confusion, Some in the Fake News Media are Saying that It Is the Governors Decision to Open Up the States, Not that of the President of the United States & the Federal Government. Let It be Fully Understood that This Is Incorrect . . ." April 13, 2020, 10:53 AM. https://twitter.com/realdonaldtrump/status/12497124042604 21633?s=21.

Twagilimana, Aimable. "Civil Rights Act of 1875." In *Federalism in America: Volume 1*, edited by Joseph R. Marbach, Ellis Katz and Troy E. Smith, 80–81. Westport, CT: Greenwood Press, 2006.

Urofsky, Melvin. *Lethal Judgments: Assisted Suicide & American Law*. Lawrence, KS: University Press of Kansas, 2000.

U.S. Constitution, amend. 13.

U.S. Constitution, amend. 14, sec. 1.

U.S. Constitution, amend. 15, sec. 1.

U.S. Constitution, art. I, sec. 8.

United States House of Representatives. "The Civil Rights Bill of 1866." Accessed January 8, 2020. https://history.house.gov/Historical-Highlights/1851-1900/The -Civil-Rights-Bill-of-1866.

―――. "National Defense Education Act." Accessed February 27, 2020. https://hi story.house.gov/HouseRecord/Detail/15032436195.

United States President, Executive Order. "Presidential Executive Order on Enforcing Statutory Prohibitions on Federal Control of Education." April 26, 2017. https:// www.whitehouse.gov/presidential-actions/presidential-executive-order-enforcing -statutory-prohibitions-federal-control-education/.

United States Senate. "Landmark Legislation: The Enforcement Acts of 1870 and 1871." Accessed February 12, 2020. https://www.senate.gov/artandhistory/history/ common/generic/EnforcementActs.htm.

United States v. Windsor, 570 U.S. 744 (2013).

Valdes, Francisco. "From Law Reform to Lived Justice: Marriage Equality, Personal Praxis, and Queer Normativity in the United States." *Tulane Journal of Law & Sexuality* 26 (2017): 1–52.

Van Der Silk, Jack R. "Civil Rights Act of 1964." In *Federalism in America: Volume 1*, edited by Joseph R. Marbach, Ellis Katz and Troy E. Smith, 81–82. Westport, CT: Greenwood Press, 2006.

Vergari, Sandra. "Federalism and Market-Based Education Policy: The Supplemental Educational Services Mandate." *American Journal of Education* 113, no. 2 (2007): 311–339.

―――. "Safeguarding Federalism in Education Policy in Canada and the United States." *Publius* 40, no. 3 (2010): 534–557.

Walker, David B. "American Federalism from Johnson to Bush." *Publius* 21, no. 1 (1991): 105–119.

―――. "The Advent of an Ambiguous Federalism and the Emergence of New Federalism III." *Public Administration Review* 56, no. 3 (1996): 271–280.

―――. *The Rebirth of Federalism*. Chatham, NJ: Chatham House, 1995.

Walls, Stephanie M. *Individualism in the Unites States: A Transformation in American Political Thought*. New York, NY: Bloomsbury, 2015.

Weeden, L. Darnell. "Marriage Equality Laws are a Threat to Religious Liberty." *Southern Illinois University Law Journal* 41, no. 2 (2017): 211–236.

Weiss, Joanne and Patrick McGuinn. "States as Change Agents Under ESSA." *Phi Delta Kappan* 97, no. 8 (2016): 28–33.

White House. "Franklin D. Roosevelt." Accessed January 16, 2020. https://www.whi tehouse.gov/about-the-white-house/presidents/franklin-d-roosevelt/.

Williams, Mary Frase. "American Education and Federalism." *Proceedings of the Academy of Political Science* 33, no. 2 (1978): 1–7.

Williams, Reginald. "Same-Sex Marriage and Equality." *Ethical Theory and Moral Practice* 14, no. 5 (2011): 589–595.

Wood, Gordon. *The Creation of the American Republic, 1776–1787.* Chapel Hill, NC: The University of North Carolina Press, 1969.

Woodward, C. Vann. *The Strange Career of Jim Crow.* New York: Oxford University Press, 1974.

Wyatt-Brown, Bertram. "The Civil Rights Act of 1875." *The Western Political Quarterly* 18, no. 4 (1965): 763–775.

Yarbrough, Jean. "Federalism and Rights in the American Founding." In *Federalism and Rights*, edited by Ellis Katz and G. Alan Tarr, 57–73. Lanham, MD: Rowman & Littlefield Publishers, Inc., 1996.

Yoshino, Kenji. "A New Birth of Freedom?: Obergefell v. Hodges." *Harvard Law Review* 129, no. 1 (2015): 147–179.

Yu, Chung-En, Jun Wen and Fang Meng. "Defining Physician-Assisted Suicide Tourism and Travel." *Journal of Hospitality & Tourism Research* 44, no. 1 (2020): 1–10.

Zimmerman, Joseph F. *Contemporary American Federalism.* Albany, NY: State University of New York Press, 2008.

Zuckert, Michael P. "Toward a Theory of Corrective Federalism: The United States Constitution, Federalism, and Rights." In *Federalism and Rights*, edited by Ellis Katz and G. Alan Tarr, 75–100. Lanham, MD: Rowman & Littlefield Publishers, Inc., 1996.

Index

241

About the Author

Stephanie M. Walls is associate professor of political science at Bowling Green State University—Firelands College. She is the author of *Individualism in the United States: A Transformation in American Political Thought* (2015).

Lightning Source UK Ltd.
Milton Keynes UK
UKHW041321230222
399126UK00001B/58

9 781498 589444